DARKENING THE DOORWAYS

DARKENING THE DOORWAYS

Black Trailblazers and Missed Opportunities in Unitarian Universalism

Mark D. Morrison-Reed, Editor

Skinner House Books
Boston

 Published by Skinner House Books, an imprint of the Unitarian Universalist Association, a liberal religious organization with more than 1,000 congregations in the U.S. and Canada, 24 Farnsworth St., Boston, MA 02210-1409.

Printed in the United States

Cover design by Kathryn Sky-Peck
Text design by Suzanne Morgan

Print ISBN: 978-1-55896-610-9
eBook ISBN: 978-1-55896-754-0

6 5 4 3
20 19 18 17

We gratefully acknowledge permission to reprint the following copyrighted materials: "Pioneering Minister Is Helping Troubled Area" by Ernest Tucker (March 26, 2006, Metro 16A) and "First Unitarian Uses Brotherhood Idea" by James O. Supple (February 25, 1949) from the *Chicago Sun Times,* used with permission.

Library of Congress Cataloging-in-Publication Data

Darkening the doorways : Black trailblazers and missed opportunities in Unitarian Universalism / [edited by] Mark Morrison-Reed.

p. cm.
Includes bibliographical references (p.) and index.
ISBN-13: 978-1-55896-610-9 (pbk. : alk. paper)
ISBN-10: 1-55896-610-2 (pbk. : alk. paper)
1. African American Unitarian Universalists—History. I. Morrison-Reed, Mark D., 1949-
BX9833.48.A47D37 2011
289.1092'396073--dc22

2010042305

To my companions in this quest
Nancy Doughty
Willard Frank
Walter Herz
and Richard Morris

CONTENTS

PREFACE

When this project began in 1977, I was a young man; I am no longer. I aged and it grew as I tried to answer a perennial question: Why are there so few African-American Unitarian Universalists?

This question arose from my existential situation. As an African-American child growing up during the 1950s in the First Unitarian Society of Chicago, I saw so few of my hue that I could not help but be conscious of the only other African American in the children's choir, my first black Sunday school teacher, the UU seminarian who was my youth group advisor. The feelings of self-consciousness and relief churned within until they formulated themselves into the question "Why?"

As the twentieth century progressed, many in our faith community grew ill at ease over the absence of significant numbers of black folks and other people of color within Unitarian Universalism. Sometimes, when awareness of this uncomfortable reality breaks through, Euro-Americans feel bewildered. They cannot reconcile it with a self-conception that holds Unitarian Universalists up as liberal, progressive people. So, from different perspectives, we end up sharing the feeling of confusion—and a yearning that it might be otherwise.

This book aims to dispel that confusion. The story told by the biographies, memoirs, documents, and essays gathered here is painful but not befuddling. On one hand, it is a tale of systemic paternalism and prejudice-induced failure of vision, of squandered opportunities, and of good intentions turned into tragedy more often than triumph. On the other hand, it is a tale of idealism, courage, intrepid allies, dogged determination, and steadfast loyalty in the face of rejection. This exploration of the tainted reality behind Unitarian Universalism's espoused liberalism is heartwrenching but leads to an important truth: The premise that liberal religion has not and cannot attract African Americans is false.

In exploring Universalism and Unitarianism, we are talking about two separate religions. Both have roots in New England, rejected Calvinism, and espoused heretical—sometimes different, sometimes overlapping—beliefs. Both demanded freedom of conscience and championed tolerance. Yet they were separated by class and religious sentiment. This book, built upon a series of narratives, endeavors to weave episodes from these two histories into a whole. We grasp the sense of something through narrative. By linking seemingly unrelated events, disparate biographies, and fragments of text, we catch glimpses of our communal life story as part of a drama in which African Americans always played a role. My intention is to correct and recast the Unitarian Universalist narrative. My hope is that from now on, when Unitarian Universalists describe who we are, African Americans will be intrinsic to that identity.

This book is divided into four sections: The Unitarians, The Universalists, The Empowerment Saga, and Still Seeking a Way. The latter two focus on post-consolidation Unitarian Universalism. Each begins with an introduction that provides historical context, an overview of the materials, and why each was selected. Several essays focus on a particular event; however, most are either biographies or primary documents. Each primary document is preceded by a preface that introduces the author and places the document in context. Each also serves to get the current writers out of the way and let the reader have a firsthand sense of what was going on.

In part, I have organized the book this way to draw upon the scholarship of more than a dozen people who, over the past two decades, have unearthed important parts of the story of the African-American experience within Universalism, Unitarianism, and Unitarian Universalism. Although most of these stories can be read independently, the reader will enter more deeply into this experience if she or he reads the book from front to back. The introductory essays and primary documents weave the individual narratives into the larger story. The use of narrative makes this book accessible and usable as a resource that one can revisit. However, its episodic nature challenges the reader to look for the interpersonal and institutional connections, cultural patterns, and pervasive themes.

The most obvious theme is that, feeling the powerful pull of religious freedom, these individuals were drawn to liberal religion and chose a faith community that was white in every way and often—despite its espoused humanitarian values—racially bigoted. This choice required that they navigate between largely segregated worlds, one black, the other white.

The most important theme is the central role education played in their lives. Literate and well-read, these individuals often worked as teachers and administrators, writers and speakers; moreover, those who lived at the turn of the nineteenth century had to stake out a position in the great debate between Booker T. Washington and W.E.B. DuBois over the purpose and content of black education.

The significance of education is closely related to a third theme, another area in which Washington, the accommodator, and DuBois, the crusader, disagreed: social activism. In an aggressively and systemically racist society, these women and men were concerned with justice and freedom. Some became involved in politics, several became socialists, but all, through various means, were dedicated to "uplifting the Negro race," to use the language of an earlier era. Their experience of racism enabled them to understand, in a way most Euro-American religious liberals do not, that human liberation is a communal undertaking, and its achievement a collective reality.

There are many more African-American Universalists, Unitarians, and Unitarian Universalists than have been chronicled to date; nevertheless, overall there are few. Their history is disturbing, the stories enraging, shameful, and poignant, but in assembling them, I began to wonder: How could they have been ignored for so long? An entire remarkable history—a substantial one, a rich one, an old one—and only a handful of people know anything about it. And no one—white, brown, yellow, red, or black—has an inkling of its scope. Why was it disregarded? Did we all, Afro- and Euro-Americans and others, assume there was no such history? Why, in a denomination that revels in the hero worship of Benjamin Rush, Thomas Jefferson, John Adams, Ralph Waldo Emerson, Lydia Maria Child, P. T. Barnum, Susan B. Anthony, Albert Schweitzer, and Linus Pauling, to invoke a few, did we ignore our black forebears? Why this silence? Could it be that religious liberalism as an icon of enlightened progressivism simply could not survive a reckoning with this truth?

Yet these essays also tell us how far we have come—the 2001 election of the first African-American president of the Unitarian Universalist Association. We make a mistake when we measure events and progress primarily in regard to our own life span. When we discuss geology, paleontology, or archeology, we speak in terms of epochs or ages. Taking the longer view, change seems self-evident, and the direction easily discerned. In the often paraphrased words of Unitarian Theodore Parker, "I do not pretend to understand the moral universe; the arc is a long one, my eye reaches but little ways; I cannot calculate the curve and complete the figure by the experience of sight; I can divine it by conscience. And from what I see I am sure it bends towards justice."

With new information constantly emerging, this book is far from an exhaustive exploration; nonetheless, the life stories and achievements of the African Americans you will discover in these pages are remarkable. That they chose our faith traditions as their religious home should fill us with pride; that they suffered the indignities that they did, at the hands of our spiritual ancestors, will fill us with shame. What I learned as I divined and despaired over the fate of these black trailblazers is that there will be other opportunities: New women and men will come forward. African

THE UNITARIANS

The American Unitarian Association (AUA) was founded on May 26, 1825, as an association of individuals whose sole purpose was to promote liberal Christianity through publishing tracts and sending out "agents." Some participants even protested these activities. Historian Earl Morse Wilbur wrote that, "Belonging generally to the conservative class, socially and politically, they were disposed to be complaisant and self-confident, and felt moved by no eager desire to make converts to their religion or to urge it upon others."[1] The divide between those who wanted to spread the faith and those who were reticent was still evident thirty-five years later in the proceedings of the AUA 1860 autumnal convention, described in the first essay of this collection. Titled "A Cold Shoulder for William Jackson," it recounts an event that could have radically changed the course of Unitarian history and its relationship to African Americans. The lack of outreach to the black community is best understood in the context of this ambivalence and the prejudice and elitism that lay behind it—a prejudice so entrenched that the most radical minister of that era, Theodore Parker, wrote in 1859, "An Anglo-Saxon with common sense does not like the Africanization of America; he wishes the superior race to multiply rather than the inferior."[2] Yet this belief did not keep him from being an outspoken abolitionist.

The abolition of slavery was another point of contention among Unitarians of that era. Broad support for abolition did not exist. Indeed, amidst strong anti-Negro prejudice and sometimes mob violence, Unitarian positions were diverse and the fledgling denomination was reluctant to take a stand. In the South, where there were only a handful of Unitarian congregations, ministers remained silent on the issue, although Charles A. Farley in Richmond and Theodore Clapp in New Orleans defended slavery. In the North, Daniel Webster and a few prominent ministers had been early supporters of the American Colonization Society's efforts to return free blacks to Africa. Others judged the discussion divisive and out of place in a free religious movement. Some, like Ezra Stiles Gannett, were as passionate in their desire to preserve the Union as the abolitionists were in their efforts to end slavery. Indeed, along with William Lloyd Garrison, they made up the leadership of the Massachusetts Antislavery Society. Yet even among the abolitionists, there were significant divisions. In 1854, Theodore Parker, a member of the Secret Six—which later financed John Brown's raid on Harper's Ferry—participated in the failed effort to forcefully stop the rendition of the slave Anthony Burns under the Fugitive Slave Law. Many more, while antislavery, were not abolitionist; they counseled moderation and argued for gradual emancipation. Moderate ministers, often men of principle trying to steer unsympathetic parishioners toward condemning slavery, were denounced as traitors by the more radical.

This was the context in which African-American abolitionists William Jackson, Frances Ellen Watkins Harper, and Peter H. Clark came into contact with Unitarians and developed an appreciation of Unitarianism. The essays about these three figures and Fannie Barrier Williams, who was a child during the Civil War, show how their lives were interwoven. Clark lived in Ohio, as did Harper, during the early 1850s, and later Clark worked with Harper's brother for Frederick Douglass in Rochester, New York. Harper knew Jackson, and it is difficult to imagine that Jackson's and Douglass's paths did not cross. Williams first met Douglass when she was a child, and he would call on her parents in Brockport, New York. In later years, she spoke at the 1893 Columbian Exposition World Congress of Representative Women, as did Harper and Susan B. Anthony. Douglass, who attended the first Women's Rights Convention in 1848 in Seneca Falls, New York, knew Anthony. Anthony, in turn, was a friend of Hester C. Whitehurst Jeffrey, an African-American suffragette, organizer, and Unitarian. She and Anthony were members of the Unitarian Church in Rochester. Indeed, Jeffrey was the only local layperson to deliver a eulogy at Anthony's funeral. Jeffrey, having moved to Rochester in 1891, was instrumental in erecting a statue of Frederick Douglass in that city, where he was buried. She, Harper, and Williams were involved in the 1896 formation of the National Association of Colored Women (NACW), whose motto was "Lifting as We Climb." The NACW was a merger of the National Federation of Afro-American Women, the National League of Colored Women, and the Women's Era Club, which was founded by Unitarians Florida Ruffin Ridley and Maria Baldwin, and Florida's mother, Josephine St. Pierre Ruffin, who sat on the Board of the National Association for the Advancement of Colored People with white Unitarian Mary White Ovington. Jeffrey, like Williams, Harper, Clark, the Ruffins and Baldwin, was part of a web of values, relationships, and institutions that connected these individuals to one another and to liberal religion.

Although Don Speed Smith Goodloe was born on the other side of the Civil War and the Emancipation Proclamation, he nonetheless followed in the path of those who preceded him. Like them, his concern was improving the conditions of African Americans, an endeavor that led him to enroll in Meadville Theological School. Founded in Meadville, Pennsylvania, in 1844, the seminary's mission was to spread liberal Christianity by training ministers to serve in the West. In this spirit, Meadville's president, Franklin Southworth, wrote to Jamaican Egbert Ethelred Brown about admitting Goodloe, "I believe myself that liberal Christianity has a mission to the blacks, whether it be labeled Unitarianism or not, and I want Meadville to help in solving the race problem."[3] By this time in its history, Meadville had already enrolled four African Methodist Episcopal (AME) students, the first in 1871. Between then and 2003, at least thirty-two people of color, about half of them black, would attend. Southworth's letter was written at the same time the AUA was trying to dissuade Brown from entering the ministry, but enter he did. Goodloe's story is followed by one about the first-ever African-American Unitarian minister, Clarence Bertrand Thompson. Between 1906, when Goodloe graduated from Meadville, and 1910, when Brown arrived, Thompson enrolled at Harvard, served a congregation for three years, and resigned.

Graduating in 1912, Brown returned to Jamaica, but by 1920 had emigrated to New York City. A newspaper article describes the unique ministry Brown founded in Harlem. In 1929, the AUA withdrew Brown's ministerial fellowship, and in 1938 refused the fellowship of William H. G. Carter or to recognize the Church of the Unitarian Brotherhood in Cincinnati, a congregation he started in 1932. The choices Goodloe made and the success he experienced as an educator and later as a businessman provide an instructive counterpoint to both Brown and Carter, who chose politics and ministry. How far might Unitarianism have come with the help of these able individuals had the AUA possessed the imagination to envision a more culturally diverse future?

Despite the indifference, paternalism, and, at times, outright hostility of the AUA administrations under Samuel A. Eliot and Louis C. Cornish, liberal religion continued to appeal to progressive, free-thinking blacks. Throughout the 1920s, 1930s, and 1940s, in what many considered the capital of the black world, Brown's Harlem Unitarian Church was a center of black radical discourse. In 1937, under the AUA presidency of Frederick May Eliot, the association's attitude toward African Americans began to change. This reformation, which grew stronger throughout the 1940s, is evident in the 1942 AUA General Assembly Resolution on Race Relations and the accompanying *Christian Register* article, "Basic Steps to Ethnic Democracy: WHAT CAN WE DO To Carry Out the Unitarian Resolution on Race Relations." "I Have Two Dreams," written by Brown in 1947, and "Why Brotherhood Week?" written a year later by Edward D. Smith-Green, a black member of the Fourth Unitarian Society of Brooklyn, are challenging but ultimately hopeful. So is a *Chicago Sun-Times* article about a sermon Rev. Lewis A. McGee delivered during Brotherhood Week in 1949. However, Eugene Sparrow's experience seeking settlement in 1950 was quite the opposite. His story is recounted in "The Candidacy of Eugene Sparrow." This section concludes with "On the Eve of Merger," which summarizes the situation within the AUA in 1961, as it was about to unite with the Universalist Church of America.

A COLD SHOULDER FOR WILLIAM JACKSON

On Thursday, October 11, 1860, a key incident of Unitarian history occurred in New Bedford, Massachusetts. The American Unitarian Association (AUA) was holding its annual autumnal convention there, discussing among other topics how the AUA might spread the good news about Unitarianism to more people. On the last morning of the three-day convention, African-American minister William Jackson stood and addressed the convention. What Jackson said was unprecedented; and the way the AUA responded prefigured the course of Unitarian race relations for the next century.

William Jackson was born in Norfolk, Virginia, on August 16, 1818, the youngest of ten children. His father, Captain Henry Jackson, was a pilot at the port of Norfolk, and his father's father owned ships that sailed to the West Indies, so it is not surprising that William went to sea while still a boy. Subsequently, his mother and father moved to Philadelphia, the city that William considered home. They had forsaken Virginia when, following the Nat Turner insurrection in 1831, draconian restrictions were placed upon "free colored people."

At sixteen, William began serving aboard the U.S. sloop of war *Vandalia*. After three years of hardship aboard the vessel, he was moved by a growing religious feeling to join a Baptist church. Soon after, he began preparing for the ministry, and in 1842, was ordained by the Oak Street Baptist Church in Philadelphia. He later served Baptist churches in New York and Delaware, before returning to the Oak Street Church. During his second tenure at the Oak Street Church, the Fugitive Slave Law was enacted.

The Fugitive Slave Law was part of the Compromise of 1850, an ultimately futile attempt to maintain national unity. Unitarian legislators argued on all sides—pro, con, and evasive—as the bill made its way into law. Joseph Grinnell, the U.S. representative from New Bedford from 1843 to 1850 and a lifelong member of the New Bedford Unitarian church, was conspicuously absent during the vote on the law—he didn't want to vote against it because he owned a cotton mill and depended on good relations with the southern states for a supply of cheap cotton. Unitarian Charles Sumner, senator from Massachusetts, was one of the law's most vociferous opponents. John C. Calhoun, vice president of the United States and a founder of All Souls Church, Unitarian, in Washington DC, staunchly defended slavery and states' rights. He literally rose from his deathbed to hear his friend Daniel Webster's address to the Senate. Webster, another senator and Unitarian, delivered a speech titled "Liberty and Union, One and Inseparable, Now and Forever," defending the rights of southern states to pursue fugitive slaves into the free states. And when Congress passed the Fugitive Slave Law, President Millard Fillmore, another Unitarian, signed it into law, hoping it would stave off war.

Soon afterward, fugitive slave William Taylor was arrested in Philadelphia, and in an act of civil disobedience, William Jackson led a group of men to rescue Taylor from jail. The story, as told by Jackson years later, reveals a good deal about his character:

> One William Taylor was the first fugitive slave that had been arrested following the passage of this law. Recognizing the "Higher Law" as being in force by Divine Authority and being superior to the Decree of a wicked Judge, and feeling a kindred sympathy with my brother as being bound with him, I felt morally and religiously impelled to strike for his freedom. The whole community had been thrown into the most terrible excitement over the arrest of Taylor, the fugitive slave. Whereupon I felt myself nerved with moral and physical courage to do my duty, and save a brother man from perpetual and

cruel bondage. Hence, as the leader of a band of brave men, we went forth and rescued the prisoner from the clutches of the Marshall. We arrayed him in the attire of a woman, and successfully landed him in a few hours on the shores of Canada, where he found shelter and friends in the city of Toronto. As the leader of the rescuing party, I was duly arrested and incarcerated in the city jail.

On learning of my imprisonment the colored people immediately assembled themselves together in their Churches, like those of old when Peter was imprisoned, where prayer was offered for my deliverance. A party of my friends and the members of my Church had met at the Parsonage . . . where they fervently invoked the blessing of God upon their imprisoned pastor, and earnestly prayed for his deliverance. Strange as this remarkable interposition of Providence in answer to the prayer may appear to some, I was soon released from the Jail by a writ of Habeas Corpus from Judge [King] obtained through the efforts of the Rev. Edgar [Levy] of the First Baptist Church, West Philadelphia, and [William W.] Keene and [Major] James M. Linnard, and presented to my people at the very time they were praying for my deliverance. It was certainly the most remarkable coincidence, how God in his mercy seemed to manifest himself in my behalf by putting it in to the hearts of these men to use every effort, at this unusual hour of the night, to secure my release from prison. Though it had been indicated by the officer at the time of my arrest that I should try to get bail, I surrendered myself up at once and made no effort in that direction, for I regarded it as no disgrace to be arrested and imprisoned under this infamous and inhuman law, or for advising my fellow men "that if they would be free themselves they must first strike the blow."[1]

In 1851, Jackson accepted the invitation of Second Baptist Church in New Bedford to come preach to them as their settled minister. For the first few months, William's wife, Jane Major Jackson, stayed in Philadelphia because three of their children were ill. While William was in New Bedford, one of their daughters died, but because of his responsibilities with his new church, he was unable to travel back to Philadelphia for her funeral. Indeed, only three of William and Jane's nine children survived to adulthood. Familiarity with personal tragedy must also have shaped his character.

At some point, William met a dynamic young woman named Frances Ellen Watkins who, after her marriage in 1860, would take on the name by which she is now best known, Frances Ellen Watkins Harper. As an abolitionist, she had lectured in New Bedford several times, beginning in 1854. She was also a well-known poet—America's first real protest poet. While living in Ohio, she had gotten to know some Unitarian abolitionists and conductors on the Underground Railroad. It was she who may have first introduced Jackson to Unitarianism.[2]

In 1858, a group of about ninety people decided to leave Second Baptist Church and form a new congregation. They invited William Jackson to be their minister, and after some consideration, he agreed. The new congregation was so successful that they soon purchased the old Centre Church building on North Sixth Street for $4,500. It had been built and used by a Unitarian congregation until 1854.

Salem Baptist Church was successful, yet Jackson kept thinking about Unitarianism. As an abolitionist, he likely would have known John Weiss, another abolitionist and minister of the New Bedford Unitarians until 1859; whether these two liberal New Bedford ministers ever met or talked about religion is not known. Weiss left New Bedford, and a new Unitarian minister named William J. Potter came to the city in late 1859. Evidence indicates that Jackson and Potter knew each other at least by reputation. All the while, Jackson edged closer to publicly declaring himself a Unitarian.

Then in 1860, the American Unitarian Association scheduled its autumnal convention to take place in New Bedford from Tuesday evening, October 9, through Thursday, October 11. William Jackson attended the convention and was moved by the sermon delivered by Rev. William Greenleaf Eliot on Wednesday evening. Jackson decided to make a public statement. On Thursday morning, he rose to address the autumnal convention of the American Unitarian Association, intending to declare his conversion to Unitarianism.

The autumnal conventions had been gathering only since 1842; indeed, the Unitarians had refused to organize themselves at a denominational level until 1825, when the AUA began as an association of individuals. Joining was completely optional. Most Unitarians were not members, and there was no requirement that a Unitarian church had to have AUA members in order to call itself Unitarian.

One of the AUA's earliest purposes was to publish tracts defending the Unitarian position against attacks from orthodox trinitarians. Over time the AUA, which held its annual business meetings in May, gradually began to do more than just publish tracts. By 1842, some ministers felt the need to meet "in the autumn for the purpose of awakening mutual sympathy and considering the wants of the Unitarian body."[3] These ministers instituted the autumnal conventions. From the beginning, practical subjects were addressed at these conventions, and both lay leaders and ministers were involved. The conventions continued until 1863, when they were disrupted by the Civil War. After the war, the autumnal conventions were replaced by a more efficient national organization, the National Conference of Unitarian Churches.

The 1860 convention in New Bedford had opened on Tuesday evening with a sermon by the renowned Rev. Dr. Frederick Henry Hedge, who spoke about the use of reason in religion. On Wednesday morning, Tracy Howe, a lay leader from the Cambridge, Massachusetts, Unitarian church, talked about the importance of spreading religion in the recently settled lands of the West. What kind of religion was needed? Any religion based on authority or fear would not do. No, the West needed the regenerating influences of a religion based on freedom; the West needed Unitarianism. Howe's talk prompted much discussion about the West and about Unitarian mission work in general. Daniel Foster, a minister from Kansas, agreed with Howe, saying that Unitarians must at once occupy the vast mission field of the West. The Unitarian minister from Haverhill, Massachusetts, disagreed, arguing that Unitarians simply did not do missionary work, and that Unitarians should remember that they had not come into being through missionary efforts. But then a Mr. Livermore from New York proposed that a collection be taken up then and there to support Foster and the Kansas mission field, and the leadership of the convention agreed.

Edward Everett Hale, a member of the executive committee that planned the convention, rose to say that the executive committee wanted the convention to think about broader efforts to spread Unitarianism. So Thomas Hill, president of Antioch College, told the story of what had happened to him when he visited one Unitarian church in Boston—he was given "an ill-kept stranger's seat by the side of the organ." Hill added that "such things chill the heart." And James Freeman Clarke spoke, saying that Unitarianism needed churches where all people, whether poor or rich, could come and feel at home.[4]

Thus ran the discussion on Wednesday, a discussion that tried to determine how Unitarianism could be welcoming to more people. The church building was filled to capacity. In addition to the official delegates to the convention, people from New Bedford who were not delegates also attended. They included Rev. William Jackson, who may have been the only African American at the convention.

Then, on Wednesday evening, came the sermon by William Greenleaf Eliot. Eliot had been born in New Bedford in 1811 to a Unitarian family. In 1834, he had been ordained as a Unitarian evangelist in Boston, and immediately went west, where he had founded a Unitarian church in St. Louis, Missouri; he was still the minister in St. Louis when he spoke to the autumnal convention in 1860. Saying that he was a Unitarian born, bred, and baptized, he asked how the Unitarian churches might be revived. His answer, perhaps unfamiliar to our ears today, resonated with at least one person in the audience that evening. Eliot said that Unitarian churches should be revived by "preaching Christ and him crucified."[5] Years later, William Jackson would write almost the same thing: that he always tried to preach "Christ & him crucified."[6] Eliot went on to put a Unitarian spin on this point. He said that Unitarians must always adhere to the principles of the use of reason and private judgment; that they could use the example of Jesus giving freely of himself in order to encourage Unitarians to contribute money towards establishing new Unitarian churches; and that the example of Jesus would lead Unitarians to engage in philanthropy and social justice.

After Eliot's sermon, it was time for dinner. According to the *New Bedford Evening Standard*, "the people proceeded to City Hall where the festival was to be held. The hall was thronged, and a very pleasant season was enjoyed. Tables were laid upon either side of the hall, which were loaded with the choicest of viands, fruits, &c."[7] The *New Bedford Mercury* reported that over a thousand people went to this festival to eat dinner.[8] Given the racial attitudes of the day, William Jackson probably did not attend.

The final business session of the meeting took place Thursday morning. The most important item of business was drafting a response to the West Christian Unitarian Union of England. The British Unitarians took their American co-religionists to task for not being aggressive enough in fighting slavery. In the past, the AUA had given lukewarm support, or no support at all, to antislavery efforts. But by 1860, the AUA had changed. Historian Douglas Stange wrote that "remarkably, the autumnal convention of the American Unitarian Association assigned two abolitionists to answer [the British Unitarians], a clear sign that abolitionism in America and in the Unitarian denomination had gained respectability."[9] Rev. Samuel J. May, a well-known Unitarian minister, was one of those two abolitionists who drafted the reply.

Perhaps William Jackson knew or recognized Samuel May; perhaps May's apparent respectability encouraged Jackson to think the AUA might be ready to welcome African Americans into their ranks. Certainly, the discussion on Thursday morning would have encouraged him. Several ministers and laypeople had spoken in support of increased funding for spreading Unitarianism. Then William Jackson rose to address the 1860 autumnal convention.

There he stood, a distinguished-looking man of forty-two, an experienced minister, an African-American man addressing a sea of white faces. He was about to tell these white Unitarians that he was one of them, that he too was a Unitarian.

There are three slightly different firsthand accounts of what Jackson said to the AUA. Because this is such a crucial moment for Unitarian history, we will consider all three. The *Christian Inquirer*, a Unitarian newspaper, reported,

> Rev. Mr. Jackson, the colored minister of New Bedford, had been converted [to Unitarianism]. He was converted yesterday by the essay. He should preach the Broad Church. He had learned that the religion of Jesus was universal, and gave all the right and privilege of thinking for themselves. As he was perhaps the only colored Unitarian minister, he hoped they would hear from him patiently. He then presented the claims of his church, which was in debt, and desired that some aid might be afforded him to discharge this debt. After some further remarks, a contribution of $49 was taken up, to which more was afterward added to lift the debt on Mr. Jackson's church.[10]

Let us give full credit to the gathered members of the AUA: In 2007 dollars, their contribution to Jackson's church would have amounted to about $1,100. They did give him a reasonably large sum of money. But the *Christian Inquirer* did not report that the AUA gave Jackson any encouragement along with the money.

The second firsthand account of this historic moment comes from the *New Bedford Mercury*:

> Rev. Mr. Jackson of New Bedford (colored) presented the claims of his own church and made an appeal for help as a recent convert to Unitarianism. . . .

> A contribution was taken up on behalf of Rev. Mr. Jackson's society, and the President announced that the sum of $49 was raised for that purpose, and $300 at [sic] the contribution of yesterday for Rev. Messrs. Foster and Brown of Kansas.[11]

This report puts into perspective how much money was raised for Jackson's church. According to the *New Bedford Mercury*, the white Unitarians from Kansas got six times as much money as the black Unitarians from New Bedford.

The final account of this historic moment gives a key piece of information that is not in the first two accounts, and therefore provides a more nuanced perspective. The *New Bedford Evening Standard* reported,

> Rev. Mr. Jackson, pastor of the Salem Baptist Church, (colored) of this city, addressed the Convention saying that he subscribed entirely to the doctrines advanced in the discourses which had been delivered before the body. He avowed himself as a convert to the doctrines of liberal Christianity, and should endeavor in the future to advocate those sentiments from his pulpit.
>
> Rev. Mr. [William J.] Potter, of this city, bore testimony to the character and integrity of Mr. Jackson. He suggested that a collection be taken up in aid of Mr. J.'s church, which was somewhat in debt.[12]

In this account, the key piece of information appears in the second paragraph—that William Potter publicly supported William Jackson, and Potter asked that a collection be taken. Potter, who had often emphasized intellectual freedom at the expense of political freedom, came through for Jackson. White William Potter stood up in front of the AUA and voiced his support for black William Jackson. Jackson testified to his conversion to Unitarianism, to the use of reason in religion, to the universality of Jesus. But it was Potter who told the AUA that they should contribute money to William Jackson and the very first African-American Unitarian church.

The rest of the white delegates at the autumnal convention, however, could not find it in themselves to voice their support for Jackson. Historian Douglas Stange described the historic moment in this widely quoted passage: "The Unitarians took a collection . . . and Mr. Jackson was sent on his way. No discussion, no welcome, no expression of praise and satisfaction was uttered, that the Unitarian gospel had reached the 'colored.' In truth, the antislavery forces had lost the battle, perhaps because many of them had never begun to wage it."[13]

William Jackson was indeed sent on his way. It seems probable that William J. Potter and other New Bedford Unitarians had expressed some sort of welcome, and they may have told Jackson about the convention and even encouraged him to attend. But the AUA, representing the denomination as a whole, declined to do anything more for Jackson than to give him some money. In 1860, the AUA simply wasn't ready to welcome people of color.

After the lack of enthusiasm shown by the AUA, William Jackson did not become a Unitarian. He stayed at Salem Baptist Church, and Salem Baptist Church remained Baptist. By 1863, the church was entirely free from debt. Jackson then asked for a leave of absence and joined the Union Army to participate in the Civil War. He became a chaplain to the famous Fifty-fourth Massachusetts Volunteer Infantry Regiment, commanded by the Unitarian colonel Robert Gould Shaw, and was the first person of color to receive a commission as an officer in the United States Army. He was then transferred to the newly formed Fifty-fifth Regiment, which participated in the assault on Fort Wagner while William Jackson was attached to it.

Following his military service, Jackson returned to the Salem Baptist Church, staying there until 1870. At about the time he left, Salem Baptist Church had some two hundred members, with seventy-five in the Sunday school. He served a Baptist congregation in New Jersey until his retirement in 1885, when he returned to live out his life in New Bedford. In retirement, he became a familiar figure at Cottage City on Martha's Vineyard, now known as Oak Bluffs. There he held the honorary position of town crier during the summer season. He died on May 19, 1909.

We can only regret that such a man as William Jackson was lost to Unitarianism, lament the loss of what might have been, and take a modicum of pride in the fact that Jackson thought enough of liberal religion to publicly declare himself a Unitarian.

—Dan Harper

Sources

Very little published material exists about William Jackson. I found primary source material in a few libraries and in private collections. Jackson's descendants have loaned a small but significant collection of correspondence to the research library of the Old Dartmouth Historical Society. A member of the New Bedford Historical Society loaned me a photocopy of the typescript "Memoir of Rev. William Jackson," dated 1899. "Fifty Years a Pastor: Interesting Career of Rev. William Jackson of This City," an article in the New Bedford Standard, *May 7, 1892, includes information from later in Jackson's life. Several newspapers of the day carried accounts of the 1860 autumnal convention. These include* New Bedford Mercury, *October 10, 11, and 12, 1860;* New Bedford Evening Standard, *October 11, 1860; and* Christian Inquirer, *October 20, 1860. A conversation with Joan Beaubion, director of the New Bedford Historical Society, also proved helpful in understanding Jackson's Unitarian connection. Jackson's service as a military chaplain is mentioned in several published works on the Fifty-fourth and Fifty-fifth Massachusetts Regiments.*

FRANCES ELLEN WATKINS HARPER
1825–1911

There is one aristocracy which must ever outrank them all, and that is the aristocracy of character; and it is the women of a country who help to mold its character, and to influence if not determine its destiny; and in the political future of our nation woman will not have done what she could if she does not endeavor to have our republic stand foremost among the nations of the earth, wearing sobriety as a crown and righteousness as a garment and a girdle.

—Frances Ellen Watkins Harper

On September 24, 1825, the same year that the American Unitarian Association (AUA) was founded, Frances Ellen Watkins Harper was born to free black parents in the slave state of Maryland. After losing her mother at the age of three and later her father, Harper came under the protection and tutelage of her abolitionist uncle, William Watkins of Baltimore. Watkins, a noted writer and orator, was also the founder and director of the Academy for Negro Youth. Harper's life reveals the unmistakable stamp of her uncle's early mentoring, academically and philosophically. Harper was educated at his academy until the age of thirteen, when she was forced to seek employment as a housekeeper and seamstress from 1838 to 1849. Until then, Harper's life had been that of a middle-class black female with the full benefits of education in the protective environment of her family. Taking advantage of her new situation,

Harper used the library of her employer—a Baltimore bookstore owner—and assembled her own writings. By 1846, she had published her first book of poetry, *Forest Leaves.*

In her lifetime, Frances Ellen Watkins Harper, the Bronze Muse, effectively integrated her passion for social justice in six different movements: abolitionism, suffrage, and temperance, as well as in the black literary, children's rights, and women's movements. One of the first black women to earn a living from her published writings, Harper was a shrewd businesswoman. Her lectures included excerpts from her poetry and copies of her books offered for sale. By the end of the century, Harper's prolific writings had produced a conservative estimate of over 100,000 books in print. Nonetheless, in 1866, following the death of her husband, Fenton Harper, after just six years of marriage, Harper was so destitute that her belongings were seized and auctioned. This financial crisis forced her to send her husband's children from his first marriage to his family and her daughter, Mary, to her own kin. Harper barely had time to grieve her husband's death and the departure of her stepchildren and daughter before setting out upon a grueling lecture tour through thirteen southern states that lasted from 1867 to 1871. She traveled at her own expense, "buttressed by meager audience collections and sales of her poetry."[1]

A staunch supporter of numerous institutions, Harper participated in all aspects of Sunday schools, YMCAs, women's clubs, and a wide variety of organizations—assuming leadership roles in many.[2] Her oratorical skills provided an entrée to the World Congress of Representative Women, the National Council of Women of the United States, and other high profile conferences. In her long career, she shared the platform with her friend Frederick Douglass, as well as Sojourner Truth, William L. Garrison, and Unitarian Lydia Maria Child. Equally impressive was her network of friends, which included Henry Highland Garner; John Brown and his wife, Mary; William C. Nell; Susan B. Anthony; Elizabeth Stanton; Fannie Barrier Williams; and Ida B. Wells. Harper counted William Still, one of the most notable black conductors of the Underground Railroad, as a friend; and she may have even been a conductor herself.

Harper's many "firsts" included her appointment in 1850 as the first female instructor at Union Seminary, the precursor to Wilberforce University in Columbus, Ohio, an African Methodist Episcopal (AME) school established for free blacks.

She was awarded a day on the Red Letter Calendar of the World Women's Christian Temperance Union, posthumously in 1922, the only black woman to receive the honor. In 1854, she published *Poems on Miscellaneous Subjects*. The same year, Harper was employed by the Maine Anti-Slavery Society to carry their message across the Northeast. For the next six years, she toured eight states, representing several different antislavery societies.

Harper's contributions were ground-breaking as a "doer of the word," dedicated to freedom and elevation of her race.[3] Her oratorical skills were legendary. Some attendees, having never heard a woman speak in public, were astounded by her eloquence and articulate delivery. Harper never charged blacks at her lectures, presumably to encourage black attendance. Her close friend William Still wrote in the introduction to her first novel, *Iola Leroy*,

> The kind of meetings she took greatest interest in were meetings called exclusively for women. In this attitude she could pour out her sympathies to them as she could not do before a mixed audience; and indeed she felt their needs were far more pressing than any other class.[4]

Harper's lectures, poetry, and novels challenged people by utilizing Judeo-Christian teachings and the moral codes of Protestantism. Her writings often depicted historical biblical figures struggling with right and wrong; this effort to transfer and superimpose biblical figures and their struggles onto the issue of slavery is obvious in all her writings. By doing so, Harper, a Christian-inspired writer, astutely drew on a long tradition that connected the travails of others to blacks suffering under slavery:

> What I ask of American Christianity is not to show us more creeds, but more of Christ; not more rites and ceremonies, but more religion glowing with love and replete with life,—religion which will be to all weaker races an uplifting power, and not a degrading influence. Jesus Christ has given us a platform of life and duty from which all oppression and selfishness is necessarily excluded. While politicians may stumble on the barren mountains of fretful controversy and ask in strange bewilderment, "What shall we do with the weaker races?" I hold that Jesus Christ answered that question nearly two thousand years since. "Whatsoever ye would that men should do to you, do you even so to them."[5]

Harper located blacks in Christian sacred history and emphasized the Christian belief in human frailty, suffering, and human redemption. She focused on the experiences of blacks in slavery—a people struggling to survive while at the same time grappling with issues of social identity. Often she wrote about characters who learned of their mixed heritage and then were forced to choose along racial lines because of prevailing social norms. This approach allowed Harper to demonstrate the false imposition of race as a social construct. She also depicted the ethical issues faced by both blacks and whites living with the reality of slavery.

Three works by Harper were rediscovered in the last few decades: *Minnie's Sacrifice*, *Sowing and Reaping*, and *Trial and Triumph*—originally serialized in the *Christian Recorder*, the official journal of the AME Church. These texts appeared in approximately ten-year intervals in the Recorder. They are significant because they represent the first substantial body of fiction known to have been written specifically for a black audience, and primarily, a newly literate one. Blacks were clearly Harper's audience, but it can be argued that she also used her writings and certainly her speaking to bridge the racial divide between whites and blacks. While her writings contained binary good and evil, white and black characters, Harper strove to render a range of personalities and stories that included both compassionate and evil whites along with both virtuous and scandalous blacks. Furthermore, Harper used her writings to educate whites about slavery and its effects.

Frances Ellen Watkins Harper maintained religious affiliations in two very different worlds, the AME church and Unitarianism. Pew rental payments document that she was a member of the Unitarian church on Chestnut Street in Philadelphia from 1870 until her death in 1911, with Rev. William Henry Furness serving as minister at the time of her membership.[6] However, for reasons still unknown, Harper failed to write about or otherwise document her relationship to Unitarianism.

Harper first became acquainted with Unitarians before the Civil War, as a result of mutual interests in both the abolitionist movement and the Underground Railroad. Her friend, Peter H. Clark, noted abolitionist and educator in Ohio, had become a Unitarian in 1868. When Harper and her daughter settled in Philadelphia in 1870, she joined the First Unitarian Church. She navigated the boundary in her religious expressions, defying denominational affiliations and sectarianism, and challenging the social norms of her day in every area of her life, including religion. Harper also maintained membership at (Mother) Bethel AME Church. She worked with a number of black churches in North Philadelphia, her community. She also joined forces with Rev. Henry L. Phillips at the Church of the Crucifixion to fight juvenile delinquency. Her daughter, Mary, emulated her mother and taught Sunday school at the Church of the Crucifixion. Harper was a member of the Sarah Allen Missionary Association, which fed the poor and children, and she taught Sunday school at Mother Bethel AME Church while a member of the Unitarian Church. When Harper died on February 22, 1911, her funeral services were held at the Unitarian Church.

Frances Ellen Watkins Harper's life exemplified free black antebellum women who used literacy, one of their primary class privileges, to write and speak about issues of justice and freedom. Her writings, while primarily directed towards blacks, also helped whites by providing personal accounts of the suffering blacks experienced under slavery. Her ability to build empathy utilizing Protestant rhetoric and biblical narratives to make linkages and connections in whites' lives demonstrated a rare creative gift. Her works, spanning more than six decades, have become required reading in literature and gender studies.

On September 27, 1992, at the end of the Continental Congress of African American Unitarian Universalists, Rev. Daniel Aldridge organized a group to place a headstone on the unmarked grave of this woman who had provided a prophetic voice in the wilderness of our country's early years. The event occurred one hundred years after the publication of *Iola Leroy*, Harper's best-known novel. During preparations for the ceremony, the original headstone was found sunk beneath the soil. Nevertheless, the new headstone was placed upon her grave as a salute and in appreciation of Frances Ellen Watkins Harper.

—Qiyamah Rahman

Sources

The main sources of information on Frances Ellen Watkins Harper include Melba Joyce Boyd's book, Discarded Legacy: Politics and Poetics in the Life of Frances E. W. Harper 1825–1911, *and Frances Foster's* A Brighter Coming Day: A Frances Ellen Watkins Harper Reader. *The A.M.E. Church Review contained installments of her writings that were helpful background reading, as was Jane E. Rosecrans's paper "Between Black and White: Frances Ellen Watkins Harper and Philadelphia Unitarianism," which she graciously shared. Individuals who attended the Continental Congress of African-American Unitarian Universalists in Philadelphia in 1992 and participated in a ceremony placing a headstone on Harper's gravesite provided a contemporary link between my research and her life.*

PETER H. CLARK
1828–1925

In Greenwood Hall, by the politicians and religious friends of Thomas Paine, in this city, Mr. Peter Clark, a colored teacher in the schools, was one of the orators, and made public avowal of his full belief in the religious and political tenants of that Philosopher. In his presence, a number of toasts and sentiments were given to an unknown god, which gave friends of the children in the schools which he taught, great pain and dissatisfaction, the more so when he publicly proclaimed that his only hopes for the ultimate happiness of the colored race, were based on the full and final triumph of the Tom Paine doctrines, religious and political. The colored board of trustees immediately removed him from the school as teacher, but replaced him on the written agreement by him that he would not publicly participate further in the movements of the "Liberals," an Infidel Association then meeting weekly.

—Daily Cincinnati Gazette

Peter Humphries Clark was a gifted educator, abolitionist, writer, and speaker, whose Unitarian faith and radical ideas about black education and equality often collided with the prejudice and politics of his day. He was a man of mixed-race heritage. Betty, his paternal grandmother, "belonged to" John Clark, a slave trader in Harrison County, Kentucky, who was his paternal grandfather.[1] Freed after John's death, Betty and her children moved to Cincinnati. Peter's father, Michael Clark, was a successful barber and community activist. He established the Colored Orphan Asylum of Cincinnati in 1845 to house and feed black children, a cause which Peter supported throughout much of his life.

Knowing the value of a good education, Michael sent his son to private schools and secured him a job as an apprentice in a printing shop owned by a white abolitionist. However, when the shop owner sold the business, the new owner refused to have a black apprentice and fired Peter.

At about the same time, his father passed away, and Clark took over the family barber business but found this work abhorrent. Required to cater to the prejudices of white customers, particularly their insistence that he not allow other blacks in the shop, Clark quit the business. According to biographer Walter Herz, Clark declared that "he would never shave another white man, and, if he did, he would cut his throat."[2]

In 1849, the Ohio Legislature approved the creation of the state's first "colored" public high school. Clark's uncle and close friend, John I. Gaines, had led the campaign to establish the school, and Clark was hired as its first African-American teacher. The scandal over his religious and political views led to his dismissal in 1852. Rehired in 1857, he went on to serve as principal of Gaines High School from 1866 to 1886. During his tenure, the institution became nationally recognized for its achievements in educating African-American youth. Many of the graduates of the school stayed in the area and became the foundation of Cincinnati's black middle class.

Between the time of his firing and his return to Cincinnati's school system, Clark had become deeply involved in abolitionist efforts. He was active in the Ohio Conventions of Colored Men, editing and publishing its weekly newsletter and briefly publishing his own abolitionist newspaper called the *Herald to Freedom*. He moved to Rochester, New York, in 1855 to join Frederick Douglass as assistant editor of Douglass's widely-circulated abolitionist newspaper. The following year, he was appointed secretary of the

National Convention of Colored Men and traveled the Midwest making abolitionist speeches. Through his relationship with Douglass, Clark became friends with Frances Ellen Watkins Harper, a popular African-American poet, abolitionist speaker, and later, member of the First Unitarian Church of Philadelphia.

Clark married Francis Ann Williams in 1854. The couple had two sons and a daughter, all of whom attended the Gaines School and went on to successful careers in politics and the arts. Clark's family and extended family were active members of the Allen Temple, Cincinnati's largest African Methodist Episcopal (AME) church.

Around 1857, he became friends with Alphonso Taft and George Hoadly, two prominent local attorneys who were members of Cincinnati's First Congregational Unitarian Church. These men introduced Clark to their liberal faith, and he began regularly attending services with them. Attracted by the abolitionist sermons and deist theology of the church's minister, Clark became a member of First Unitarian Church in 1868, its first and only black member until 1952. Clark joined the church's Unity Club and served as its treasurer for almost two decades. The club presented well-received lectures about abolitionist topics, and Clark used these occasions to help raise money for the Black Orphan Asylum. In 1871, Clark traveled with Rev. Thomas Vickers and a delegation from Cincinnati's First Church to the annual meeting of the National Conference of Unitarian Churches in New York City, making him one of the first blacks to represent a congregation at a Unitarian convention.

Throughout this time, Clark remained a member of the Allen Temple, and records show that both congregations were aware of his involvement with the other. Like his friend Frances Ellen Watkins Harper and other liberal religious African Americans of the day, he retained his connections to the black church as a way of keeping important ties to the community.

Membership in the Unitarian church gave him access to many political leaders who were sympathetic to the cause of black citizens.

As one of the most prominent black Republican figures in the Ohio Valley, Clark concentrated his political efforts on securing a national civil rights law, which would enforce the rights guaranteed to black citizens in the Fourteenth and Fifteenth Amendments to the U.S. Constitution. In 1873, he organized Ohio's black leaders in an effort to pressure the Republican Party to move forward with promised civil rights legislation. When the Republicans failed to deliver, these leaders began encouraging black voters to support only candidates who were responsive to their cause, regardless of political party.

Clark came to embrace socialism as a political philosophy and worked with the Workingman's Party, speaking publicly in support of the workers and against federal intervention during the Great Railroad Strike of 1877. That same year, he ran for Ohio commissioner of education as a candidate of the Socialist Party. Such political views made him unpopular not only with whites but also with many in the African-American community.

In 1882, Clark switched his allegiance to the Democratic Party and played an important role in the election of his friend George Hoadley as Ohio's first Democratic governor since the end of the Civil War. Within six months, Hoadley secured the repeal of most of Ohio's Black Laws and nominated prominent black leaders to several state offices, including appointing Clark as the first black trustee of the Ohio State University.

Clark had long been an advocate of mixed-race schools, believing that blacks would receive a better education in a mixed environment. But when all-white boards took over control of Ohio's black schools in 1885 and began advocating for mixed-race school legislation, Clark opposed the bill based on his concern that white parents would not allow blacks to serve as teachers for their children. He feared that without mixed-race authority, black students would become targets for insults and harassment. He ultimately lost this battle, and over the next decade, graduation rates for African-American students in Ohio schools decreased dramatically.

The following year, Republicans took control of the Cincinnati School Board and summarily fired Clark from his long-held position as principal of Gaines High School. This dismissal was seen by many as retribution for his support of Democratic candidates. It also sent a strong message to other black leaders that they would receive the same treatment if they attempted to wield too much political power.

Clark and his wife relocated to Huntsville, Alabama, where he took a job as principal of the State Normal School for one year before moving on to St. Louis to teach at the Sumner School, the first high school for African-American students west of the Mississippi River. He retired in 1908.

Clark remained unchurched from the time he left Cincinnati until his death in 1925 at the age of ninety-six. In his will, he did not designate any religious rituals for his burial but did request that "Thanatopsis," a poem by Unitarian William Cullen Bryant, be read at his graveside. Clark's Unitarian faith was shared by only one other member of his immediate family, his daughter Consuelo, who became an active member of the Unitarian Church of Youngstown, Ohio.

Throughout his life, Clark believed that full citizenship for blacks was the key to ending discrimination, and that social equality would follow if race-based laws were repealed. Constantly encountering the harsh realities of the "color bar," he used his frustration and great talents as a writer, speaker, and organizer to build support for changing attitudes about race in public education and in the wider society.

In an 1885 letter to President Grover Cleveland, then Ohio governor George Hoadley said of his friend Peter Clark, "His color has kept him in the shadows; had he been a white man, there is no position in the state to which he might not have aspired."[3]

—Bruce Beisner

Sources

A prime source of information on Peter H. Clark is Walter Herz's essay in the Unitarian Universalist Historical Society's "Dictionary of Unitarian Universalist Biography." Other sources I drew on for this article are "In His Veins Coursed No Bootlicking Blood: The Career of Peter H. Clark," by Lawrence Grossman, from Ohio History *(Vol. 86), writings by Clark posted at BlackPost.org, and two unpublished essays by Walter Herz in the archives of First Unitarian Church of Cincinnati.*

FANNIE BARRIER WILLIAMS
1855–1944

I have still many white friends and the old home and school associations are still sweet and delightful and always renewed with pleasure, yet I have never quite recovered from the shock and pain of my first bitter realization that to be a colored woman is to be discredited, mistrusted, and often meanly hated.

—Fannie Barrier Williams

Fannie Barrier had a pleasant upbringing in a mostly white town in upstate New York, where racism did not impinge on her family life. She was born in Brockport in 1855, ten years before the end of the Civil War. Her parents' friend, the fiery abolitionist Frederick Douglass, would sometimes visit from nearby Rochester, but the conversations about terrible conditions for black people in other places had no personal meaning for her until later.

The three Barrier children were the only African Americans in their public school. Fannie, the youngest, was a bright, personable, attractive child, popular with teachers and classmates. A talented artist and musician, she often sang and played the piano in the First Baptist Church, where her well-respected parents were leaders. Christian religion was an important part of her youth.

Fannie's brother George became an inspector for Detroit's Public Works, and sister Ella became a teacher and principal in Washington DC. Fannie entered the classical program at Brockton Normal School, and in 1870 was the first African American to graduate. Inspired by reports of women going to former slave states to teach in the new Freedmen's Bureau schools during Reconstruction, Fannie joined the movement so she could contribute to the uplifting of black children and adults, and widen her cultural awareness. There for the first time, she felt the degrading force of segregation. In defiance, she took advantage of her light skin and genteel manner when in the South and sat in train cars reserved for whites. In one incident, she spoke French to a questioning conductor and calmed herself by remembering that she had French ancestry and that "their barbarous laws did not allow a lady to be both comfortable and honest."[1]

Wanting to advance her artistic skills while teaching in the South, Fannie persuaded a painting teacher to let her take lessons in her spare time, only to be humiliated when she found herself screened off from the white students in the class. She took a hiatus from teaching to enroll in the Boston Music Conservatory to study piano. But when forced to leave because Southern white students objected to her presence, she learned that the phenomenon of racial prejudice was national, though usually less brutal in the North. Because of these experiences, she dedicated her life to seeking fair treatment and equal justice, especially for black women.

For a number of years, Fannie Barrier also taught school in Washington DC. There she studied painting at the School of Fine Arts, excelling in portraiture. She socialized with educated blacks and met a brilliant law student named S. Laing Williams. After their marriage in 1887, they moved to Chicago to a closely knit African-American community on the South Side, where Laing began a successful law practice. In addition, he established the Prudence Crandall Study Club, named for the white woman attacked for opening a school for black girls. It was limited to twenty-five couples from the city's African-American elite. Fannie served as director of art and music.

Laing and Fannie Williams, who had no children, were an asset to Chicago's burgeoning reform movements. They fostered not only cultural activities for African Americans but also humanitarian aid for those in need. Though forced to live in segregated housing, they became friends with white activists such as Jane Addams, founder of Hull House, and Mary MacDowell, director of the University of Chicago Settlement. Meatpacker Philip D. Armour gave generously to the biracial Provident Hospital that the Williamses helped establish, which included a training school for black nurses barred from other institutions.

Searching for a religious community to join, the Williamses were attracted to the Unitarian Church of All Souls. The free-thinking white minister, Jenkin Lloyd Jones, was a strong supporter of civil rights for all, women's suffrage, and the ordination of female preachers. In 1905, Jones was instrumental in the church's establishment of the Abraham Lincoln Centre, an integrated welfare agency that still exists. A fervent pacifist, he was also a founder of the World's Parliament of Religions, which played an important role in Fannie Barrier Williams's rise to national fame. Considered radical even by many Unitarians, Jones's harsh criticisms of traditional Christianity and his vigorous social activism influenced Williams's increasingly progressive ideas regarding religion and her desire to help improve the lives of struggling African Americans.

At All Souls Church, Williams met Celia Parker Woolley. A white Unitarian minister, at that moment without a pulpit, Woolley was nonetheless involved in many causes. The two formed a close friendship that lasted until Woolley's death in 1918. Together they founded the Frederick Douglass Centre, modeled after Hull House, which fostered cordial race relations and offered lectures, discussions, concerts, and classes of all kinds. A popular place for middle-class whites and blacks across Chicago to socialize, it also provided support services and education for those less fortunate.[2] Woolley served as the institution's first director with Williams's active support.

Twelve years earlier, in 1893, the Columbian Exposition had come to South Side Chicago. No black women were asked to help with the exhibits, so to appease protestors, thirty-eight-year-old

Fannie Williams was appointed to use her organizing and artistic skills in the women's hall. More important, she was invited to speak at the World's Congress of Representative Women. And perhaps at the urging of Rev. Jones and Rev. Woolley, she gave a talk at the World's Parliament of Religions. She greatly impressed both audiences with her self-confidence, eloquence, and courageous remarks on highly sensitive topics. Her petite beauty and vitality also charmed the listeners.

In her first speech, "The Intellectual Progress of the Colored Women of the United States since the Emancipation Proclamation," Williams stressed how far former slaves had come in thirty years, despite painful hindrances of discrimination, particularly in employment. These women, determined to support themselves and their families, were hard-working, responsible, and eager for the education and skills denied them during bondage and still in the 1890s. Williams praised white people who aided those striving to better their lives and begged all to judge individuals by worth rather than race and to help "avert the arrows of prejudice that pierce the soul because of the color of our bodies."[3] In the audience was seventy-five-year-old Frederick Douglass. Moved by her remarks and those of the other "refined, educated, colored ladies" who spoke to the Congress, he predicted that "a new heaven is dawning upon us, and a new earth is ours."[4]

In her second speech, "Religious Duty to the Negro," Williams excoriated Christians who enslaved Africans and preached a "false, pernicious, demoralizing Gospel" to make them dependent and docile. The masters dared not "open the Bible too wide" and expose the hypocrisy of their atrocious acts. She extolled, however, those Christian churches after the Civil War that "came instantly, heroically, and powerfully to the rescue" of newly freed people, especially with education resources they desperately needed and desired.[5]

"What can religion further do for the colored people?" she asked her audience. Her provocative answer—"More religion and less church. . . . Less theology and more of human brotherhood, less declamation and more common sense and love for truth"—undoubtedly sprang from Jenkin Lloyd Jones's liberal Unitarianism. The advancement of African Americans had been obstructed, she continued, by the "tendency of creeds and doctrine to obscure religion, to make complex that which is elemental and simple, to suggest partisanship and doubt in that which is universal and certain."[6]

After her highly acclaimed talks, Fannie Williams was invited to speak in venues across the land, and these sometimes included a piano concert as part of the presentation. But even with her new fame, racism still impacted Williams's life. In 1894, she was nominated for membership in the prestigious eight-hundred-member Chicago Woman's Club by its former president Celia Parker Woolley and two other white friends. A minority vociferously objected. Clearly, she met the eligibility requirements. The only problem was her color. The dispute, widely publicized, continued for fourteen months. Williams was dismayed but refused to withdraw her name and was finally voted in by a strong majority, causing some members to resign. Years later, in 1924, she was honored to be the first African American and first woman appointed to the board of the Chicago Public Library.

In addition, Williams wrote many articles for African-American publications and, with Booker T. Washington, co-edited *A New Negro for a New Century: An Accurate and Up-to-Date Record of the Upward Struggles of the Negro Races.* She and her husband also worked closely with Washington on a biography of Frederick Douglass. They were early members of the National Association for the Advancement of Colored People and had a good relationship with one of its founders, W.E.B. DuBois, despite his feud with their close friend Washington over how to best educate free blacks.

For the most part, Fannie Williams enjoyed a privileged, cultured life, but her heart ached for all the black women who struggled to survive in a society that barred them from education and employment for which they were capable. Even for herself, she wrote, "whether I live in the North or the South, I cannot be counted for my full value."[7] With persistent zeal, she urged businessmen to hire competent black females, sometimes quoting scripture to prick their moral consciences, and she challenged real-estate segregation codes as well. A major contribution was her leadership in founding a federation of clubs, which later became the National Association of Colored Women, that taught literacy, homemaking, and job skills, and provided child care, savings banks, employment bureaus, and mutual support for black women across the land. She also worked for the right to vote. After Susan B. Anthony died in 1906, Williams was the only African American invited to give a eulogy at the national suffrage convention.

In 1926, five years after her husband's death, Fannie Barrier Williams, at age seventy-one, returned to Brockport, New York, and lived the next eighteen years in the Barrier family home with her sister Ella. Their brother George had died in Detroit in 1907; Fannie died in 1944, and Ella a year later. The sisters were buried alongside their parents in the town's small High Street Cemetery. The home was designated a New York state historical site in 1998.

When Williams's activism and health declined, so did her recognition. An impassioned advocate, she had fought hard for equal rights and opportunities, especially for black women born into slavery or born free but faced with blatant discrimination. Even though her faith was "often strained to the breaking point," she wrote, "I dare not cease to hope and aspire and believe in human love and justice."[8]

—June Edwards

Sources

"A Northern Negro's Autobiography" and other articles by Fannie Barrier Williams, reprinted in The New Woman of Color: The Collected Writings of Fannie Barrier Williams, 1893–1918, *by Mary Jo Deegan, were primary sources on Williams's life, theology, and beliefs about the plight of African Americans. Some others I consulted were Wanda Hendricks's article on Williams in* Black Women in America:

An Historical Encyclopedia; *Koby Lee's "Friendship Across the Color Line: Celia Parker Woolley and Fannie Barrier Williams," a 1997 occasional paper for the Unitarian Universalist Women's Heritage Society; and family obituaries and newspaper articles in the archives at Drake Memorial Library at the State University of New York at Brockport.*

DON SPEED SMITH GOODLOE
1878–1959

I find this morning in putting the possibilities squarely before him that he has come here with his eyes open, knowing that it is not a good way into the orthodox ministry, but ready to take the consequences. . . . What the Negroes need in his judgment more than emotionalism in religion and more even than industrialism in education, is moral teaching and preaching. He proposes, with the help of his wife, to start a small school composed of carefully selected and choice students, and to run the school along with his Sunday preaching. . . . And he will succeed.

—Franklin Southworth

Don Speed Smith Goodloe was born in Lowell, in the Appalachian foothills of eastern Kentucky, in 1878. When he was fifteen, he enrolled in nearby Berea College. Attending their Grammar School and Academy from 1893 to 1898, he completed his sophomore year in the academy in the literary curriculum.

Berea College was founded in 1855 by Presbyterian abolitionist John G. Fee. Believing that God had made all peoples of the earth of one blood, he shaped the school to reflect the values of love, human dignity, equality, and peace with justice. He opened its doors to all races, colors, genders, and classes, and never charged tuition—all students were expected to work. About half the Berea students were black and half white until 1904, when Kentucky passed a law requiring schools to be segregated, as permitted by the 1896 landmark U.S. Supreme Court *Plessy v. Ferguson* decision, which upheld the constitutionality of segregation under the doctrine of "separate but equal." This Supreme Court ruling drove a wedge between black and white societies until the 1954 *Brown v. Board of Education of Topeka*, when the Court, in a 9–0 decision, overturned *Plessy* and other rulings by declaring that separate public schools for black and white students were "inherently unequal," and denied black children equal educational opportunities.

From 1898 to 1899, Goodloe attended Knoxville College, a historically black college in Tennessee founded by the United Presbyterian Church. There he met Fannie Carey, and they married after she graduated in 1899. At Knoxville, Goodloe observed firsthand the educational philosophy he would later follow in Bowie, Maryland. Knoxville College, founded in 1875 as a normal school for training black teachers, followed the self-help philosophy of General Samuel Armstrong at Hampton Institute in Virginia, which was later spread by Booker T. Washington, a Hampton graduate, as head of Tuskegee Institute in Alabama. The philosophy was that blacks should receive moral training and a practical industrial education, obtaining skills such as brick making, carpentry, and agriculture, as well as business and teacher training. At Knoxville, students built most of the buildings on campus, cut the timber, and made a million bricks on site. When, in 1877, the school was designated a college, it began offering classics, science, theology, agriculture, industrial arts, and medicine in addition to industrial training.

Goodloe began his career as principal of a black public school at Newport, Tennessee, fifty miles east of Knoxville, from 1899 to 1900. It was there that Don Burrowes, the Goodloes' first son, was born. In 1900, they moved to Greenville, Tennessee, where Goodloe became teacher and principal of Greenville College, a black normal school. The next year, they moved back to Lowell, Kentucky. Goodloe taught again from 1901 to 1903, and Fannie gave birth to Wallis.

An avid reader of newspapers of the day, Goodloe no doubt watched Booker T. Washington's success in raising money from white donors, educating black students, and even being invited by Teddy Roosevelt to eat dinner at the White House in 1901. He also would have followed news of Washington's acceptance of segregation in his 1895 Atlanta Exposition speech. W.E.B. DuBois labeled the speech "The Atlanta Compromise" and Washington, "the Great Accommodator."[1] Washington appealed to middle-class whites across the South, asking them to give blacks a chance to work and develop separately, while implicitly promising not to demand the vote. White leaders across the North, from politicians to industrialists, from philanthropists to churchmen, enthusiastically supported Washington, as did most middle-class blacks.

After being a student at two normal schools and further schooled as a teacher and principal in two other normal schools and a black public school, Goodloe felt the need to continue his formal education by studying for his bachelor's degree. Berea College was no longer an option because of the school segregation law, so he moved his family once again, this time to Meadville, Pennsylvania. It was there that their third son, Carey, was born. In Meadville, Goodloe could earn not only his bachelor's degree from Allegheny College, a liberal arts school founded in 1815, but also a divinity degree from Meadville Theological School. But first he found employment to support his family, now two sons and a pregnant wife. Then he set himself the formidable task of enrolling simultaneously in both schools.

He entered Meadville realizing that it was unlikely a Unitarian church would ordain him—no Unitarian congregation had ever ordained a black minister. He also knew that a degree from a Unitarian seminary was not the best way to find work as a preacher in the Methodist Church, in which he was an elder, or among other mainstream Christians. Indeed, his son Wallis stated that his father never considered the possibility of becoming a minister.[2] And as Meadville president Franklin Southworth explained in a letter, Goodloe wanted to prepare for his dream of starting his own school with Fannie, where he would provide members of his race with less "emotionalism in religion" and more "moral teaching and preaching."[3] Goodloe graduated from both schools in 1906. He was the second black student to graduate from Allegheny. The college yearbook, in its roast of Goodloe, stated that he was "Bound to displace Booker T. Washington."[4]

After graduating, his first job was teacher at Danville (Kentucky) Normal School, just twenty miles west of his family home in Lowell. In addition to teaching, he also engaged in business to support his family. Then, in 1910, he was hired as vice principal of Manassas Industrial School for Colored Youth in Virginia.

When he heard that the Maryland Board of Education was relocating its normal school for black students from Baltimore to a 187-acre farm in Bowie, and was looking for a principal, he applied.

In 1911, at age thirty-three, Goodloe became the first principal of the Maryland Normal and Industrial School at Bowie for the Training of Colored Youth, now Bowie State University. The family moved again, this time into a newly constructed administration building. Female students lived upstairs, and Fannie was their matron. Boys lived in the barn. Goodloe began a ten-year stint developing the school to provide instruction in carpentry, blacksmithing, plastering, papering, and shoemaking for the male students, and domestic science, such as sewing and millinery work, for the women—along with preparing students to teach in the black-only elementary schools. The academic curriculum was equal to the ordinary high school course and included English, arithmetic, algebra, history, geography, geometry, music, government, physics, botany, Latin, and German.

Each year, Goodloe prepared a report to the board of education about the condition of the school. Often, he would address the state legislature on the needs of the school, and according to his son Wallis, Goodloe was a persuasive speaker. In May 1912, he reported, "While the school is like all State institutions, strictly undenominational and unsectarian, the atmosphere is Christian . . . and every effort is bent towards influencing and molding their characters to the end that the highest ideals of service to race and country may obtain. D.S.S. Goodloe, Principal."[5]

During his decade-long tenure, Goodloe established a faculty of ten members, student enrollment of eighty, an admission requirement of completion of seventh grade, a model elementary school for student teachers, a summer session, a new dormitory for women, and renovation of the living quarters for men, and he added an additional year to the course. He made many pleas for increased funding before the legislature in Annapolis. These would have enabled a more rapid development of the school and the possibility of upgrading the curriculum to the standards used at Maryland's two white normal schools, but the legislature's appropriations continued to favor the latter.

In 1916, Goodloe and Fanny built a house of their own, utilizing an African-American architect. They hired local black workers, who cut lumber and made bricks on the property. Some seventy years later, it would be listed in the National Register of Historic Places.

In 1918, as a result of World War I, the worldwide outbreak of influenza, and the high cost of living, Bowie enrollment plunged to thirty-six students. Following the war, however, the number of students rebounded to sixty-nine.

Little is known about why Goodloe resigned his post in 1921 at the age of forty-three. He told one friend that he was simply tired of being principal. His sons believed that the state board may not have renewed his contract because of his criticism of the county school superintendent for failing to provide adequate elementary and secondary education to black children. Perhaps he had struggled too aggressively to improve black education in Maryland, and in doing so, ruffled many feathers at a time when Jim Crow prevailed. Indeed, white mobs had lynched at least fourteen blacks in Maryland in the twenty years before Goodloe arrived, and two during his tenure at Bowie. But on December 28, 1920, he must have been gratified to receive a letter from the annual meeting of the Maryland State Colored Teachers' Association saying, "We commend Dr. D.S.S. Goodloe for the constant and progressive fight he has made toward enriching of the curriculum and the uplifting of the standards of the Bowie State Normal School."[6]

The year after leaving the school, he became vice president, general manager, auditor, and actuary of the Standard Benefit Society of (Baltimore) Maryland, which issued "sick, accident, whole life and endowment policies,"[7] a year later becoming its president. He grew prosperous and later moved to Washington DC.

Goodloe died there in 1959, having achieved his goal of helping children of his race with "moral teaching and preaching," not in a school of his own, but in a public normal school that later became Bowie State University. His memorial service was held at All Souls Church, Unitarian, where his son, Don B. Goodloe, was a member.

—Richard Morris

Sources

Primary sources of information on Don Speed Smith Goodloe are Who's Who of the Colored Race: A General Biographical Dictionary of Men and Women of African Descent, *Vol. 1, 1915, p. 117, by Frank Lincoln Mather, and the "At-a-Glance History" of Bowie State University (www.bowiestate.edu/about/AtAGlance). Other sources for this article are the Meadville Lombard Theological School Archives, annual reports of Bowie Normal School that Goodloe prepared for the state Board of Education, college archives, and U.S. census records. Copies of most articles reside in the Goodloe Archives at Goodloe Memorial Unitarian Universalist Congregation in Bowie, Maryland.*

CLARENCE BERTRAND THOMPSON
1882–1969

The church, in fact virtually all churches in all denominations, perpetuate practices quite apart from the teaching of "The Church," which is a spiritual construct of belief. The churches alienate wage earners through their superiority attitudes and indifference. This behavior is self-destructive for the church and a calamity for society as a whole. . . . Underlying this is the insistence on social distinctions which is so objectionable to all people who are discriminated against. . . . There is an apparent exception to this rule in the Negro Churches in America, in which . . . the people as a whole are struggling together for justice and the antagonism of their environment drives them together to the consolations and hopes of religion, also, the usually superior education of their clergy leads all classes to look naturally to them for leadership.

—Clarence Bertrand Thompson

Clarence Bertrand Thompson was the first African American in ministerial fellowship with the American Unitarian Association (AUA). He had earned a law degree before he was old enough to practice. He earned bachelor's and master's degrees from Harvard University in sociology and economics by age twenty-six. During that time, from 1906 to 1909, he was also the minister of the Unitarian Church of Peabody, Massachusetts. His sermons on social and economic issues were often printed in the *Salem Eve-*

ning News. At twenty-seven, he published his first important book, *The Churches and the Wage-Earners: A Study of the Causes and the Cures of Their Separation*.

As an early member of the faculty of the Harvard Business School, he pioneered the case study method. He then consulted around the world on positive management. During and after World War II, in the final third of his long life, he devoted himself to scientific work on the biochemistry of enzymes, particularly in relation to cancer studies. Despite this remarkable threefold career, Thompson was entirely forgotten within Unitarian circles until his story was rediscovered almost a century after his brief career in ministry ended. How did this amnesia happen?

Thompson's story could be called a case study in color. Both his parents were of mixed racial ancestry. Although they clearly identified as "of color," the same may not always have been the case for their son. His niece, Anita Thompson Reynolds, called her family memoir *The Tan Experience*. Thompson's Peabody pastorate was both brief and not entirely happy. The church he served later merged with several other Unitarian and Universalist congregations in the area to form what is now the Northshore Unitarian Universalist Society in Danvers, Massachusetts. After he joined the Harvard Business School faculty, there is no record of Thompson continuing to function or identify as a Unitarian minister. Moreover, once he began to consult abroad after 1916, he was gradually forgotten in the United States, even in the field of management. His second book, *Scientific Management*, was occasionally noted as pioneering but was rather too critical of accepted practices. Thompson's life and career were rediscovered in 1998 by two African-American professors of management, Otey M. Scruggs and Lawrence Howard. A chance meeting between the latter and the present author in 2003 led to exploring the full story of Thompson's Unitarian connections.

Those connections begin with his parents. They met as members of Boston's small black community in the years following the Civil War. James Beauregard Thompson had been a free man even before that war. He served in the Union Navy aboard the U.S.S. *Eutaw*, reportedly as an officer. Family tradition, as recorded by his granddaughter, also said that he was the child of an unnamed woman of color and a grandson of Napoleon's brother, Jerome Bonaparte, who after fleeing Haiti, had settled in Baltimore. After 1865, James apprenticed with a Boston jeweler, and went to Paris in 1867 to help assemble a bejeweled fountain that was part of the U.S. pavilion at the first Paris Exposition. He also became part of the Essex Club, an organization for mutual aid and education led by Boston's black elite. There he met Medora Gertrude Reed, the child of a white Virginia slaveholder and a slave of Native-American and African-American ancestry. Medora and her mother had come to Boston in 1862. She married Thompson in 1868.

James and Medora clearly knew and worked with Boston Unitarians. According to family report, their first-born child, Beatrice Sumner Thompson, was given that name because U.S. Senator Charles Sumner, a Unitarian abolitionist, attended her christening in 1874. This story is plausible. Sumner's townhouse on Beacon Hill was close to the African Meeting House. Beatrice even named her son Sumner.

In 1880, the Thompson family took the classic advice to "go West." They settled in Denver. Homesteading in a frontier city, James invested in real estate that remained in the family long after his death in 1901. Clarence was born in Denver in 1882. His sister graduated from high school there in 1892. She applied for work in the county treasurer's office. According to the local black newspaper, she obtained the job only "after much discouragement and many troubles."[1] James Thompson by then was earning his living not as a jeweler, but as a railway porter. His marriage to Medora ended in divorce in 1890. She moved to Los Angeles with eight-year-old Clarence. There she married Peter Mitchell, a railway cook who opened a restaurant in the black community. Prodded by a mother described as "intelligent and ambitious,"[2] Clarence finished high school at the age of fifteen. In 1900, at eighteen, he graduated from the University of Southern California School of Law. Unable to practice law until he reached twenty-one, he studied and taught French, the language of his European ancestors; studied piano; and wrote articles for the *Cyclopedia of Evidence*. After finally beginning legal practice, he soon left "the legal profession on account of the corruption and trickery associated with it," as a reporter later interpreted his motivations.[3] Certainly he was a young idealist.

In 1904, at twenty-two, Thompson became part of an ethical and Transcendentalist group called the Fellowship. A Unitarian congregation in all but name, it aspired to transcend sectarian distinctions. Classes on Emerson were offered to newcomers. Its minister was Benjamin Fay Mills, a former Presbyterian. The associate minister was his wife, Mary Russell Mills. Chartered with eight hundred people already enrolled, the Fellowship was so radically egalitarian that regular attendees were asked to rotate their seating from the front of the rented hall to the back, lest anyone seem to have precedence. Clarence Thompson was elected assistant minister.

During this time, he met Maravene Kennedy. The daughter of an Ohio Methodist minister, she had been married at only seventeen to a man who tried to suppress her independence and intellectual life. After her divorce, she studied social settlement work, philosophy, and economics in New York. Still in her early twenties, she was already a writer and lecturer. Family connections may have helped. A first cousin, James M. Cox, became governor of Ohio and Republican candidate for U.S. president in 1920. Maravene was white.

Thompson applied to Harvard to study sociology and economics and began in the fall of 1905. Maravene had settled in Boston. Introduced by Mills to the Unitarians, Thompson also applied for AUA ministerial fellowship and did some pulpit supply. Having accepted a call to be installed as minister of the Peabody Unitarian Church, in November 1906, he received fellowship. Evidently Thompson did not mention his mixed racial heritage. His Peabody sermons were on themes such as "The Pragmatic Test Applied to Religion" and "Who or What Is God?" One series addressed controversial social and economic issues: "Labor and Labor Unions," "Corporations, Trusts, and Monopolies," and "Socialism." But none referred to race.

According to a fragment of a 1907 clipping from the Sunday edition of Boston's *The American*, in which Mavarene Kennedy announced her engagement to Thompson, rumors came from the West about his mixed racial heritage. She was said to be "crossing the color line," at least by the press, but in the church, she was described as "fashionable."[4] Although his sermons continued to be well received, Thompson noted that at least one parish family had sought out another minister for some pastoral service. He asked the board to pass a resolution against the practice. The lay leaders declined and advised Thompson to drop the entire matter. It is unclear whether he did or not. He tendered his resignation in May 1908, to take effect on October 1. Then, at the last minute, he withdrew it for a year. The lay leaders seem to have accepted that. A final letter of resignation, effective October 1, 1909, thanks "my many friends for their loyal support of the church during this last year."[5]

Thompson left to finish work on *The Churches and the Wage Earners*. Aware that he had no real experience as one of the latter himself, he worked a bit unloading trucks. He was also an assistant to Professor Carver at Harvard. Edwin Gay, first dean of the Harvard School of Business Administration, invited Thompson to take an instructor position in "industrial organization." He then worked with Edward Filene, president of the Boston Chamber of Commerce, on a project known as the Boston 1915 Movement. Others involved were activist journalist Lincoln Steffens and architect Daniel Burnham, known as the father of city planning. Thompson was organizational secretary and chaired the committee on educational, civic, and philanthropic organizations.

The overall theme was cooperation between labor and capital. Both need one another, Thompson had said in his sermons and book. Class warfare is destructive. Socialism, in the limited sense of social control over efforts like public transport or utilities, is good. Beyond that, it offends human nature and self-reliance, setting up insoluble problems of equitable distribution. Managers need to learn to listen to workers. It was in this context that he met Frederick Taylor, the then-current guru of shared or scientific management. Thompson's 1914 book interpreted Taylor's theories. Later, Taylorism was perhaps justifiably pilloried by labor for its time and motion studies, and for its emphasis on efficiency. But Thompson put the accent on Taylor's call for management and labor to cooperate in determining the best future for any enterprise. In 1916, he wrote *The Taylor System of Management.*

Offered a full professorship at Harvard Business School, Thompson declined. As with all questions of human motivation, it's hard to know why. Scruggs and Howard, in their studies of Thompson as a pioneering African-American management teacher, say that he was always more interested in practice than in theory. He took an opportunity to consult abroad. It's also possible that questions of race mattered far less overseas. The atmosphere for Thompson at Harvard Business School may also be reflected in the fact that the first history of that institution, covering the years from 1908 to 1945, contains not one indication that he had ever been there. Thompson consulted widely, applying his positive management theories in the Philippines, China, and France (where in 1934, he was made a Chevalier of the Legion of Honor), and traveled through North Africa to Kenya to see the effects of European colonialism.

The collapse of France to Nazi aggression and internal Fascism in 1940, when Thompson was fifty-eight, seems to have caused a profound vocational crisis. Positive management and cooperation by capital and labor had been defeated and co-opted by racialist socialism. On the front page of the business section of the *New York Times* for December 8, 1940, Thompson wrote, "France fell a victim to all the political and industrial evils which can flourish in a democracy unless and until they are checked by a genuine patriotism based on confidence in a government of justice and fair play, equal opportunity, general interest in individual welfare, competence and honesty."[6]

Scruggs and Howard's work on Thompson's life is unclear about when Maravene Kennedy Thompson died and when he met Lisbeth, his second wife. In 1940, he began studies at the University of California at Berkeley in biochemistry and the role of enzymes in cancer. Continuing his work at Harvard, he learned enough so that in 1946 he had his own laboratory at Berkeley. Forced into retirement at sixty-five, Thompson moved again and spent his last years in Montevideo, Uruguay, with Lisabeth, pursuing this research. Continuing to send notes to his Harvard graduating class, he asked when, for example, the principles of efficiency and cooperation in production he championed would be applied to the urgent issue of equitable global social distribution. He wrote scientific papers. He wrote to his sister, Dora Mitchell, in a U.S. nursing home. Sadly, whether justifiably or not, he seems to have felt that his scientific results were being blacklisted. When he died in 1969, not a single Unitarian, nor any of his colleagues in positive management or biochemistry, seem to have noted his passing. All the more important that we should remember him here—as a poignant, human, Unitarian "case study in color."

—John Buehrens

Sources

In 2005, I was in El Salvador with my wife, Gwen, herself a trailblazer among ordained women in the Episcopal Church. The Board of Episcopal Relief and Development was meeting. Her fellow Board member, Dr. Lawrence Howard, an African-American professor of management, asked me if I knew about an African-American Unitarian minister, C. Bertrand Thompson. I assured him that Mark Morrison-Reed had chronicled all the early African-American pioneers in our denomination. He then sent me his research on Thompson's life as a Unitarian minister, Harvard Business School professor, management consultant, and cancer researcher—work done with his colleague, Dr. Otey Scruggs. Confirming documentation was obtained through the Northshore UU Church of Danvers, Massachusetts, successor to the Unitarian Church of Peabody, Massachusetts, where Thompson became the first African-American Unitarian minister in fellowship—even if he is not recognized as such.

"REV. ETHELRED BROWN IS SYMBOL OF RADICALISM IN PULPITS IN HARLEM"

1934

Egbert Ethelred Brown (1875–1956) was born in Falmouth, Jamaica. His dismissal from the civil service, where he worked as an accountant, brought about a spiritual crisis and a decision to pursue a long-dormant desire to enter the ministry. After attending Meadville Theological School from 1910 to 1912, he was ordained and returned to Jamaica. For two years, he labored as a Unitarian missionary in Montego Bay and for six in Kingston before emigrating to New York City in 1920 and founding the Harlem Unitarian Church (HUC).

The HUC, which at its inception was named the Harlem Community Church and later the Hubert Harrison Memorial Church, was a center of radicalism in Harlem. Among its founding members —Grace Campbell, W. A. Domingo, Robert B. Moore, and Frank Crosswaith—were socialists, like Brown, who himself once ran for the New York State Assembly, and some were members of the African Blood Brotherhood (ABB), which Brown served as chaplain. Founded in 1914, the secretive ABB called for black self-defense and self-determination. Many HUC members also supported Marcus Garvey and the United Negro Improvement Association and its emphasis on race consciousness and self-sufficiency. But as Garvey turned toward demagoguery, most of them, including Brown, a former assistant treasurer of Garvey's Black Star Line, became vocal opponents. Brown's politics must have left AUA officials aghast, but the correspondence indicates little awareness of his status in Harlem. Rather, its officials, annoyed with his ongoing solicitation for support, viewed him as such a nuisance that in 1929, after several earlier attempts, he was dropped from fellowship.

The leadership of the AUA under both Samuel A. Eliot and Louis C. Cornish, who thought African Americans to be of the "lower classes," "shiftless rascals,"[1] and to have "an extraordinary histrionic vein,"[2] argued that it was an "impertinence"[3] to spread Unitarianism among them. Thus, a year after Brown's fellowship as a Unitarian minister was withdrawn, Harry V. Richardson, an African American studying at Harvard Divinity School (HDS), was refused admission by the AUA. Graduating from HDS in 1932, he later attended Drew University Theological Seminary, where he earned a doctorate in 1945. In 1958, Richardson was one of the founders, and first president, of the Interdenominational Theological Center in Atlanta.

In 1935, Brown's fellowship was reinstated when, with the support of the American Civil Liberties Union and represented by, as an AUA official wrote, "a Jewish lawyer of the type you might expect," legal action was threatened. The following article from a Jamaica newspaper contrasts with the way Brown was viewed by the AUA.

One of the most unusual pulpit figures in Harlem is the Rev. Ethelred Brown, whose name has become synonymous with religious radicalism. He is said to be the only Negro Unitarian minister in America.

Over his Bible stand in the Hubert Harrison [sic] Memorial Church, 14 West 136th Street, organized some thirteen years ago by a group of radicals under the leadership of the present pastor, an amazing number of thought-provoking topics are analyzed and discussed every Sunday night of the year.

As a matter of fact the Hubert Harrison Memorial Church is not exactly a church, and neither is it a forum. It has been aptly described as a church-forum where the honey-in-heaven and harassment-in-hades type religion is never tolerated. There are no "amen corners" in this church, and no "sob sister bench."

Likes Debate

The Rev. Ethelred Brown is a thinker. He loves a debate. He doesn't suffer from any form of inferiority complex. That's why, off and on, he invites to his pulpit such men as Bertram Wolf [sic],[5] Hodge Kirnon and J. B. Matthews. Like a long procession of others they propose or oppose some of the most unusual viewpoints ever expressed in a church.

It would be nothing strange, for example, to walk in on a Sunday night while the complexion of the Christ Savior was being discussed. Or, the topic might be, "Straw in the land of the Pharaohs and Cotton in Alabama." Hodge Kirnon and the Rev. Ethelred Brown once criticized and praised the Savior in a heated and highly interesting debate.

Obviously, the pastor is an avid newspaper reader. If the Jews are being persecuted in Europe, he invites a speaker of the caliber of Bertram Wolf from the white race, and the topic might very well be "The Jews in Germany and the Negroes in America."

Ordained in 1910

The Rev. Ethelred Brown received his theological education at the Meadville Theological School at Meadville, Pa., and was ordained in the Meadville Unitarian Church in 1910. He returned to Jamaica in the British West Indies immediately after his ordination and worked under the American Unitarian Association in the island until 1920. He then returned to America to organize the Harlem Community Church, later re-named the Hubert Harrison Memorial.

The pastor's brother, the Rev. Walter Launcelot Brown, was the first Negro minister to be placed in charge of the metropolitan Episcopalian Church in the island of Jamaica. He is now priest-in-charge of a church in the city of Kingston with a membership of 1,500 Negroes and whites.

—"Rev. Ethelred Brown Is Symbol of Radicalism in Pulpits in Harlem," Daily Gleaner, *Jan. 20, 1934, p. 16.*

WILLIAM H. G. CARTER
1877–1962

Rev. Carter is a kindly man, quite intelligent. But his storefront church is in the wrong place. The neighborhood surrounding it is poor and characterized by rowdiness. . . . I do not recommend fellowship for Rev. Carter.

—Lon Ray Call

It is 1934. In one of the poorest neighborhoods of Cincinnati, Ohio, a group of thirty-five people assemble for worship. Their church is a rented storefront in an aging brick tenement on Fifth Street, in what locals call the West End, meaning the "colored" area of downtown. Crowded alongside old wooden pews and folding chairs are a coal stove, hat rack, several bookcases, a piano, radio, clock, and a bulletin board covered with announcements of political rallies and community events. In the rear sit two idle printing presses and an architect's desk. On one wall hangs a roughly rendered drawing of Jesus, showing him at the end of an evolutionary line from apes to man. Outside on the windows of this storefront is painted, in vivid color, "Unitarian Brotherhood Church."

Presiding is Rev. William Henry Grey Carter, a tall, handsome, learned man whose life had led him from Arkansas and deeply Christian religious roots to community activism and Unitarian ministry in southwestern Ohio.

William H. G. Carter was born in Arkansas in 1877. His maternal grandfather, William Henry Grey, was a former slave who had served as a cabin boy on steamers plying up and down the Mississippi and Ohio rivers. After Emancipation, Grey became a Baptist minister and prominent politician, serving as land commissioner of the state of Arkansas and U.S. ambassador to Madagascar. Carter's father, James, attended Howard University and served as a minister in churches in Mississippi, Kentucky, and Arkansas before becoming the dean of Shorter University, an African Methodist Episcopal (AME) school in Arkansas.

In his autobiography, Carter recalls being an avid reader, who by age six had mastered *Aesop's Fables*, *Robinson Crusoe*, Paine's *Age of Reason*, and other classics. He attended Shorter University with aspirations of following his father and grandfather into the ministry. However, upon completion of his doctor of divinity degree, he found himself unable to serve in the AME Church because he could not accept the divinity of Jesus.

He worked as superintendent of a Methodist Sunday school in Arkadelphia, Arkansas, before enlisting in the army in 1898 to fight in the Spanish-American War. Upon returning home, he married Beulah Grey, a woman of short stature and strong character. Although a devout Christian herself, she was a steadfast supporter of Carter's endeavors and a devoted mother to their children. Beulah often used her skill as a pianist to comfort her husband through times of frustration and difficulty, of which there were many.

The couple moved to Mississippi, and Carter took work as a photographer and artist. After the family's home and studio were destroyed by fire, they moved to Memphis, where Carter became known as the city's first "Snap Shot King." A skilled entrepreneur, Carter bought and sold real estate, worked for the post office, and opened a successful carnival-style funhouse on famous Beale Street. Harassment by local law enforcement over trumped-up charges of receiving stolen goods and the ever-present threat of racial violence against his family led Carter to sell his business interests and move his wife and fifteen children up river to Cincinnati in 1918.

Carter, a self-declared Unitarian, came to this identity not by attending a service at a Unitarian church or by knowing other Unitarians, but by studying the world's great religious traditions and reading about Arius, Francis David, Socinus of Poland, and Henry David Thoreau. Troubled by what he saw as the errors of Christianity, he wrote, "Our churches today have changed from worship of the Father to worship of the Son."[1] For him, Jesus was a mortal, a brother with great spiritual wisdom who had been unwisely turned into a god by his later followers. "Abraham Lincoln did more for the black man than did Jesus or Moses and yet I don't idolize Lincoln."[2] He rejected the doctrines of original sin, the immaculate conception, and eternal damnation, believing less in the miracles of the New Testament and more in a God of love and compassion. While never belittling the Bible or Jesus, his study of scripture led him to reject much Christian dogma as false, and to assert that "I have to throw out the filth and am trying with all my heart to refill it with God's blessed and everlasting heavenly truth."[3]

His brand of liberal faith led Carter to become a community activist and advocate for the poor in Cincinnati. He helped provide food and shelter for thousands of West End residents. In 1933, he organized a march of 250 people, white and black, to the county courthouse, demanding that the government provide food and clothing to those in need for the coming winter. When the group was turned away, they marched across town to city hall and made their case before the city council for a bill to be placed on the fall ballot; the result was the passage of a $1,119,000 bond issue for "poor relief."[4]

Carter ran for Cincinnati city council in 1935, 1939, and 1945 and—despite numerous invitations from the powerful local Republican Party to join them—in each campaign he remained an independent and unsuccessful. He founded a fraternal organization called the Grand Order of Denizens, G.O.D. for short, which sponsored well-attended lectures on liberal religious theology and ethics. Wishing to provide wholesome recreation for the young, Carter opened a nonalcoholic pool hall with "no swearing allowed" and offered informal instruction in black art and history to children in the community.

Of his many endeavors, the Church of the Unitarian Brotherhood was one of the most passionate. Believed to have opened around 1932, the membership in this storefront congregation totaled fifty to sixty, with an average attendance between twenty-five and forty. From the pulpit and in his writings, Carter advocated daily meditation and diary writing as a path to moral living and extolled the virtues of what he called "drugless healing," a combination of deep breathing, daily exercise, and adequate fluid intake.

The church was a labor of love for Carter, who lived with his wife and sizable family in several apartments on the second floor of the building. Receiving little or no compensation for his pastoral work, he often kept the doors open using his own funds.

The church operated independently, without affiliation or recognition by the larger Unitarian denomination. The leaders of the other Unitarian churches in Cincinnati knew of Carter's congregation, but there was minimal contact. Both Rev. Julius Krolfifer, minister of St. John's Unitarian Church, and Rev. John Malick, minister of First Unitarian Church of Cincinnati, spoke just one time before Carter's group. And although both established churches donated Unitarian tracts and a small number of hymnals to the church, the hymnals were so out-of-date that Carter made little use of them because, as he said, they contained "too much Jesus."[5] Carter never attended a Unitarian convention, and was unaware that the American Unitarian Association (AUA) General Conference, under the leadership of fellow Cincinnatian William Howard Taft, had met in his city in 1938.

Word of this small congregation eventually leaked out into the wider Unitarian world, all the way to Boston. Late in 1938, AUA field staff member Lon Ray Call came to Cincinnati to visit Carter and his church. Call attended a Sunday service and interviewed both Carter and Beulah. He also spoke with the other local Unitarian ministers, who reported that the reception to their lectures before Carter's church had been "not very intelligent." While speaking highly of Carter's personal character and of his many humanitarian efforts, these white Unitarians characterized the neighborhood surrounding his church as "poor and rowdy."[6]

Carter was never admitted into ministerial fellowship by the AUA, nor did his church receive official recognition or financial support from the association. Based on the report Call submitted, the AUA judged that the congregation was "in the wrong place" and its leadership unqualified. The decision to withhold support was taken by officials in Boston at a time when the AUA policy was to discourage the formation of what it called "sporadic personal movements."[7]

The imposed isolation of Carter left him believing that the Church of the Unitarian Brotherhood was the only "colored" Unitarian Church in the United States. There was, however, another: the Harlem Unitarian Church, which had been founded in 1920 by Rev. Egbert Ethelred Brown. Brown was Jamaican, and his congregation was largely of Caribbean descent. His church, like Carter's, was rebuffed by the AUA. However, unlike Carter, Brown found a few allies within the denomination.

Carter's congregation—founded for and attended by African Americans—was unique in being indigenous. At a time when Unitarianism was almost exclusively a religion of the white, middle-class, and well-educated, Carter invented his own brand of liberal religion and created an autonomous fellowship of Unitarian faith for the people of his segregated community.

The church closed its doors in 1940. Carter passed away in 1962 at the age of eighty-five. He and Beulah are buried in an African Methodist Episcopal cemetery in Cincinnati's northern suburbs. By strange coincidence, in 1967 the Northern Hills UU Fellowship was built next door, but William H. G. Carter and the Church of the Unitarian Brotherhood remained unknown to it and to the larger Unitarian Universalist community until 2000, when leaders of two Cincinnati UU congregations began looking into the story. What resulted was a fitting tribute to a man and his ministry, too long dismissed and forgotten.

—Bruce Beisner and Walter Herz

Sources

Much of the information in this article comes directly from Rev. Carter's self-published autobiography, My Father's Business. *Other sources we drew on were "Descendants of W.H.G. Carter," an essay by Carter's grandson, Leslie Edwards, and "His Rightful Place," an essay by Carter's great-granddaughter, Starita Smith, published in the* UU World. *This article also includes information from correspondence in the Unitarian Universalist Association archives and sermons by Rev. Morris Hudgins and Richard Bozian.*

"RESOLUTION ON RACE RELATIONS"
1942

AUA president Frederick May Eliot was elected to his second four-year term with a mandate to revitalize Unitarianism, but the Second World War and its consequences had to become his focus. In the January 1942 issue of the Christian Register, *Eliot wrote, "our Association stands together in full commitment to the overthrow of totalitarian power wherever it seeks to dominate free people or destroy the institutions of free nations." And so it was. The Unitarian Service Committee was established in order to assist refugees. Dozens of ministers served as chaplains. With a substantial number of the young men serving in the armed service, churches struggled to cope with this new reality. But the threat of Nazism and awareness of its racist ideology also brought about self-examination.*

A year later, the Register *had a new editor, Stephen H. Fritchman. He writes in* Heretic: A Partisan Autobiography *that the January 1943 issue was the first under his editorship in which*

> *I did not feel any obligation to use the stack of hold-over articles. . . . Since the American Unitarian Association . . . had passed a fairly tough and fresh statement on race relations I devoted an entire issue to that theme. . . . The Race Issue included articles by Dr. Franz Boas, of Columbia, American's leading anthropologist at that time; by George B. Murphy, Jr., secretary of the National Negro Congress . . . and by our sole Black Unitarian minister, Rev. Ethelred Brown, of Harlem. The issue aimed to alert Uni-*

> *tarian churches to their unrecognized institutional racism as well as to indicate the personal astigmatism of individual members.*[1]

This was the context in which the 1942 AUA Resolution on Race Relations and accompanying suggestions for its implementation appeared.

Whereas: All race prejudice, particularly anti-Semitism and anti-Negro feeling and anti-Orientalism, threaten not only our national morale but also our unity as a people in this grave hour of crisis; and

Whereas: Such prejudice and fanaticism are fundamentally opposed to all high morality, to the spirit of true religion, and to every principle of democracy, and therefore cannot be condoned nor tolerated by a free people committed to the proposition that "All men are created free and equal"; and

Whereas: It must be a major concern of all religion to oppose all enemies of freedom and democracy; therefore, be it

Resolved: That the American Unitarian Association assembled in its 117th annual meeting again voices with solemn emphasis and profound conviction its faith in the universal Brotherhood of Man, and in the complete equality of all men before God and the Law; and be it further

Resolved: That the Association call upon all its member churches and affiliated organizations to implement this declaration of principle by effective action in promoting interfaith and inter-racial solidarity through the means of

1. the practice in all their relationships of those principles of brotherhood on which the liberal church is founded;
2. special study of the sociological, psychological, and religious factors involved in racial discrimination;

3. the development of special techniques of action adapted to particular local and special conditions;
4. public commendation and support of government or other action which furthers racial and religious equality and brotherhood; and
5. public condemnation and effective counter-agitation against all forms of racial discrimination and religious prejudice.

Basic Steps to Ethnic Democracy

WHAT CAN WE DO

To Carry Out the Unitarian Resolution on Race Relations. . . .

FIND OUT whether Negroes in your town are adequately represented on the following community agencies, and if not, secure such representation: school boards, teaching staffs, juries, Civilian Defense committees, Community Chest committees, U.S.O., Red Cross, hospital staffs.

START an inter-racial council in your community.

WRITE your Senators, Congressmen, Secretaries Knox and Stimson protesting segregation in the armed forces, asking for a mixed regiment of servicemen willing to join. Demand protection for Negroes in uniform from violence and insults.

DEMAND that Negro doctors and nurses be used in the Medical Corps without segregation.

PROTEST Jim Crow conditions (i.e. segregation in or exclusion from restaurants, hotels, theatres, public vehicles, hospitals, schools, day nurseries) in your town.

GO TO SEE under what conditions Negroes live in your town. Observe restricted areas, higher rents, poor health conditions, tuberculosis rates, juvenile delinquency.

REGISTER a protest against the unscientific segregation of Negro blood plasma when you make your blood donation at the local Red Cross center.

WELCOME Negro children in the day nursery your church sets up for children of war workers.

START a study group in your church on race problems and their origin. Start with Dr. Boas' article page 461. . . .

GIVE a church school party for the children of a Negro or Mexican church school, without patronizing them.

PLAN joint services and friendly relations with neighborhood Negro churches. This would be a good way of observing Race Relations Sunday. . . .

VISIT the local USO and find out whether Negro servicemen are welcome on a basis of equality. . . .

INVESTIGATE discrimination in employment, report any to Fair Employment Practices Committee and publicly support this committee.

COMMEND either personally by letter, or by resolutions of your organizations, action by Congressmen, government officials, trade unions, employers, which "further racial equality and brotherhood." Get adequate publicity for such commendations.

MAKE SURE that Negroes are made welcome in your church . . . and as members of your church.

MAKE FRIENDS with members of others races, this is the only sure way of overcoming prejudice.

REFUSE to laugh at or to repeat anti-Semitic, anti-Negro and other jokes which create an attitude of contempt.

TRACK DOWN rumors and slanders in your community about racial groups. They probably started with an Axis short-wave broadcast.

BE VERY RELUCTANT to join or maintain membership in organizations that exclude other races. Change their policy if possible.

SUBSTITUTE the name of whatever minority group in your community, racial or national, is most clearly a victim of prejudice, discrimination or neglect in the place of "Negro" on this page. These might be: Portuguese, Filipino, Chinese, Japanese, Mexican, Italian, or others.

WRITE to the following agencies for information and suggestion for action:

Fair Employment Practices Committee, Washington, DC.

National Association for the Advancement of Colored People, 69 Fifth Ave., New York City

National Negro Congress, 290 Lenox Avenue, New York City

National Urban League, 1133 Broadway, New York City, or the branch in your town

National Conference of Christians and Jews, 381 Fourth Avenue, New York City

—*"AUA General Assembly Resolution on Race Relations,"* Christian Register *(Race Issue), January 1943, pp. 4, 10.*

"I HAVE TWO DREAMS"
1947

Egbert Ethelred Brown's relationship with the American Unitarian Association (AUA) changed for the better when Frederick May Eliot became president in 1937. Denominational officials took note of Brown's prominence in Harlem, where he was the chair of the Board of the Jamaica Benevolent Association, the president of the Jamaican Progressive League—a political organization that helped to secure self-rule for Jamaica—and an occasional speaker at Adam Clayton Powell's Abyssinian Baptist Church, one of the oldest and most prominent African-American Baptist churches in the North.

The following article appeared in the Christian Register *three years after the Harlem Unitarian Church (HUC) announced that it was an interracial congregation. The announcement was made on October 1, 1944, the Sunday before the inaugural service of another interracial church, the nondenominational Church for the Fellowship of All Peoples, where Rev. Howard Thurman, an African American, served as co-minister. That service was held at the First Unitarian Church of San Francisco. During the 1944–1945 church year at HUC, Brown and white ministers preached on alternate Sundays. Don Harrington, the minister of the Community Church of New York, and his wife, Velma, joined the congregation and later another white man and woman. Fellowship Church and HUC were not alone in moving in this direction. In 1945 the Chicago Unitarian Council expressed interest in forming an interracial congregation in the Chicago area. That same year in Dallas, after two African Americans began attending, the Board of the Unitarian Church voted to wel-*

come black people into membership. In 1948, when the First Unitarian Society of Chicago did the same, two Board members resigned. In the same year, when Stephen Fritchman proposed to the Board of the First Unitarian Church of Los Angeles that it affirm the congregation's openness to all races in its by-laws, a Board member resigned.

At the beginning of my ministry it was my task to keep the flag of Unitarianism flying in a segregated city-within-a-city—to prove not to the world, but to Unitarians, that Negroes are capable of becoming Unitarians, and that therefore Unitarianism is a universal religion.

What we had to do was to show that the principles of our free faith are understandable and acceptable to all men, regardless of race. Negroes are not committed to voodoo, fundamentalism, the drum of the jungle: they are thinking, critical, exacting men in their religion—just as some white men are. . . .

Maybe all this sounds like mere truism today; but even Unitarians, whatever they may have said in easy words, found these truths hard to accept when I began my work more than a quarter of a century ago. It was one thing to try to show the world; but it was quite a different thing to show the Unitarian Fellowship, already verbally dedicated to the principles of the brotherhood of all men. The principle sounded good. Behind them was little conviction. Even in the Unitarian leadership—official Unitarianism—the words had a question-mark in the dark backward and abyss of thought. . . .

This initial phase of my task I have been lucky enough to have somewhat accomplished: Unitarians themselves now admit Negroes to the brotherhood of man on grounds of full and unhesitating equality because of their basic humanity. There are still, however, my two dreams to be fulfilled.

The first dream of mine is within this same sphere of racial relations within our church.

When a majority group enforces segregation on a minority, this enforced segregation is in effect the stamping of the segregated group with the stigma of inferiority; and if that implication is not justified by the facts, a real and serious injustice is perpetuated.

This enforced segregation is the unhappy lot of Negroes in this country, and there is no doubt whatever that segregation is thus imposed because the overwhelming majority of the white people of this nation believes that Negroes are not only inferior—but inherently and unalterable inferior.

The disturbing fact is that the churches of America approve segregation in the continuing existence of separate churches for whites and Negroes. Our Unitarian churches are a current partner in this sorry business. My first dream is that one day in the not distant future our Unitarian churches will be genuinely interracial—and I mean in their pulpits as well as in their pews.

This must be our goal. For us, this must be the imperative minimum.

I know too well—and from a poignantly personal standpoint—as you know from a well-read, well-informed, but less personal view—that as a denomination we are not ready yet even to take the minimum step. There are some of our churches which characterize the suggestion of interracial churches as "impractical" and "fantastic."

Only yesterday after supper a woman seriously asked me how it is that, in the face of the fact that Unitarian churches have been and are the leaders in the fight for racial equality, there are no Negroes applying to enter the Unitarian ministry. A nice point! Can we rationalize some answer? Can fact be set aside by neat phrases? Is there some happy generalization which will set this question at rest?

I replied that we are not ready. And when I set out to speak of the necessity of genuine interracial relationships in our churches I discovered that my questioner was only interested in Negro Unitarian ministers who would organize segregated Negro churches. "Negroes should work out their own peculiar problems within their own group." That is up-to-date Unitarianism. . . .

We are not ready.

But we had better be! If we are fighting for social justice in the world around us, then we must be consistent and remove the barrier which keeps colored people from our churches. Such a barrier implies—as it was intended to imply—Negro inferiority. Unitarians are followers of science. Science has proved the generalization of Negro inferiority untrue. No doubts about this remain any longer. . . . No race, color, creed or nationality is "inferior" to the scientific anthropologist. Argument in this field is no longer possible—except to the emotionally enslaved.

I call upon Unitarians to make a start toward the dream which I have tried to make verbal. Which one of our 348 active churches will be the first to pave the way by accepting a Negro as its assistant minister? This imperative minimum must not be dodged.

Unfortunately we have lost the glorious opportunity to be the pioneers here. Were we afraid? Doubtful of our principles? Too much engaged with things as they were? In any event, the distinction has been won by others. Liberals out-liberalled! Therefore, if we move in this direction, we must follow now. But follow we must! Either that or lose the name of active Unitarians. This is my first dream.

I am ashamed of the results of twenty-seven years of work in Harlem. I am bewildered. I have not made progress as I should have. We speak—but even good words come cheap. When shall we begin to act?

In Harlem, we have not lost courage. In January 1946 we dared to launch a campaign to raise $15,000 to purchase a building. We had a concert in All Souls Church on January 27, and a rally in the Y.M.C.A. on May 5. As a result of these two projects, we deposited $1,260 in the bank for our building fund. Nothing is more realistic than the little blue figures in our bank-book. Theory or no theory, here is truth! Truth in financial terms. . . .

A Unitarian church in Harlem—remember well: in Harlem—will be the first church of its type in this country of ours. Have faith, we say to the AUA and to the readers of *The Register*. Help us build the church and the congregation will be assured. This is my second dream—the dream of a man no longer young—of a man on the way out.

Two dreams—genuine interracial churches in America and a Unitarian church in Harlem! Dreams? Yes; but some dreams come true. These may.

—*Ethelred Brown, "I Have Two Dreams,"* Christian Register, *Dec. 1947, pp. 471–72.*

"WHY BROTHERHOOD WEEK?"
1948

Born in British Guiana (now Guyana), Edward D. Smith-Green graduated from Queens College and was employed as an officer in the British Customs Service. After ten years, he moved to the United States, where he became a founding member of the Harlem chapter of the United Negro Improvement Association. Marcus Garvey asked him to serve as the secretary of the Black Star Line, Inc. His tenure, however, was brief. By 1929, he had split with Garvey over financial irregularities.

Smith-Green, who was also an inventor and a widely read man, wrote several manuscripts. One was titled Christianity, White Supremacy and the Black Man, *another* An Analysis of Race Prejudice. *Neither was published.*[1] *He was also a member of the Fourth Unitarian Society of Brooklyn. He wrote the following article for the* Christian Register.

THE PURPOSE of celebrating Brotherhood Week is, I take it, to give to the citizens of this great nation the opportunity to consecrate themselves anew, individually and collectively, to the ideals of the brotherhood of MAN which the acceptance of God as the universal father implies. The very stressing of this objective points to the determination of America to translate into reality those high principles, enunciated both in the creed it professes and the charter of its destiny as a nation, which will contribute to the ultimate establishment of freedom, justice and peace among its people. . . .

I wish every American could spend some time in my native land, British Guiana. There, within the precincts of those sacred institutions, he would witness the practical application of brotherhood. For it is in them that the children of the settlers who came there from England, Portugal, China, India, Holland, Java, the Cape-de-Verde islands, Ireland, Africa, or Scotland study, play and worship together. There, too, he would discover that they are taught that, theoretically and practically, they are, each and everyone, regardless of race or national origin, important links in the chain of destiny wrought in the forge on his country's history. It is with the full sense of the social responsibilities entailed that he assumes, subsequently, his status as the equal of his peers before the law, exercises his prerogatives as a citizen, becomes jealous of the dignity of his manhood, and accepts as his, by right, the equality of opportunity without which all other professions are iniquitous. . . .

Then I came to the United States of America.

It should be readily understood how difficult it was for me to grasp the significance of the ethical code of the new social order in which I found myself. To have my liberty circumscribed; to be denied the opportunity for using my natural talents and acquired skills in the field where I could be socially efficient; to be tethered within the narrow confines of what was designated "my place" in the otherwise extensive domain of American life for no other reason than the fact of my racial origin, was as incomprehensible as it was shocking . . . incomprehensible because of the sheer novelty of the experience; shocking because of my unanticipated discovery of the existence of the wide gulf which separated the great promise of American democracy and the letter of its accomplishment.

But within the span of the years I have lived in this country there has come to me, through an objective and intensive study of the history of its birth and growth, the realization that, as in the case of every other society, this nation can achieve an approximation of its ideals only through the slow processes of the evolutions of its institutions.

No longer am I a Britisher. I could not be. No one who experiences the throb of America's travail toward its destined maturity can remain deaf to its insistent call to action for the daily reaffirmation of the self evident truths of "The Declaration." And I am proud of being an American citizen whose sons' shoulder to shoulder with their compatriots recently risked their lives in defense of those freedoms which I am confident they will, eventually, fully enjoy.

That confidence is born of my belief that, in "the pursuit of happiness" which their God-given and "unalienable rights" entitle them, my fellow citizens of all races and creeds, will in time come to know that brotherhood is implicit in the very acceptance of "the kingdom" for which they pray and work . . . that confraternity of free men known as American can continue to be the beacon of hope to other and less privileged peoples only as it demonstrates, in word and deed, that its citizens are, truly members of the same household enjoying equally its blessings, accepting equally their responsibilities and duties toward their fellows, and offering on the altar of their fellowship their diverse gifts for the common good.

Further, I do not hesitate to express the conviction that, in spite of its fears, unfounded as they are, America will yet recognize that Brotherhood does not mean "the erasure of the individuality in the man, the family or the race." Its unity is truer and richer because not run in one or expressed in monotony of form. Like all vital unities, it is a composite. It is consistent with the individuality of the man; it is consistent with the full individuality and the separate integrity of the races. It does not mean fusion of the races any more than it involves the fusion of the creeds or the fusion of the arts. It means cooperation, individual integrity, peace. "Fitness, not race, is the test. Opportunity, not fusion, is the aim."

—Edward D. Smith-Green, "Why Brotherhood Week?" Christian Register, *Feb. 1948, p. 48.*

"1ST UNITARIAN USES BROTHERHOOD IDEA"

1949

A year after the First Unitarian Society of Chicago voted "to invite our friends of other races and colors who are interested in Unitarianism to join our church," the congregation held a joint service with the interracial Free Religious Fellowship where Lewis A. McGee was minister. A newspaper report on that service appears below.

During that same month, the Tennessee Valley Unitarian Church in Knoxville was chartered. Jim Person, an African American, was an early attendee who held off joining until, as the minister Dick Henry put it, "he decided we were for real."[1] The congregation hired an African-American music director. By 1957, the number of black members had grown to about fifteen and by 1973, to around twenty-five. Indeed, as the 1950s commenced, more congregations welcomed racial integration. The year 1950 saw the board of the church in Richmond, Virginia, vote to welcome "Negroes," and during that same year, All Souls Church, Unitarian, in Washington DC, which was on its way to becoming the most racially diverse congregation in the UUA, welcomed its first African Americans into membership.

Members of the First Unitarian Church decided to be practical about Brotherhood Week. They invited the city's newest interracial church to join them in worship and in planning ways to making "Brotherhood" real in Chicago.

For their "Brotherhood Week" service the white people of the church decided that inviting a minister of another race to preach to them wasn't enough. So they asked not only the Rev. Lewis A. McGee, former Army chaplain and a Unitarian minister of the Negro race, but also his congregation of 16 white people and 53 Negroes who have dedicated themselves to the idea of constructing a church on an interracial basis—the Free Religious Fellowship.

Members of the First Unitarian Church . . . already had a racial consciousness. Their minister, the Rev. Dr. Leslie Pennington, has been a leader in the promotion of interracial justice within the city's church life. His sermons include an occasional frank blast at racial restrictive covenants and frequent high praise for fair employment practices and non-discriminatory housing legislation.

Big crowd

The Woodlawn Ave. church was crowded for the "Brotherhood" service and Dr. McGee [sic] made use of the opportunity, avoiding platitudes and vague references to "goodness" and "peace." He stood before the crowd and pointed out that the 18,000,000 American citizens who are not of the white race are both legally and in the law of God, entitled to full equality on the basis of their individual worth.

His sermon covered the range of racism on the international, national and local levels. American [sic] must back the international charter of human rights both at home and abroad. "The best way to fight Communism is to out do Communism" in the application of the principles of brotherhood, he said.

Truman report

On the national level the American citizen, regardless of what his own race might be, should seek realization of the reports of the President's Commission on Civil Rights and Education. And in Chicago the truly American citizen is the man who works for the breaking down of ghettoes whether in housing or industry or schools.

Then after the service the two congregations attended a "ways and means" discussion led by two members of Dr. McGee's church . . . and two members of Dr. Pennington's. . . .

By the time "Brotherhood Week" rolls around next year the two groups would have concrete evidence, they vowed, to show that they had tried to make "Brotherhood" a reality and not just a word.

—James O. Supple, "1st Unitarian Uses Brotherhood Idea," Chicago Sun-Times, *Feb. 25, 1949, p. 18.*

THE CANDIDACY OF EUGENE SPARROW

There are stories in which you sense the story line before you read to the end. Such is the saga of Eugene Sparrow when, in 1950, he was a candidate for assistant minister at Church of Our Father (later known as First Unitarian Universalist Church) in Detroit, Michigan.

Gene Sparrow was not the first African-American man to be ordained into the Unitarian or Universalist ministry, but he was the first to graduate from Harvard Divinity School with the intention of becoming a Unitarian minister.

June 1949 was an eventful month for Mr. Sparrow. On the seventh, he was appointed to the position of dean of students at Jarvis Christian College in Texas. The next day, the American Unitarian Association (AUA) granted him preliminary fellowship as a Unitarian minister, and on June 23, he graduated from Harvard Divinity School—a hopeful situation for a twenty-eight-year-old African American.

Born in 1921, Eugene Sparrow was an adopted only child. As a youth growing up in Boston, he was raised in a Congregational church, yet his natural interest in religion led him to closely observe the activities at a nearby Catholic church and a Jewish synagogue. He exhibited his gifts of intellectual and musical talents early, and by excelling academically, he gained admission to the prestigious high school, Boston Latin School. In 1941, after graduating from Boston Latin and spending one year in college, Sparrow enlisted in the army.

After World War II, he attended the University of Michigan in Ann Arbor; his fields of concentration were Spanish and sociology. Newly married, he rented a room in the Ann Arbor Unitarian Church parsonage and developed a friendship with Edward Redmond, its minister. This friendship played a significant role in leading Sparrow to Unitarianism and, following his graduation, to study at Harvard for the ministry. The AUA Department of Ministry first interviewed Sparrow in 1946.

A year earlier the Iowa Association had voted to support Grant Butler, the minister of the First Unitarian Church of Des Moines, in exploring the feasibility of organizing a "Negro Unitarian Church" there.[1] AUA officials had conducted exploratory conversations with two African-American men about entering the Unitarian ministry and had also sought recommendations from Dr. Leon Wright of Howard University. When no other candidate emerged, they reluctantly settled on a recent, black graduate of Starr King School for the Ministry, Alvin Neeley Cannon. Cannon did not hit it off with the black community in Des Moines and by June it was clear the effort would not succeed.[2]

The situation within Unitarianism was indeed bleak if you were black and studying for the ministry. Egbert Ethelred Brown was marshaling on in Harlem as he had since 1920; Lewis McGee was birthing a new interracial congregation on Chicago's South Side; Jeffrey Campbell, unable to find parish settlement, had forsaken ministry for teaching and the United States for England; and in Cincinnati, William H. G. Carter had given up and let the Church of Unitarian Brotherhood die.

A January 1950 AUA Department of Ministry chronology of its interaction with Mr. Sparrow lists many churches he was recommended to in Massachusetts during his student days. Only Somerville took him on as an assistant from 1948 to 1949. A list of fifteen urban churches in the AUA was mentioned as possible settlements for him as assistant minister. As his graduation approached in 1949, he received no offers, and so with a wife and two children to support and despite their reluctance to move south, he took a position at Jarvis Christian as dean of men.

At the 1949 mid-winter conference at Meadville Theological School, a petition drafted and signed by twenty-six ministers, supported by the Unitarian Ministers Association, and addressed to AUA President Frederick May Eliot, urged the Department of Ministry to aggressively explore avenues for Sparrow's settlement. President Eliot's reply challenged the Western Unitarian Conference to find a place within its boundaries for Sparrow, "to demonstrate . . . its capacity for leadership not only in idealistic thought but in practical churchmanship."[3]

Among the several churches the AUA courted for Sparrow's settlement, it seems that only Church of Our Father seriously candidated him. Ministers of churches in Minneapolis, Madison, Chicago, Indianapolis, Kansas City, Philadelphia, Providence, and Washington DC, were approached, but nothing materialized. Even the Ann Arbor church, with Redman as minister, did not pursue settlement.

In 1950, Church of Our Father had about 370 members, and its church school registration stood at 280. Matilda "Tillie" Moore was director of religious education, and the church was celebrating the tenth anniversary of Tracy Pullman's ministry. Church newsletters indicated they were a dynamic team, each being involved in Detroit-wide religious and civic organizations, including interracial and interfaith ones. Dr. Pullman had been branded the "pink pastor" for his criticism of Joseph McCarthy, and the church was frequently picketed.

In January 1950, Dr. Pullman read a letter to the Church Council that stated, "The AUA is anxious to have us take on our staff as Director of Youth Activities a young Negro recently graduated from Harvard Divinity School, Eugene Sparrow."[4] The AUA had sweetened the arrangement by offering $3,600 for the first year in order to place Mr. Sparrow. The minutes reflect that Dr. Pullman and Ms. Moore were supportive of Sparrow's coming because of the possibility to expand the youth program and to develop a campus program at Wayne State University, which was only a few blocks from the church.

However, not until the March council meeting was a special committee appointed to gather information about Mr. Sparrow and ascertain the sentiments of the congregation about employing him as youth director. Then in April, Tillie Moore's resignation further complicated the matter.

The May council meeting minutes indicate that even though there was sentiment within the church for dropping the issue, the Special Committee prevailed in a vote to invite Mr. Sparrow to Detroit over a weekend. The expenses for his visit were to be defrayed, not out of the church's funds, but "by personal subscription."[5] The congregation would be informed of the council's action through the newsletter and from the pulpit. The special committee solicited funds, arranged for Mr. Sparrow to preach on Sunday, June 4, and publicized his coming in the church newsletter. The Pullmans provided overnight lodging and hosted a reception to which members of the council were invited. About twenty-five people attended.

At a church council meeting the Monday after Sparrow had preached, the special committee proposed that a congregational meeting be held later in June, with a panel speaking to six questions: What are the needs of the church? What is the story of the AUA offer? What are Sparrow's qualifications? What are the financial aspects? What are the social and religious aspects? What effects on the church may be anticipated? Over objections to the suggested format, it was eventually agreed to proceed with a special congregational meeting the evening of June 21, 1950.

The minutes of the June 21 congregational meeting have not been uncovered, nor was there a report of that meeting in the June 25 church newsletter; perhaps it was past deadline for a story. Then the newsletter publication ends because of summer vacation. The first newsletter in September 1950 also reports nothing about the Sparrow matter, and there is no mention of Sparrow or the outcome of the June congregational meeting in the minutes of the first fall council meeting. Why the silence?

Fifty-seven years later, eight people, who were all members of Church of Our Father in 1950, were interviewed about their recollection of the Sparrow candidacy. Only one, Dores McCree, had not attended the meeting; paradoxically, she is the only person who remembers meeting and hearing Mr. Sparrow preach. McCree and her late husband, Judge Wade McCree, were among a handful of African-American church members in 1950.

Wade McCree and Sparrow had been boyhood friends in West Roxbury, Massachusetts. They attended a Congregational Sunday school and Boy Scouts together, and were students at Boston Latin School concurrently. But on the Sunday when his friend preached at Church of Our Father, Judge McCree was out of town.

Helen Riebling, who had just joined, recalls, "I was thrilled because the young man in question was a Negro . . . we did have congregational meetings. Just informal ones at first. Two or three I don't remember much about, because they were affable and were friendly."[6]

No one remembers that a panel presentation was made at the June 21 meeting. What is vividly remembered is that feelings ran high. Verbal animosity and venomous remarks poured from members, shocking those later interviewed. One person said,

> The meeting itself was terrible. I have never seen anything quite so bad around the church. I know we are vocal and I know that people have strong feelings but it was terrible. People were screaming at one another. . . . We wanted to hear what was being offered and we were more in favor than we were against, but it was a very, very difficult meeting.[7]

Another remarked,

> I was shocked at the discrimination. I was shocked at racism and I was very shocked at some of the people that I regard very highly.[8]

And another member frankly stated,

> They did not feel that it was appropriate to have a Negro coming in such a responsible job. This was after all a white congre-

> gation and they would be very uncomfortable with the whole thing. They didn't want him. I didn't want it. People said they would leave the church if he came. They would withdraw their pledge. They were voting simply on his color. I admit that I would not have liked it at the time. I wasn't ready for it and voted against. Now I would be more willing to accept, but I would not have wanted to have been known as belonging to the church with a colored minister.[9]

Four members clearly remember that Andee Seegar, who had been a student at the University of Michigan when she first met Gene Sparrow and his wife Donna, delivered an impassioned speech in his support. She recalled, "In my naiveté I thought I would surely convince people to bring him in after all that had been said against him. I had to get up and at least give a character reference, which I did, and I don't think it influenced anybody."[8]

There is no record stating whether the vote was taken with a show of hands or ballot and no unanimity among those interviewed of its outcome. Some interviewed recalled it was close, others say it was overwhelmingly against calling Sparrow, and one person recalled a one-vote majority against.

The shock was followed by deafening silence. People simply did not want to talk about what had happened. Jo Birdsall, who was chairperson of the special committee, is remembered as being very disillusioned with the church. Seegar remarked that the decision had "something to do with my reluctance to take an active part in the church for many years thereafter."[9] Another person recalled, "The reason I felt violated is because my whole reason for joining the Unitarian Church was a profound belief that it had an umbrella that took in everybody and didn't discriminate. I was perhaps too idealistic about that at the time. I assumed everybody believed in these kinds of things. It seemed to me that the way the congregation reacted that night was totally anti-Unitarian."[10]

Another member concluded, "People were rather ashamed of themselves by the way they acted, especially the way they were charging against one another. I think what they really sort of did was say, 'Well, this is past and I am sorry I shouted at you.' And then went on. I don't recall any crisis as there might be today."[11]

The silence in Church of Our Fathers' records about the Sparrow vote is a powerful statement of the shock and shame that reverberated throughout a community that had failed to live up to its professed principles.

The voyage ahead for the Sparrows would prove rough. Records indicate that Gene Sparrow moved from one employer to another throughout the 1950s, attempting to find a niche for himself. He was acting director of the Urban League in Springfield, Massachusetts; director of Camp Atwater in Massachusetts, serving as chaplain and music director; then director of a recreational center in Connecticut.

Although he was ordained by the Ann Arbor Unitarian Church and carried on its roster as minister-at-large, he was never settled in a Unitarian congregation. His mentor and friend Rev. Edward Redman facilitated his employment as director of field service for the Western Unitarian Conference, a position that was abolished in 1962 after the consolidation of the Unitarians and Universalists.

During the 1960s, Sparrow held positions with Human Relations Councils, first as assistant director in Cincinnati, Ohio, and later as director in Grand Rapids, Michigan. In 1968, he settled into teaching anthropology and sociology as associate professor at Widener College in Chester, Pennsylvania. There, he collaborated in the development of Project Prepare, designed to aid academically able but financially disadvantaged students succeed in college.

His memorial service was held at Widener College in 1978. Eulogizing his friend, Rev. Edward Redman said, "Looking back on those days I know that we were too far out front, ahead of our times by a dozen years." Summing up, he said, "I have heard him speak of his longing to motivate his students to ever higher levels of accomplishment, not only for the sake of new opportunities opened, but to awaken in them an appreciation for the goals and values which possessed him."[14]

In 1990, Harvard Divinity School classmate and Unitarian Universalist colleague John Evans lamented, "I have no way of knowing whether he would have succeeded in the parish ministry, or even have been happy in the effort. But I regret, times and policies being what they were, that he never had a chance to find out."[15] Thwarted by Unitarian Universalism, Sparrow nonetheless found a way. Believing as he did that "the love of one's fellow humans is not just a passive intellectual concern for their welfare, it should manifest itself as an active effort to improve their lot,"[16] it was through teaching that he expressed his love.

—Nancy J. Doughty and Mark D. Morrison-Reed

Sources

Nancy Doughty first heard of Eugene Sparrow in 1962 when she was the minister of education at the First Unitarian Universalist Church of Detroit. Mark Morrison-Reed learned about him when he interviewed Rev. Edward Redman in 1978. The primary resource for this essay are eight interviews with people who were members of the Detroit congregation in 1950, carried out by Nancy in 1997. These were augmented by reviewing church minutes, newsletters, and correspondence, and conducting subsequent interviews. In 2005 Sparrow's family donated his papers to Meadville Lombard Theological School. In this trove of material the authors found "In Memory of Rev. Eugene Sparrow" by Redman, which succinctly described Sparrow's experience. Also helpful in understanding the roots of Sparrow's religiosity is his essay in Why I Believe There Is a God *(1965).*

ON THE EVE OF MERGER

One of those attending the American Unitarian Association (AUA) autumnal convention in 1860, at which Rev. William Jackson proclaimed his conversion to Unitarianism, was Rev. Samuel J. May. A supporter of William Lloyd Garrison—who many considered among the most radical of abolitionists—May was nonetheless held in high regard by everyone as "a brave, wise, eloquent, warm-hearted prophet and pastor."[1] At that gathering, May had spoken up to remind the audience of the importance of women in the advance of Unitarianism westward and to attest to their ability to perform good works, holding up the efforts of Lucy Stone and Angelina Grimke in "antislavery reform." Soon thereafter, he read to the convention a letter from British Unitarian colleagues, chastising the AUA for its fainted-hearted efforts against slavery. What is curious is that May is not recorded to have spoken up on behalf of Jackson. When he did rise, very soon after Jackson's testimony, it was to speak about fund-raising for missionary efforts in the West and a little later to table a response he had written to their British brethren. May was a kind, thoughtful visionary with a deep concern for the common good, yet Jackson seems to have been beneath his notice. May's silence presages a denominational pattern of speaking out against injustice but not reaching out to African Americans.

Ninety years later, in 1950, Eugene Sparrow's experience paralleled that of William Jackson. "I still remember," said Sparrow's mentor, Ed Redman, "some of the callousness and indifference of colleagues who a decade later prided themselves on their freedom-riding exploits and their closeness to CORE [Congress of Racial Equality] and to Martin Luther King."[2] In 1956, the vote for Lewis McGee in Flint, Michigan, had been so weak that he chose not to accept the call. By 1960, one hundred years after Jackson's testimony, on the eve of merger with the Universalists, progress had been made. But the old pattern of rhetorical moral outrage and reticent outreach still prevailed.

As a new decade began, signs were hopeful. In spring 1961, while America was still enthralled by President Kennedy's inaugural call, "Ask not what your country can do for you; ask what you can do for your country," Lewis McGee was the associate minister in Los Angeles. Rev. Benjamin Richardson, the youngest brother of Harry V. Richardson (whom the AUA had denied fellowship in 1930), was serving the Free Religious Fellowship that McGee had help found in 1948. Eugene Sparrow was director of field service for the Western Unitarian Conference. Pauline Warfield Lewis had been serving as the director of religious education at the First Unitarian Church of Cincinnati since 1956, and Bernice Bell Just had held that same position at All Souls Church, Unitarian, in Washington DC since 1957. Brown had died in 1956 and with him the Harlem church; Jeffrey Campbell still had not been settled; and William R. Jones, who had been fellowshipped in 1958 and served as an assistant minister in Providence, Rhode Island, until 1960, was working toward his PhD at Brown University.

In 1954, the AUA Commission on Intergroup Relations, which included two blacks—Rev. Howard Thurman and Dr. Errold D. Collymore, DDS—reported (with a response rate of one-third of the congregations) that of 170 societies, 52 had African-American members, with 13 having more than 5.[3] The report recommended that the AUA annual meeting be held at Fisk University following the annual race relations conference, a recommendation that was not pursued. Later that year, an African American, William Y. Bell, Jr., was appointed director of adult education and social relations for the Council of Liberal Churches (Universalist-Unitarian). The CLC was an intermediate step on the way to merger, and Bell served for several years before moving on.[4]

Beginning in 1955 the AUA and UUA concern for the issue of race and racial justice can also be seen in the books published by its wholly-owned subsidiary, Beacon Press. Some were provocative, seminal works. Foremost among the early titles were James Baldwin's *Notes of a Native Son* (1955) and Kenneth B. Clark's *Prejudice and Your Child* (1955).

By 1956, according to a *Christian Register* survey with a 55.8 percent response rate (i.e., 287 of 514 congregations), 80 had African-American members, and in 49 of those, African Americans were active as officers; that meant nearly 10 percent of Unitarian congregations had African-American members holding positions of leadership.[5] Indeed, by 1961, several congregations claimed memberships that were as much as 10 percent African American. This positive sign at the local level was less apparent nationally. At that level, Barbadian-born Collymore, an activist who had integrated the White Plains, New York, congregation in 1927 and later chaired its board, had served as an AUA Trustee from 1954 to 1957. But at the time of merger, there were no black department directors nor was there a black presence on the board. The lone African American sitting at the national level seems to have been Marcella McGee (the wife of Lewis McGee), who was a member of the joint board of the Alliance of Unitarian Women and Association of Universalist Women.

There was, however, one local congregation which would have a national scope and enduring impact. In 1959, the North Shore Unitarian Society (NSUS) on Long Island passed the Veatch Resolution which, with a bequest left to NSUS, established the Caroline Veatch Assistance and Extension Program (later renamed the Unitarian Universalist Veatch Program at Shelter Rock). As the Veatch Program grew, it and its UU Funding Program would become key players in promoting programs that addressed diversity, racial justice, and institutional change. The 2005 NSUS bylaws state, "The purposes of the Program are to foster and promote religious, charitable, benevolent or educational activities . . . which share our beliefs in the democratic process, the ideal of human kinship or the individual's potential for growth and dignity."[6] In the ensuing years, as it funded programs that a denomination chronically short of financial resources would not have been able to pay for, Veatch became the invisible hand supporting denominational diversity and racial justice efforts.

Individual Unitarian Universalists were also important constituents in the racial activism the UUA would be swept up in. After the success of the Montgomery Bus Boycott in 1956, civil rights actions increased. Members of local Unitarian congregations in Denver; Chicago; Kansas City; St. Paul; Barnstable, Massachusetts; and elsewhere were broadly involved in the issues of fair housing and equal access, but the focus was outward not inward. Religious outreach to African Americans was still not on the national Unitarian agenda. Nonetheless, the engagement of members of the new denomination in the civil rights movement was attracting African Americans. Thus, as merger approached, Unitarians and Universalists were cognizant of racism and their moral obligation to speak out and act against it—but this reality had no bearing regarding the birthing of the UUA. That was about to change.

—Mark D. Morrison-Reed

Sources

The primary resources for this essay are the denominational journals the Christian Register *and the* Universalist Leader. *In addition, the author drew on his experience of having visited over a hundred Unitarian Universalist congregations. Information about the UU Veatch Program at Shelter Rock can be found on its website: www.uucsr.org/veatch.*

THE UNIVERSALISTS

When John Murray founded the first Universalist meeting house in America, historian Russell Miller states, "among the eighty-five signatories of the Charter of the Compact of the Gloucester Society in 1785 [was] Gloster Dalton, an African brought to America as a slave."[1] In 1813, Thomas Jones, Murray's successor, reporting Dalton's death, wrote, "In this country from a youth. Supposed to be 90 years old, or upwards. The [sic] said Gloster Dalton was an honest, industrious man. . . . He was a believer in Jesus Christ, the Saviour of the world, and belonged to the independent Christian Society many years. He was a native of Africa, and brought away as a slave (so called). For there are no slaves! All men are born free!!!"[2] Dalton was not an anomaly. In 1801, Amy Scott, a black woman, was one of the incorporators of the First Universalist Society organized in Philadelphia. In the 1830s, Nathan Johnson, a prominent African-American citizen of New Bedford, Massachusetts, and conductor on the Underground Railroad, became a member of its Universalist church when John Murray Spears, an abolitionist, was its minister.

In 1784, the Universalist Benjamin Rush, who was among the first to call for the abolition of slavery, helped to organize and later served as president of the Pennsylvania Society for Promoting the Abolition of Slavery. The core of the Universalist argument against slavery was to emphasize "the fatherhood of God and the brotherhood of man"[3] and to decry slavery as not distinguishing between "man and property."[4] Elhanan Winchester, an early Universalist itinerant preacher, who spent considerable time preaching to slaves, found the institution wholly inconsistent with a belief in "one great family." His message to those held in bondage was that Jesus "loved them, and died for them as well as for us white people."[5]

Universalism, like Unitarianism, began as a form of anti-Calvinism, and similarly, its strength was in the Northeast. Nonetheless, there were Universalist ministers, state conventions, and journals in the South that defended slavery. The editor of the *Evangelical Universalist* wrote in 1839, "We do not admit slavery to be evil, but the greatest blessing that ever happened to the Negro race."[6] Southerners constituted a small portion of the denomination but Northerners, wary of causing a split as had happened in other denominations, kept antislavery resolutions from reaching the floor of their assemblies. When in 1837, Adin Ballou adopted a radical abolitionist stand, many members of his congregation in Mendon, Massachusetts, left.

Notwithstanding, advocates of abolition kept the pressure up until—as the tension continued to mount nationally—the Vermont, the Massachusetts, and the General Conventions all adopted antislavery resolutions in 1843 and 1844. In response, the Georgia Convention proposed withdrawing from the General Convention, but nothing came of it. Leading antislavery laypersons were Maine Congressman Israel Washburn Jr. and Horace Greeley, the editor of the *New York Tribune*. However, in general, Universalists were not among the leaders in antislavery societies, and their debates and organizations remained internal to their movement. This insularity could explain why Universalism did not attract the caliber of African-American abolitionists that Unitarianism did.

Following the Civil War, only a few African Americans were drawn to Universalism, the missionary efforts being slight. The exception is significant. The Universalist mission in Virginia's Tidewater region spanned nearly one hundred years. Five essays in this section recount the rise and decline of that unique endeavor and the dominant role its educational objectives played. The story is told through the lives of Joseph Jordan, Thomas E. Wise, Mary J. Jordan, Joseph Fletcher Jordan, and Annie B. Willis.

Elsewhere, evidence of African-American involvement in Universalism is scant but does exist. The most important of these stories is that of Jeffrey Campbell and his sister, Marguerite, of Nashua, New Hampshire. Jeff would attend St. Lawrence, the Universalist's theological school in Canton, New York and become a minister, while Marguerite would spend thirty-three years working first for the Universalist Church of America (UCA) and after 1961, the UUA. Their story includes excerpts from an article written by Jeff that appeared in the *Christian Leader* in 1940 after its editor attacked Marguerite's marriage to a Euro-American Universalist seminary student. The 1943 UCA's "Affirmation of Social Principles" is also included. It provides a point of comparison to the 1942 AUA General Assembly's "Resolution on Race Relations," as the two denominations were within a few years of renewing a skittish courtship that would lead to the consolidation of the UCA and AUA in 1961. The section ends with "Universalism's Theological Conundrum." After reviewing Universalist efforts, it reflects on possible factors that limited Universalism's appeal to African Americans.

JOSEPH JORDAN
1842–1901

The first speaker, a genuine representative of the race once enslaved, was . . . Rev. Joseph Jordan of Virginia, his topic being "Our Mission Among the Colored People." Tall, straight as an arrow, stalwart of muscle, his presence evoked applause.

—Christian Leader

Joseph Jordan, the first African American to be ordained as a minister by the Universalist denomination, founded the First Universalist Church of Norfolk, Virginia, in 1887, and led an ever-expanding educational effort for African-American children in Norfolk and vicinity. The mission and schools born of his vision and efforts served thousands of children and families in eastern Virginia until 1984.

Joseph Jordan (pronounced "Jerden," and sometimes mistakenly referred to as "Joseph H. Jordan" in historical writing) was born free in June 1842, in the settlement of West Norfolk in Norfolk County, Virginia, on the Elizabeth River, downstream from the city of Norfolk. One of several children of Elizabeth Jordan, he took up at an early age the trade of oysterman, as did many free blacks of the time. When he was twenty-one, Joseph moved to Norfolk to seek greater opportunity. There he married Indianna Brown, also free-born. The couple had three children. Some years later, Indianna left to go on her own, taking their only surviving child with her. Joseph frequently changed occupations—oysterman, laborer, grocer, and finally carpenter. At this trade, he was quite successful, earning enough money to buy or build several houses in the Norfolk suburb of Huntersville and to live off the rent. Literate, skilled, and a property owner, he was among the elite of his race and poised to become a leader in his community.

Religion was a deeply felt calling to Jordan. By 1880, he had been ordained a Baptist minister and become a preacher in that faith alongside his trade as a carpenter. A few years later, a Methodist colleague gave Jordan a book that had come into his possession and asked him what he thought of it. The book, Thomas Whittemore's *The Plain Guide to Universalism*, made an immediate, powerful, and lasting impression. While it is not known what passages particularly attracted Jordan, Whittemore's book explained the goodness of the universe, the loving parental guidance of the Almighty for all of humanity, and the promise of salvation for all. Universalism was not a religion of the bigoted but for those who could accept that God's love extended to all equally and that God encouraged toward holiness both the powerless and the powerful, the oppressed and their oppressors. This rejection of "partialism" contrasted starkly with the prevailing attitude among blacks in the 1880s who, as subjugation and segregation became increasingly implanted in Southern society, believed that white oppressors would surely suffer in hell. Whatever the specific cast of the Universalist faith for Joseph Jordan, he was ready to devour all he could find on Universalism, and soon acquired John Bovee Dods's sermons to add to the Whittemore volume for what would be a growing library of his new faith.

No longer able to preach the Baptist faith because his conscience wouldn't allow him, Jordan continued plying the carpenter's trade while he pondered what his new discovery would call him to do. It came to him to go to Philadelphia, where he knew Universalists formed a significant community. Once there, he went straight to Rev. Edwin C. Sweetser, minister of the Church of the Messiah. The Universalist movement had been searching for a way to reach out to the vast population of blacks in the South, now that they were supposedly free and no longer under the restrictive slave laws of the past. Sweetser was alive to this urge within the white denomination to reach out. It was a propitious meeting, and Joseph Jordan remained in Philadelphia for seven months, studying and worshiping with Sweetser as his spiritual mentor. Their mutual respect deepened and reached toward friendship, even if within the limits of the social restrictions of the era. Studying with Sweetser deepened Joseph Jordan's faith and led him to the writings of other Universalists. Those of Alonso Ames Miner and Thomas B. Thayer made an especially deep impression.

Returning to Norfolk, Jordan began to preach the Universalist faith to anyone who would listen. He rented a room at 42 Lincoln Street as a chapel, which shortly became packed with worshipers. Employing his skill as a carpenter, he fashioned a pulpit for his makeshift chapel. Ever more certain of his calling, Jordan and his congregation of twenty families formally organized themselves as a Universalist mission on June 29, 1887. Jordan had a double vision, of a full-time ministry among his people and the establishment of a day school to meet the needs of the educationally denied black children of Norfolk. To Jordan, church and education went hand in hand to help one live life with dignity, purpose, and effectiveness, and to empower oneself and one's community. He then raised the question with Edwin Sweetser whether he could become a recognized Universalist minister. Sweetser referred the issue to the Universalist General Convention, which, in 1888, issued Jordan a formal license to preach for one year, the normal step toward ordination.

On March 30, 1889, the formal Universalist Ordaining Council of three distinguished ministers (Sweetser, James Shrigley, and Gerhardus L. Demarest) and four laypersons met with Jordan in the Church of the Messiah to examine his fitness for the Universalist ministry. The council found his candidacy satisfactory. Upon a unanimous recommendation, the next day, March 31, 1889, Jordan was ordained as a Universalist minister in full standing at a ceremony in the Church of the Messiah. The Universalist denomination had now welcomed its first African-American minister just as, in 1863, it was the first denomination to welcome a woman minister, Rev. Olympia Brown.

Jordan returned to Norfolk with crates of books and the hope that the Universalist faith would spread ever more widely and deeply in the African-American communities of the South. His church was quickly admitted into fellowship by the Universalist General Convention, and the Lincoln Street house soon bore a sign proclaiming itself the First Universalist Church of Norfolk.

Jordan engaged in his work with zeal, and the rented chapel room became so crowded with worshipers that a larger space was needed. The financial ability of the congregation and the $491 contribution from the denomination were completely insufficient to build a church and school building. In 1893, Jordan journeyed to Washington DC for the meeting of the General Convention, where he addressed the delighted delegates on the need to fund an adequate building. Donations quickly added up to $2,758, enough to build a church and provide for some of its necessary furnishings. In November 1894, the new building was dedicated. It contained a separate sanctuary and church schoolroom, and was located on Princess Anne Avenue in the heart of Norfolk's black community. Jordan and his assistants taught day school to 90–100 children during the week, fully utilizing both rooms, while Sunday evening worship attracted up to thirty-five congregants. Occasionally, white Universalists, without a church of their own in Norfolk, attended. Universalist missionary Quillen Shinn organized a chapter of the Young People's Christian Union and envisioned great plans for expansion of the "mission to the Colored people."

By 1900, the day-school attendance settled down to an average of fifty pupils, served by a staff of three teachers, while participation in worship services declined. The desire for education by African-American parents in Norfolk remained high, and despite other private and church-sponsored schools for blacks, the demand always outstripped the opportunities. Universalism as a faith, however, was radical in social implications, controversial in the local black press, a challenge to the established black churches, and a white-run national institution. Congregants tended to be from among the independent-minded residents of Norfolk, just the kind of people who were attracted to the city from the rural South, and also more likely to move to northern cities in search of even greater opportunity. Regular subsidies by the Universalist General Convention kept the church open and the day school going. Nevertheless, while the day school remained strong, the church congregation lost key laypeople and withered.

In February 1896, Jordan had married Mary Elizabeth Clark, twenty-seven years his junior, and a teacher in Jordan's school. In October 1896, she gave birth to a son they named Richard Sweetser Jordan, his middle name in honor of Joseph's Universalist mentor and supporter in Philadelphia.

On June 3, 1901, Joseph Jordan died at fifty-nine of an unknown disease. The funeral was held in the church he had founded, his colleague and successor, Rev. Thomas E. Wise, officiating. Ministers from other black churches attended, suspicion about the foreign and strange Universalist faith having somewhat lessened. The following year, young Richard Sweetser Jordan died of tuberculosis, and his mother of the same disease the year after.

With the passing of Jordan's immediate family, proceeds from the Jordan estate, which Joseph Jordan had bequeathed to the Universalist General Convention, went to support the growing Universalist mission in Suffolk, Virginia, a daughter mission spawned by the Norfolk church. The First Universalist Church of Norfolk and its day school limped along without steady leadership, steadily declining until 1906, when it was closed. Attempts over the next decade to revive a Norfolk congregation of African-American Universalists failed. The church building lovingly built by Joseph Jordan was sold and became a billiard parlor. Yet the daughter Suffolk mission grew, prospered, and became, until its close in 1984, a vital legacy of Joseph Jordan's calling to the Universalist faith and to his people.

Jordan's obituary in the *Universalist Leader* said of him,

> He was a man of good mind, and wrought a good work among us. Chiefly by his presentation of the condition of affairs at Norfolk and the possibility of good work there, the people in attendance on the General Convention held in Washington, D.C. a few years ago, pledged a sum sufficient for the erection of a chapel and schoolroom for his work. He was a man of clean, pure life, and his ministry and teachings were greatly blessed to those whom he was able to reach.[1]

—Willard Frank

Sources

A prime source of information on Joseph Jordan is the denominational newspaper, the Christian Leader, *later the* Universalist Leader. *Other sources include the records of the Universalist General Convention and the Shinn papers in the Unitarian Universalist Special Collections at Andover-Harvard Theological Library, U.S. census records, and local official records.*

THOMAS E. WISE
1868–AFTER 1930

The trouble is that people have had but very little of our doctrine preached to them. They say that for several years they have heard it only when Dr. Shinn made his semi-annual visits. We left Canton, NY just one week (March 29) too late to keep eight of our members of the Norfolk Church from following Mr. Wise into the Methodist Church.

—Joseph Fletcher Jordan

Thomas E. Wise, the second African-American Universalist minister to serve the First Universalist Church and school in Norfolk, Virginia, also founded missions and schools in Suffolk and Ocean View. Yet, after having continuously endeavored to expand the missions' outreach, he left the Universalist fold, discouraged over his conflict of vision with white denominational leadership.

The son of illiterate parents—Michael and Mary Ann Wise, an oysterman and a homemaker, respectively—Thomas E. Wise was born in the settlement of Sycamore City (present-day Churchland), Virginia, on July 25, 1868, the middle of three brothers. As a child, he worked in the fields and attended school, and as his intellectual achievements grew, he found an opportunity to attend Howard University in Washington DC. There, at age twenty-two, he married Ida H. Graves; they would have and raise three sons.

Wise's scientific education led him to doubt his traditional faith, to explore Universalism, and to learn of the work of Joseph

Jordan in Norfolk. After living for a while in Delaware, the Wise family returned to southeastern Virginia and moved into the same Huntersville neighborhood where Jordan lived. In the late 1880s, Wise joined Jordan as a teacher and associate in the Norfolk church. A tireless organizer, he soon became the academic principal of the school.

In 1894, prominent black citizens of Suffolk, twenty miles southwest of Norfolk, called upon Wise to establish a school like the one he served in Norfolk. Wise rented a hall and organized a Universalist mission and church school on weekends, while serving the Norfolk school during the work week. The Suffolk mission profited from the good contacts Wise had in the community. It even benefitted from the attack on Universalism by traditional Suffolk-area black ministers and Wise's spirited defense of the faith in the pages of the black press, which brought defections from the congregations of established churches into the fold of the Universalist mission.

Also in 1894, the Universalist denomination granted Wise a preliminary license to preach, and the next year, while he was attending the Young People's Christian Union in Boston, the ordaining council, having examined him and found him fit for the Universalist ministry, approved him. The ordination ceremony took place in the Norfolk church on October 16, 1895; preaching the sermon, Jordan charged Wise to live and toil, watch and pray, being so full of the work of religion that he would have no time for trivial things. Several white Universalist ministers and laypersons attended the two days of festivities.

The Universalist General Convention, stimulated by having a second black minister and a second mission in the South, and with the hopeful vision of the wide expansion of the faith among African Americans, solicited funds for a church and school building in Suffolk, which Quillen Shinn continued as a personal challenge, raising over a thousand dollars by 1897. This was enough to purchase a lot on Tynes Street in Suffolk and build a two-story mission building, much of the labor and some of the materials donated by local craftspeople attracted to Universalism. It was dedicated as St. Paul's Universalist Mission on December 22, 1897, Shinn enthusiastically participating in the ceremony and planning an early expansion. Wise shared this vision.

Being so heavily engaged in the Norfolk school, in 1898, Wise had to hire other teachers for the Suffolk mission, including Ida, who had just received her diploma from the Norfolk school. The Suffolk day school at first included 40 pupils, but by 1901, the average attendance was 76 out of 275 on the rolls; since the children needed to work in the fields and mills to help sustain their families, attendance fluctuated with the seasons. Church attendance was never high, and the mission church remained dependent on the mission school. The community grew to accept the Universalist faith and school, however, and Wise became a welcome guest in the pulpits and church schools of the established churches as well as a lecturer at community clubs.

After the death of Joseph Jordan in 1901, Wise and his family moved from Norfolk to Suffolk and occupied the apartment on the second floor of the mission building, leaving the Norfolk school in the hands of less capable teachers. Attendance in Norfolk declined to an average of twenty-two, a fourth that of Suffolk. Wise acted as administrator and pastor for both missions, preaching to each congregation on alternate Sundays, and promising a great future for both. With the full support of Shinn, Wise created a third mission at Ocean View, eight miles north of Norfolk. Black residents there, employed by the white seaside resort, had no educational opportunities. In 1903, the new Ocean View mission had twenty students under a newly hired teacher. Wise promised that all three mission churches and schools would soon become self-supporting. Although Wise's primary leadership qualities were his enthusiasm, vision, and dedication, they were insufficient to sustain missions where he was not a steady presence.

In the face of Wise and Shinn's hopes for expansion, other denominational leaders—including John van Schaick Jr. of Washington DC, minister of the Universalist church closest to the

Suffolk Mission—became increasingly concerned that the missions were financially unsound and that Wise's promises were empty and his Universalist doctrinal foundation shaky. The Universalist General Convention in 1903 appointed a commission composed of Shinn, van Schaick, and General Superintendent Isaac M. Atwood to investigate. The commission concluded that Wise was overextended, that only the Suffolk mission should remain open, and that the educational focus should be on the Hampton Institute model of practical and industrial training, popularized by Booker T. Washington. Wise, however, wanted to retain all three missions and ensure that there remained academic education for the most talented young people—a position popularized by W.E.B. DuBois, in opposition to Washington.

With difficulty, Wise continued to juggle his multiple responsibilities while maintaining an outward optimism, but the strain of the work and the lack of support from denominational leaders except for Shinn took their toll. In March 1904, realizing he no longer had the denomination's backing, Wise gave up the effort, left the Universalist fold, and joined the African Methodist Episcopal Church, taking eight members of the much-weakened First Universalist Church of Norfolk with him.

Eventually the Wise family moved to Alexandria where, without the chance to follow their educational dreams, Thomas became a grocer, and Ida a laundress. By 1920, the couple had divorced. Thomas E. Wise was still listed as a grocer in Alexandria in the 1930 census. By that time, Joseph Fletcher Jordan, the successor to Wise in the Virginia mission and school in Suffolk, had died, but that school which Wise had founded, continued to thrive and serve the people of Suffolk and Nansemond County, much as Wise had envisioned it would, and did so for another fifty-four years.

—Willard Frank

Sources

Prime sources of information on Thomas E. Wise are the denominational newspaper, the Christian Leader, *later the* Universalist Leader; *records of the Universalist General Convention and the Shinn papers in the Unitarian Universalist Special Collections at Andover-Harvard Theological Library; U.S. census records; and local official records.*

MARY J. JORDAN
1865–1916

Trust in God, Be of Good Cheer, and Do the Best You Can.
—Mary J. Jordan

Mary J. Jordan was an African-American Universalist leader, teacher, and witness in North Carolina and Virginia from 1903 until her death. She was a strong partner with her husband, Rev. Joseph Fletcher Jordan, in developing the character of the children who flocked to their Suffolk Normal Training School in Virginia. Parents understood that at the Jordans' school, their children would get the best education for a quality life in the real world under Jim Crow.

Mary J. Davis was born in Clinton, North Carolina, at the end of the Civil War, the daughter of Simon and Anne Bizzell Davis, from whom she inherited French, Indian, and African ancestry. Of deep religious spirit from an early age, she nurtured an intense ambition to gain an education and become a missionary. She attended North Carolina public schools and then Shaw University in Raleigh, from which she graduated in 1884. Known for her consistently gentle and kind demeanor and for her patient and energetic spirit, she had the qualities needed to become a successful teacher. She returned to Clinton, where she dedicated herself to her new profession of service.

In 1892, she married Joseph Fletcher Jordan, an African Methodist Episcopal minister. This marriage brought together two talented and dedicated professionals in the advancement of the human spirit through religion and education. Sharing similar intellectual and moral concerns, they buoyed each other's spirits and blended their work in dedication to the welfare of others. A friend who knew them well stated that Mary was Joseph's inspiration. The couple moved to Louisburg, North Carolina, where Joseph took up the duties as pastor of a Presbyterian church. Both became teachers to local children there, winning the town's friendship. Mary Jordan bore two children, Annie Bizzell Jordan, in 1893, and Martha J. Jordan, in 1894.

During these years, both Mary and Joseph struggled with religious doubts. Joseph gave up the ministry, and the family moved to Durham, where they discovered a Bible-based Universalism that remained in the back of their minds. Then, in 1902, they heard the Universalist missionary Quillen H. Shinn preach in the Durham courthouse. Halfway through the sermon, Joseph whispered to Mary, "That's what I am." Mary replied, "Make it two."[1] Within a day, after a deep conversation with Shinn, the Jordans took up the call to embark on a new life as Universalist missionaries and teachers. In 1904, they settled in St. Paul's Universalist Church and Mission School in Suffolk, Virginia, which Thomas E. Wise had just abandoned, for what would be their life's work.

The early years in Suffolk were difficult. Building up the church and day school, with Universalism denounced from other pulpits and in the black press, took its toll on Joseph's spirits. Yet Mary always reminded him to be of good cheer and to trust in God, whereupon his hopefulness and energy were restored. Universalist general superintendent I. M. Atwood praised the Jordans for doing heroic work on slender resources. The Jordans were a close, mutually supportive team, whose work was guided by love and discipline to nurture a self-respecting, eager, and skilled person in each child.

Mary Jordan taught both academic subjects and practical skills. She never turned a child away, even if parents could not pay the five cents per week tuition. The school was its own best advertisement, due to the quality of its educational program and the care and skill of the teachers, who infused a rigorous curriculum and full school schedule with building the character and nurturing the self-worth of each child. White and black leaders of Suffolk extended their support. Among those highly impressed were the white mayor of Suffolk, the chief of police, and the superintendent of schools. Parents flocked to send their children to what the Jordans called the Suffolk Normal Training School, a bustling place seven days a week. Mary became clerk of the church, services being held in the school's main assembly room. Daughter Annie led the thirty youth of the Young People's Christian Union, while her musically talented sister Martha played the organ and piano for both church and school as well as musical events in the community. Worship service attendance averaged forty, and the school drew in increasing numbers of children walking from far and near to the mission school and church on Tynes Street.

Hundreds of children were enrolled every year, but it was an era in which children were expected to help out in the fields, allowing for most only a part-time education. Nevertheless, the Jordans made it a point to know each child's home and to encourage a loving family life. By 1911, the Jordans and their hired teachers had served 1,400 pupils, ranging in age from five to eighteen, in grades kindergarten through high school. On Fridays, all the students received a nondenominational religious education based on Universalist principles and curriculum materials. From 1907 to 1912, the property was expanded and the building increased in size, but enrollments also grew to 300 per year without solicitation, solely due to the school's reputation. Annual school graduation exercises included performances by the children and drew thousands as the main cultural event of the year.

In October 1916, Mary Jordan contracted pneumonia, and she died on November 3, at fifty-one years of age. Her funeral was held in a large Baptist church. There, from the pulpit where Universalism had once been denounced, a dedicated Universalist was eulogized as an extraordinary woman who loved life, loved children, and filled downtrodden souls with character and strength. Many who came to the funeral had to be turned away for lack of even room to stand. The school was closed for a week to honor her memory but went on to be a most respected institution dear to the hearts of the community for almost a century. Her tombstone reads, "Our trials ended, our rest won." Her legacy, however, lives on in the lives of the generations of community folk, who still today pass by the school building where Mary Jordan devoted so much of her life to so many, and pause in gratitude and respect.

—Willard Frank

Sources

Prime sources of information on Mary Jordan are the denominational newspaper, the Christian Leader, *later the* Universalist Leader; *the* Norfolk Journal and Guide; *records of the Universalist General Convention and the Shinn papers in the Unitarian Universalist Special Collections at Andover-Harvard Theological Library; U.S. census records; family records; and Suffolk official records.*

JOSEPH FLETCHER JORDAN
1863–1929

The mission is an influential factor in the uplift of the colored race in that community, and its maintenance constitutes a partial discharge, at least, of the obligation that our church, in common with all others, is undertaking to aid in the righting of a great wrong.

—H. E. Williams

Applying the Universalist principles of love, nurturing, and discipline to develop the character of his congregation and students, Joseph Fletcher Jordan—who was not related to Rev. Joseph Jordan who founded the Norfolk, Virginia, mission—was the dedicated minister of the St. Paul's Universalist Church and principal of the Suffolk Normal Training School, in Virginia, from 1904 to 1929. He believed that building character was foundational to mastering the academic subjects and living a quality life. Parents, appreciating his approach, flocked to send their children to Jordan's school, and none were turned away. Many of his students became leaders in the community, in the professions, and one the vice mayor of Suffolk.

Joseph, the child of twenty-three-year-old Mary Anne Jordan, was born into slavery in the area called Pocoson of the Great Dismal Swamp in Gates County, North Carolina. Given that Joseph listed his father's name as William, and was classified as mulatto by census takers, his father was likely William Jordan, the nineteen-year-old son of slaveholder Coston Jordan.

Joseph grew up with his mother and three siblings in this deeply rural setting. An alert and inquiring child, he went on his own to school at the age of nine; for this show of independence, his mother gave him a severe thrashing and sent him ten miles deeper into the Dismal Swamp to be the protector of an elderly woman. At fourteen, he learned bricklaying and plastering, and became the custodian of the local white Methodist church. The job required him to attend church services and Sunday school every week. Thus, he was carried into the Methodist faith and joined the African Methodist Episcopal (AME) church, but he never accepted what the minister and his elders said about hell and endless punishment.

Joseph attended the Plymouth, North Carolina, normal school, and graduated in 1885 at age twenty-two. That same year, he married eighteen-year-old Mary E. Beamon. They had two children, William Fletcher Jordan, in 1886, and Mary E. Jordan, in 1888. During this time, Joseph was ordained an AME minister and became pastor of the AME Zion church in Wilson, North Carolina. He served with distinction, despite his strong doubts about the doctrine of endless damnation, and in 1890 received a doctor of divinity degree from Barretts College. While he was "thinking hard"[1] on religion, his young wife died, leaving him with two children. But on July 26, 1892, he married college-educated Mary J. Davis. Her positive faith, gentle demeanor, and strong character provided the pillar on which Joseph would lean when his spirit flagged. Mary, all observed, was the delight of his life. Joseph and Mary brought two children into the world—Annie Bizzell Jordan, born May 30, 1893, and Martha J. Jordan, born in December 1894.

During these years, Joseph received a package from a friend in Albany, New York, containing a copy of E. H. Lake's *Key to Truth*. Lake had been the Universalist minister in Norfolk, Virginia, in the 1850s, and his book set out "arguments in favor of Universalism and objections to endless punishment."[2] Both Joseph and Mary devoured the book.

Lake put forth that Christ came to save us not from eternal punishment but from sin and unbelief. Christ came to reveal God's love for all humanity. The punishment of sin leads to repentance, which leads to forgiveness, when we are finally free of sin. Our duty is summed up in active love, which begets more love, until one is "swallowed up in the boundless ocean of God's impartial love,"[3] until God's final goal is attained, "the final holiness and happiness of all mankind."[4]

At this point, neither Joseph nor Mary had any religious affiliation, but both used Lake's book for their private devotions. Still on the path of finding a new religious foundation, Joseph took the position of minister to the Presbyterian church in Louisburg, North Carolina, while he and Mary also taught school. This halfway step, however, was not soul-satisfying, so he gave up the active ministry. Around the turn of the twentieth century, they moved to Durham, where he concentrated on reading law, passed the bar exam, and established a legal practice.

Joseph read in the newspaper that the Universalist missionary Quillen Shinn would be preaching at the Durham courthouse. The whole family of six went down to hear him. Midway through the sermon, Joseph whispered to Mary, "That's what I am." Mary whispered back, "Make it two."[5] After the service, Shinn introduced himself to the Jordans, who invited him to their home for further talk. Within a day, Joseph and Mary had found a spiritual home in the Universalist faith and a calling as missionaries in Virginia, where the overextended Thomas E. Wise, trying to serve three missions—and with a wobbly theological foundation in Universalism—was raising concerns among the denominational leadership.

The Universalist Church received Jordan as a Universalist minister in January 1903. To provide Jordan the Universalist theological foundation that Wise lacked, Shinn and the dean of the theological school of St. Lawrence University in Canton, New York, Henry Prentiss Forbes, created a special one-year course for Jordan. Otherwise well-prepared for the Universalist ministry, Jordan studied Universalist theology during the 1903–1904 academic year and interacted with Universalist leaders as well as fellow students, including Clarence Russell Skinner, who would become one of Universalism's great thinkers and advocates of social justice. In March 1904, Jordan journeyed to Virginia, only to find the Norfolk, Ocean View, and Suffolk missions in disarray, Wise having abandoned them and the Universalist faith just the week before.

Jordan closed the Norfolk and Ocean View schools, concentrating his efforts in Suffolk, where he and Mary undertook all the instruction and occupied upstairs rooms as their residence. The first years were difficult. The traditional black churches attacked Universalism. The Jordans, however, were always happy explaining their faith to others and seeing the school and the church grow. School enrollment increased from 91 in 1905 to 174 in 1911, and the church active membership from 8 in 1905 to 15 in 1912, while the Young People's Christian Union (YPCU) remained stable at between 20 and 22. Jordan disseminated a monthly newspaper, *The Colored Universalist*, which brought in quantities of donated materials from Universalists around the country. In Suffolk, daughters Mary, Annie, and Martha, and Professor James W. Wilson complemented Joseph and Mary to comprise the staff. Once this was established, Jordan made unsuccessful efforts to breathe new life into the Norfolk school, but after 1907, concentrated all his efforts on expanding the Suffolk school.

Most denominational leaders supported Jordan's dream of a greatly expanded school in Suffolk. The plan, endorsed by Universalist general superintendent William H. McGlauflin, was for the Suffolk school to expand to include all grades, the trades and academics, and a theological school for the training of black Universalist ministers to fan out in the South and propagate the faith. One prominent opponent, John van Schaick, minister of the Church of Our Father in Washington DC, argued that Universalists should operate a school temporarily only to fill a gap until local authorities would establish public schools. Jordan replied that van Schaick did not know the local circumstances or the special character of the school, which Jordan now formally named the Suffolk Normal Training School (SNTS).[6] Besides, were the school to close, the public schools could not absorb the hundreds of students. The sale of the Norfolk church building brought in $2,000. If an additional $6,000 could be raised by Universalist churches and individuals around the country, Jordan and McGlauflin could realize their dream. Meanwhile, the General Convention earmarked that much annually (and $275,000 in total by 1917) for the Japan mission,[7] while the Suffolk mission was left to be supported largely by its own efforts and those of its supporters.

Jordan traveled among the Universalist churches of the Northeast in 1911 and 1912, soliciting funds, arguing that "the Negro is as susceptible to Universalism as any other race,"[8] a proposition that many white Universalists doubted. Money was slow to accumulate. By the target date of March 1912, only $1,491 in cash and pledges of the expected $6,000 had come in. Disappointed, Jordan had to settle for only an addition to the existing building, not the campus of several buildings and increased staff as hoped.

The enlarged building, however, allowed enrollment to rise to three hundred students. Martha and Annie, both newly married, were unpaid teachers, to whose bubbly and affectionate natures the children readily responded. Mary handled the kindergarten and primary grades, and Martha taught music. Special gifts from Universalists around the country allowed the installation of indoor plumbing, new student desks, and the addition of a range for the kitchen and a phonograph, which fascinated the children.

When in 1916, Planters Nut and Chocolate Company built a large factory close by the SNTS, Jordan worked closely with the management to secure employment for the graduates of his school. In return, he kept the school open during Planters' working hours so working mothers would have a safe and educational place for their children while they worked.

The large first-floor classroom doubled as a chapel for the twenty-nine members of the St. Paul's Universalist Church. Sunday school enrollment stood at forty-two, and the YPCU at twenty-four, while on Friday mornings, the entire school had Universalist religious instruction utilizing Universalist curriculum materials, being careful that the instruction was not objectionable to Baptist or Methodist parents.

In addition to his duties with the church and school, Jordan served as the Suffolk and Nansemond County correspondent for the *Norfolk Journal and Guide*, was an agent for an insurance company, and served as juvenile probation officer. He was a vigorous supporter of the Tidewater Fair Association, which organized an annual fair with many diverse entertainments for the black community.

On November 3, 1916, at age fifty-one, Mary J. Jordan died of pneumonia. The Pine Street Baptist Church, a former opponent of Universalism, donated its large sanctuary for the funeral. Still, many were turned away for lack of seating or standing room. Within weeks, Joseph's daughter Mary was injured when the automobile in which she was riding turned over. Joseph knew the fragility of life, but his love, humor, dedication, and determination to go on sustained him. Within a year, he courted and married Viola Page.

In 1917, the General Convention challenged the racial discrimination and segregation then at a peak by adopting a social agenda, largely crafted by Clarence R. Skinner, to foster global human worth and social and economic equality. Concentration on the social meaning of Universalism, along with the disparity between the weak St. Paul's Universalist Church and the strong Suffolk Normal Training School, led the General Convention to transfer the Suffolk operation from the jurisdiction of the General Convention—which emphasized nurturing churches toward self-sustaining independence—to the General Sunday School Association (GSSA)—which emphasized nurturing Universalist values. Thus, the GSSA would support the educational efforts in Suffolk, while the Suffolk school would provide lesson materials and suggestions to Universalist Sunday schools around the country to help students learn to respect and honor African Americans.

Sunday schools raised money to support Jordan's efforts. Offerings, which totaled $440 in 1917, rose to $950 by 1919. Nevertheless, Universalists put greater emphasis on Armenian relief, which drew in $10,500 in 1920 alone. In 1922, however, the GSSA nearly equalized the previous disparity of funds going to the Japan and Suffolk missions. The first $1,000 of an American Missionary Offering (soon renamed American Friendship Offering) would go to Suffolk, and the first $1,300 of an International Missionary Offering would go to Japan. Any additional money would be allocated among other projects. In total, the SNS received from all Universalist sources in the coming years an average of $1,200 to $1,400 per year, allowing the expansion of kindergarten and other efforts. The promotion of interracial understanding and friendships by the GSSA in the 1920s was revolutionary, especially considering in these years the heightened white fear of blacks and Catholics, the rise in lynchings, and new prominence of the Ku Klux Klan.[9]

Public schools in the 1920s offered only ninth-grade education for blacks and restricted their school year to six months. Private schools had to fill the gap, primarily the Nansemond Collegiate Institute and the SNTS, with an average of four hundred and three hundred pupils respectively. Jordan was able to add to his teaching staff, and to include science and Latin to the curriculum. "Professor Jordan" insisted that his pupils dress neatly, pull their socks up, and that the boys wear a necktie (which Jordan always wore), even if it were only a strip of cloth. He kept a stick named "Betsy" in the corner, to which he would point if any child needed special encouragement to follow rules. Jordan expected the children to be on time and to be truthful, and they lived up to that expectation. To keep in touch with the community, Jordan rode a bicycle around the city. He and his daughters, Martha and Annie, created and organized special three-day school closing ceremonies each spring, where the students—the boys in suits and the girls in white—would sing, recite, and dance. Graduating students received their diplomas. For these ceremonies, he had to rent the largest available hall to hold the nine hundred to a thousand persons from the community who converged on the hall with their twenty-five-cent admission fee.

Jordan always maintained that with more resources and ministers, the black communities of the South, as they grew to understand Universalism, would embrace it. Yet he was the only black Universalist minister in the nation, and he and his family were fully engaged in running the school, leaving little opportunity to spread the Universalist message.

As Jordan's health, uncertain since the beginning of the 1920s, deteriorated, he frequently required hospitalization. Then, on November 5, 1927, Viola suddenly died, sending Jordan into a nervous breakdown. Nevertheless, his Universalist faith sustained him. He trusted being in the hands of the power of divine love, and returned to devote himself to his life's work to the degree his health allowed. With further decline, he gathered his family and friends, and to daughter Annie, he bestowed his trust. Joseph Fletcher Jordan passed into eternity on the morning of May 1, 1929.

A longtime friend published this tribute in the *Norfolk Journal and Guide*:

> Dr. Jordan was a man, truly a man. His personality was felt in every home he touched. His teachings and influence live in the hearts of his pupils. The Suffolk Training School is the pride of the community. His mouth is hushed, but his voice is heard still. He found Suffolk a wilderness of ignorance and crudeness. He leaves it a garden of intelligence and culture.[10]

—Willard Frank

Sources

Prime sources of information on Joseph Fletcher Jordan are the records of the Universalist General Convention and the Shinn papers in the Unitarian Universalist Special Collections at Andover-Harvard Theological Library; the denominational newspaper, the Christian Leader, *later the* Universalist Leader; *the* Norfolk Journal and Guide; *the* New York Age; Our Mission to the Colored People

(1912) and What the Universalist Church Is Doing *(1909), both by William H. McGlauflin; U.S. census records; family records; interviews of Jordan's family members and former students; and Norfolk and Suffolk official records.*

ANNIE B. WILLIS
1893–1977

Watch out for my children.
—Annie B. Willis

For a long while, until a month before she died, it seemed that the Universalists had forgotten about Annie B. Willis, the daughter of Mary J. and Joseph Fletcher Jordan and principal of the Jordan School in Suffolk, Virginia, from 1929 to 1974. During her forty-five years as principal, her relationship with the Universalist denomination had shifted from empowering support to disempowering, as decision making became concentrated in white Universalist hands in Boston, before the relationship was severed altogether.

Annie Bizzell Jordan was born on May 30, 1893, while her father was the minister of the Presbyterian church in Louisburg, North Carolina. Annie spent her formative years in this college-educated family that had deep religious instincts but was uneasy about the doctrine of endless punishment. Annie had three siblings, and when she was about seven years old, the family moved to Durham, North Carolina, where her father—still wrestling with his doubts—abandoned the active ministry to become a lawyer. When Annie was nine, her parents found a spiritual home in the Universalist faith, and in 1904, when she was eleven, the family moved to Suffolk, Virginia, where her parents took over leadership of the foundering Universalist mission church and school.

Joseph and Mary Jordan were full partners in life and in running the school, while Annie increasingly helped her parents as a teaching assistant. From an early age, Annie saw her parents develop character in their pupils and experienced it at home, her father by imposing an almost military discipline, her mother by a nurturing love that induced self-discipline. Annie gravitated toward her mother's methods.

Annie became the leader of around thirty young people in the Suffolk chapter of the Young People's Christian Union (YPCU). Her father had great faith in the YPCU, young people being to him the most fruitful soil for sowing the seeds of the Universalist faith in the black community. In an age of deep white prejudice and virtually impregnable racial segregation, the Suffolk YPCU sent delegates to the otherwise all-white annual national conventions, where they sometimes faced overt discrimination.

As a teenager, Annie attended the Norfolk Mission College. Back home in Suffolk, she experienced the growth of the normal (or secondary) school department, which included advanced academic subjects. Jordan even formalized the name of the school in 1911 as the Suffolk Normal Training School (SNTS), in part to emphasize that many students, not just a "talented tenth," could aspire to a high level of education. By 1911, the school had also hired an inspiring new teacher, Professor James W. Wilson, who imparted to his students his philosophy of education: that it is not ease but effort, not facility but difficulty, that builds character in the full person. All these influences shaped Annie's way of looking at the world.

Parents saw the SNTS as the best hope for their children's future, and the expanded building at once became overcrowded, as enrollment in 1915 rose to 218 and climbed to between 250 and 300 for years to come. The black population of Suffolk was growing rapidly in these years as peanut-processing factories were being built around Jordan's school. The neighborhood, once open fields, was becoming crowded, and the school's growth obliged the Jordans to ask pupils to come on alternate days so that no one would be turned away. Instruction included academic and industrial subjects. A night class in business methods attracted ambitious young men. Because the school at 179 Tynes Street had the only private telephone in the neighborhood, it also became a communications and alarm hub for blocks around.

Annie had little opportunity to consider other avenues for her life's work, because she and her sister Martha were sorely needed to respond to the growing numbers of children and youth appearing at their door. The students readily responded to the animated and tender nature of the sisters, and Annie and Martha often put in eighteen-hour days, unconcerned about working without pay. Annie had found her life's work right at home.

At twenty years of age, Annie married Richard L. Willis, whom she met while attending the Norfolk Mission College. The couple made their home in Norfolk. Annie traveled by train to Suffolk for the school week, returning on weekends. Their daughter Dorothy was born in 1915, and the Willis family moved to Suffolk in 1917. Richard helped in the school office and tried his hand in the insurance business but soon moved back to Norfolk, seeing his wife and daughter on weekends. Annie rolled with these family tensions but never flagged in her dedication to the children under her care. Living in a loving home and school, Annie and Dorothy never complained about the lack of money. The annual $1,000 subsidy by the Universalist General Convention and the five-cent weekly tuition from those parents who could afford it allowed no salaries until 1915, when Jordan was able to provide his teachers with a minimal monthly stipend of five dollars.

In 1917, the Universalist General Convention turned over jurisdiction of the SNTS to the General Sunday School Association (GSSA). The denomination would concentrate on supporting the educational work of the school, and the school would be a living model for interracial understanding and respect, especially to the Sunday school children of Universalist churches across the nation. This was a revolutionary endeavor at a time when white fears of and violence against blacks was rising. The GSSA increased its support using the American Missionary (later Friendship) Offering of Universalist Sunday Schools, and the publicity given to the Suffolk school through the Sunday schools of Universalist churches prompted many individual gifts of money or books and other useful items, bringing the total annual contributions from Universalist sources some years to nearly $2,000.

Financial support had never been better, and as support came in from Universalists far and wide, Annie and her family reciprocated. In 1922, the eighth and ninth grades raised twenty dollars, which was sent to the denomination in what became an annual tradition. Suffolk children also donated pennies or a dime to aid the even more needy children of the Near East, each child who contributed receiving a cardboard ruler as a reminder of the Golden Rule.

Annie's sister Martha moved to New York City in 1922 to pursue a career in music and theater; nevertheless, she returned each spring to prepare the students for the School Closing extravaganzas. Annie spent much of 1924 in New York City to further her own education. This continued over the next few years while Mary E. Jordan's daughter Virginia, another accomplished musician, filled the gaps in the teaching staff left by the absence of Martha and Annie. On her return, Annie taught in Suffolk while calling Norfolk home. However, Richard, who had enlisted during World War I, never recovered from his service and spent much of the next twenty-five years in the Veterans Administration hospital. Eventually, Annie was the only one of the four Jordan children who remained. William disappeared, Mary moved to Detroit, Martha to New York, and Annie back to Suffolk.

In April 1929, as Joseph Fletcher Jordan became increasingly ill, the family gathered around. To Annie, he bestowed his life's work. On the morning of May 1, he died.

As Annie Willis, now almost thirty-six, stepped into her father's shoes as principal of what many just called "the Jordan school," the General Convention bestowed its blessing. Miss Annie, as everyone called her, capped enrollment at two hundred students, offering kindergarten through the ninth grade (public schools for blacks going only through the tenth grade), for which she struggled to keep a staff of up to five teachers. The three classrooms were overcrowded, with multiple lessons going on concurrently for different grades, but Miss Annie's easy-going warmth, loving hugs, greetings to each student, and more personal words to each before the day was out, perpetuated respectful self-discipline. During cold and rainy weather, she made sure each child was buttoned up before she let them out the door. And when necessary, she administered "sugar pie"; the sting of that red rod across the palm always sufficed and was long remembered. Miss Annie allowed no discrimination by age, size, skin tone, or any other physical or mental attribute. Cleanliness, courtesy, and thoughtfulness about the welfare of others were her hallmarks. Thus nurtured, Jordan students did well on national standardized tests, some ranking among the best in the country, and all had the foundation to succeed in life as well as school.

Realizing that she was an educator, not a minister, Miss Annie gave up trying to be the lay leader of the St. Paul's Universalist Church, and it became inactive. She did, however, continue the so-called Friday Sunday School, utilizing Universalist curricula. She started attending St. Mark's Episcopal Church down the street, but to the end of her life identified as a Universalist.

As her father before her, Miss Annie became the unofficial mayor of the black community of Suffolk and "Miss Annie's" place, the cultural and values center of the black community. She would greet passersby and they would greet her. Drunks stood up straighter. City manager Woodbury was convinced that the extremely low incidence of juvenile delinquency in the black community was due entirely to her influence.

These were the years of the Great Depression; factories were closed, unemployment was rife, and many homes were cold and had empty larders. Miss Annie extended her meager resources to ensure that all the children had hot soup, milk, and bread for lunch, that children with cold homes could stay in the warm school building during daylight hours, that neglected children be bedded down in the school, and that warm clothes were provided for those children shivering in the winter cold. When the employees of Planters Peanuts went on strike, Miss Annie made sandwiches for those on the picket line.

While Annie Willis dug deeper to help the needy, the school's revenues declined. Fewer parents could pay the tuition, now ten cents a week, and fewer could afford to pay to attend the annual School Closing extravaganzas. The GSSA American Friendship Offering struggled to maintain its minimum $1,000 annual subsidy. Annie took a cut in her household allotment to ensure that her teachers received basic pay. Children climbed trees to cut mistletoe to send to Boston to be sold, with the proceeds returning to Suffolk. Yet needs constantly outstripped resources.

Economic stringency prompted the Universalist denomination to make changes. Universalism and its revenues were in steady decline, and the question arose again whether the hard-strapped Universalist church should continue to run a school. GSSA field worker Harriet G. Yates argued that since public schools were now providing basic educational services for the same grades as the Jordan School, the focus of the Suffolk operation should shift from education to social services. The new general superintendent, Rev. Robert Cummins, agreed, and in 1938, informed Miss Annie. Although Annie preferred to maintain the school and its special character, she bowed to the inevitable.

In 1941, Madelyn H. Wood and a Boston-based committee undertook to regulate what they renamed the Jordan Neighborhood House and its "workers." Miss Annie's modernized job was to make reports. The planning and authority, however, shifted to Boston. A field worker periodically appeared in Suffolk, but Wood never went to see the situation for herself or to consult directly with Annie and her staff. Miss Annie was simply to implement the instructions given her. The situation produced underlying tension, but Annie did her best to do what was asked. In place of the dropped classes, a prenatal and well-baby clinic, various clubs for older children, a parents' league, and home visitations and counseling were added. The clinic was a success, but many of the other innovations struggled.

The administration and the GSSA never recognized that these measures reinforced white haughtiness and black disempowerment. Rev. Carleton Fisher, in an article written in 1942, was alone in perceiving the arrogance with which Universalists were approaching the Suffolk operation.

Still more change arrived in 1949. The newly formed Universalist Service Committee (USC) took over jurisdiction of the Jordan Neighborhood House and the USC's first director was Fisher, a strong supporter of Miss Annie's operation. Under his leadership, the Association of Universalist Women funded a co-director, the clinic merged with others, and a renewed emphasis returned to education through building character. The kindergarten increased in 1952 to 128 pupils, once again filling the building. In 1953, Fisher turned the USC over to Dana E. Klotzle who, with his wife, frequently traveled to Suffolk and developed a close friendship with Miss Annie, the closest Annie ever had with a Universalist official. Together they built up the staff, rebuilt a quality library, sent two older students to live with a Unitarian Universalist family and work in Maine for the summer, worked on projects such as a poverty program and a plan to prepare for and hasten integration. When in the early 1960s, the hotel in the center of Suffolk desegregated its restaurant, the Klotzles invited Miss Annie to lunch there. Miss Annie in her finest dress, with hat and white gloves, chose the most conspicuous table so that everyone would not fail to notice. In 1965 and 1966, the Jordan school held a Head Start program, in which both black and white teachers prepared 70 five-year-old children for public school in the fall.

When Unitarians and Universalists merged to become the Unitarian Universalist Association in 1961, the differences between the service committees of the two denominations became clear. The larger Unitarian Service Committee focused on temporary service projects run by paid experts that promised systemic change. The smaller Universalist Service Committee was interested in people-to-people contacts and what different cultures and perspectives might learn from each other. Universalists had valued the Jordan school for decades, but in the new Unitarian Universalist Service Committee (UUSC), formed in 1963, Klotzle saw that his Unitarian colleagues had no knowledge of the seventy-eight-year history that linked the Jordan school to the Universalist denomination; nor did indefinitely running a school appeal to them. By force of personality and his dedication to Annie B. Willis, Klotzle kept the program alive but he did not have the heart to tell Miss Annie how precarious was the support.

In 1966, the UUSC tried to set up a separate corporation to oversee the school. In theory, a local corporation would empower the black community, and the UUSC would free itself from running the school. A community committee was set up, and although it went through the motions, it never became a directing force. Nor did the UUSC provide it with the long-term support that might have given it energy and direction. Miss Annie, meanwhile, had become ill and had to rely increasingly on other teachers. As opinion in the UUSC turned against Miss Annie's enterprise, a heartbroken Klotzle resigned as director of the Jordan program. In 1967, the UUSC decided to terminate its sponsorship, and 1969 marked the end of its support.

The Jordan kindergarten, still with 120 pre-school children and parents eager for it to continue, struggled on with minimal UUA support. In 1974, Miss Annie finally retired, turning the directorship over but continuing to occupy the living quarters in the school she loved.[1]

In November 1976, Miriam E. Webster of the Association of Universalist Women, having long wondered what had happened to Miss Annie, inquired at UUA headquarters. Few remembered her. She and the school were history. So Webster wrote a letter to 179 Tynes Street, Suffolk, hoping that the present owners might shed some light on the fate of Miss Annie and her school. On December 19, Webster's phone rang. It was Annie B. Willis. She had assumed that everyone had forgotten about her, but said that to hear once more from one of her own, a fellow Universalist, was the light of her Christmas season. They talked and talked. Miss Annie promised to write up her memories and thoughts, but when Miriam Webster did not hear further, she wrote another letter on February 1, 1977, begging her friend for her written memories. Annie B. Willis, however, had died that same day, the task unfulfilled.

The kindergarten had to move but continued until 1984. However, the Tynes Street building and playground—which since 1897 had rung with the voices of thousands of children—were quiet and empty.

—Willard Frank

Sources

Prime sources of information on Annie B. Willis are the denominational newspaper, the Christian Leader, *later the* Universalist Leader; *the* Norfolk Journal and Guide; *records of the Universalist General Convention, the Unitarian Universalist Association, and the Unitarian Universalist Service Committee in the Unitarian Universalist Special Collections at Andover-Harvard Theological Library, especially the correspondence between Dana E. Klotztle and Willis; U.S. census records; family records; interviews of Willis's family members and former teachers and students; and Suffolk official records.*

"AFFIRMATION OF SOCIAL PRINCIPLES"
1943

In the midst of the Second World War, the General Assembly of the Universalist Church of America met in New York City and unanimously adopted the Declaration of Social Principles and Objectives, entitled "Our Task." This was the denomination's second effort to articulate its social policy; the first, written in 1917, had been largely the work of Clarence Skinner. The following is an excerpt from the 1943 statement.

We Universalists avow our faith in the supreme worth of every human personality, and in the power of men of good will and sacrificial spirit to overcome all evil and progressively establish the Kingdom of God. This faith is being challenged on every side. We therefore reaffirm our historic stand and call upon our people to think through and act upon faith.

Now is the time for greatness. There have been few if any periods in the entire history of the human race when men have had such an opportunity to mold the future. We stand at the great divide. On one side lies a land of promise, an unprecedented opportunity to build a better world than has ever been known. On the other side lies a return to the old order with its greed, poverty and war. . . .

Partialism cannot solve the problems of today and tomorrow. Partialism limits, divides, and excludes. It emphasizes nationalism, racism, classism, sectarianism, caste, and privilege, and it inevitably issues in conflict. Partialism is the underlying philosophy of an old order which was founded on a technological and sociological isolationism which no longer exists. It is discredited and impotent. It cannot construct a unified and universalized civilization, but will lead us backward to the past. [In] that way lies disaster.

The peoples of the world have built an interdependent and integrated culture. Nations, races, classes share a common heritage of science. Airplanes have abolished boundaries. Radios have brought the voice of every people into our home. Industry has distributed far and wide the commodities of inventive genius. Music, art, and education speak a common language.

The only possible philosophy for a better world is universalism. It alone is realistic and creative. In it lies the hope of mankind; without it we are doomed.

This faith means that the whole is greater than the parts. It is the philosophy and the religion of the all-inclusive. It interprets life in terms of the universals and the unities. It levels barriers, abjures prejudice, and renounces all that sets man against his fellow man. It endeavors to integrate humanity into one harmonious co-operating unity.

This faith demands that the common humanity of all races be recognized.

This faith demands that all men of all classes, races, creeds, shall abjure war as a method of solving international disputes and shall affirm their faith in the possibility of progressively building a lasting peace.

This faith demands that we must build an international order in which sovereign power to settle international disputes resides in a league or assembly of all peoples.

This demands that the physical resources of the earth be so used that all men everywhere shall have the essentials of a good life.

This faith demands that we must build an economic order based on the abundant life for all rather than upon the acquisitive power of the few.

This faith demands that the human resources of society, such as education, culture, the arts, be made progressively available to all.

We here and now call upon all fellow Universalists to unite in a great and consecrated movement to make these things come to pass.

In the field of social welfare:

1. We must acquaint ourselves with the faith and practice of other religionists that we may help to overcome the destructive force of religious prejudice—specifically anti-Semitism and anti-Catholicism.
2. We must recognize that today Americans of Negro, Indian, and Oriental descent, and many not yet citizens, are suffering from unjust forms of discrimination. We must combat every such form of race prejudice by practical steps which shall achieve a just status for these our brethren.

—*Universalist Church of America, "Affirmation of Social Principles,"* Christian Leader, *Oct. 2, 1943, pp. 582–83.*

JEFFREY W. CAMPBELL (1910–1984)
MARGUERITE CAMPBELL DAVIS (1916–1983)

In a very real sense I have been educated by the Universalist denomination. . . . I selected its church school before I had passed my first decade. For the ten years prior to my departure for university I attended its services regularly and accepted its right hand of fellowship on the express desire to be more active in its work.

By the time I was twelve years of age the paradox between intention and action of Universalism was shaking the little church. . . . Self-satisfied, middle-class people that they were, they had nevertheless been attracted by a faith which preached the Fatherhood of God and the Universal Brotherhood of Man. That message had struck sufficiently deep for them to realize that they could not preach or accept that belief while excluding the only youngster of mixed parentage (in the Anglo-African sense) in the neighborhood. . . . Should I take a role in this or that pageant? What would a conference say if I were to represent the church?

—Jeffrey Campbell

Jeffrey Worthington Campbell and his sister Marguerite, children of a white mother and an African-American father, were raised Universalist in Nashua, New Hampshire. Jeffrey graduated from St. Lawrence University (founded by the Universalists) in 1933 and from St. Lawrence's Canton Theological School in 1935. During his six years there, he was the only black student on campus. He served as student minister in Winthrop, New York, was ordained to the Universalist ministry in 1935, and received fellowship from the Unitarians in 1938. He was president of the International Religious Fellowship from 1937 until World War II broke out in 1939. He ran for governor of Massachusetts on the Socialist ticket in 1938 (finishing fourth out of eleven names on the ballot), and in 1939, unable to find a congregation to serve, he left America to study in London. It was while there that he wrote the stunning autobiographical essay "Personality Not Pigmentation," published in the February 24, 1940, issue of the *Christian Leader*, the Universalist denominational publication.[1]

Campbell's essay responds to a series of editorials on racial matters by John van Schaick, long-time editor of the *Leader*; van Schaick's racial prejudice, however, can be traced back much further than the late 1930s. In 1903, as minister of the Universalist church in Washington DC, he was one of the three members of the committee established by the Universalist General Convention to make recommendations on the future of the Universalists' Negro missions in Norfolk and Suffolk, Virginia. The first minister to those missions, Joseph Jordan, had died in 1901, and they were struggling under the leadership of Thomas Wise, who would later forsake the Universalist ministry. Joseph Fletcher Jordan had recently emerged as the third black Universalist minister, and the committee voted 2–1 in favor of maintaining the missions until Jordan could take over. Voting in favor of supporting the missions were Quillen Shinn, Universalism's roving missionary, and Isaac Morgan Atwood, dean of Canton Theological School; van Schaick voted to discontinue support for the missions. In the years that followed, van Schaick continued to criticize the General Convention's support of the Suffolk mission, and Joseph Fletcher Jordan answered some of these criticisms in an article in the *Leader* in 1911.

In 1922 when van Schaick became editor of the *Leader*, there was a significant change in the way news from the Suffolk Mission was presented in its pages. From 1904 until 1922, news from

Suffolk was featured prominently, and the publication covered Jordan's speaking tours to raise money in the North. With van Schaick as editor, however, news about Suffolk was published far less frequently and was relegated to short blurbs at the back of the paper.

The March 25, 1939, issue of the *Leader* carries a van Schaick editorial supporting the District of Columbia Board of Education's decision to bar Marian Anderson from performing at the whites-only Central High School—a venue Anderson and her representatives had turned to after being barred from Constitution Hall by the Daughters of the American Revolution. (Anderson performed her legendary concert on the steps of the Lincoln Memorial on Easter Sunday, April 9, 1939.) Van Schaick places the blame for the controversy on the "colored people" who refused to accept conditions dictated by the Board of Education for use of the school. "We are on their side for equal rights," he writes, "but not for identical facilities. When, however, they let passion run away with judgment, we have to stand for righteous judgment."[2]

In response to the editorial, the *Leader* "received more comments than we can publish." In the April 15 issue, van Schaick repeats his views on racial separatism and, after admitting that it is wrong to hate colored people, adds his opinion on interracial marriage: "But to take the view that marriage between the members of the two races leads to unhappiness and curses the children, that interracial marriage should be discouraged and that relationships leading to marriage are to be discouraged—such things are not wrong. They are wise and they are kind."[3]

The stage was now set for what came to be called the Campbell-Davis marriage case. Marguerite Campbell had followed her brother Jeffrey to St. Lawrence University, and upon her graduation in 1939, married her white classmate, Francis Davis. They had been high school sweethearts in Nashua and now he was studying at Canton for the Universalist ministry. Jeffrey Campbell officiated at the wedding ceremony. Soon thereafter, Jeffrey went to study in London, unable to secure a pulpit in either a Universalist or Unitarian church.

The August 12, 1939, issue of the *Leader* carries van Schaick's editorial, "Idealism and Realism in Mixed Marriages," condemning the marriage of Marguerite Campbell and Francis Davis. "We believe that mixed marriages are racially unwise and morally wrong," he writes. Among other reasons, "Mixed marriages are wrong because they curse the children of such marriages. The children are brought into the world under a handicap that . . . parents have no moral right to impose upon them." In addition to being immoral, a mixed marriage disqualifies a minister from ever serving a Universalist church: "Would it be right to withhold a Universalist pulpit from a man who has contracted a marriage of this kind? It would be right because the man cannot do the work. It would be right, as it would be right not to call a man who could not read, or could not enunciate, or had met with an accident that imposed a handicap not to be overcome." Van Schaick suggests that St. Lawrence dismiss Davis, since he had so obviously disqualified himself from ever serving the Universalist ministry. Van Schaick says he had arrived at his opinions on mixed marriage and the ministry "without the slightest feeling that we are false to our ideals of human brotherhood."

Not content just to attack the Campbell-Davis marriage or undermine Davis's ability to serve a Universalist church, van Schaick also attacks Jeffrey Campbell in the editorial, though not by name. He writes that it is fine if a "young colored man desires to enter a white theological school to get an education and has as his ideal the service of his race. If, however, he despises his race, wants to have nothing to do with it, insists that he intends to join the white race, serve white churches, marry a white girl, we should tell him to go elsewhere." Any opinion to the contrary is the result of "loose hazy thought among Universalists about the relation of the races that . . . we should strive to overcome."[4]

As the product of mixed marriage himself and the only colored graduate of the Canton Theological School, Jeffrey Campbell could not have missed van Schaick's meaning. And neither did other Universalists.

The uproar was immediate. Letters pro and con flooded the offices of the *Leader*. The September 2 issue contains another editorial by van Schaick, this one headlined "Is Facing Facts Wrong?" where he acknowledges that some Universalists were upset with his views: "It would seem as if some of our people believed it to be wrong to tell these young people the truth about their situation; and wrong for a theological school to refuse to admit a man even though the faculty knows that he can not succeed." He also repeats his attacks on the Campbell-Davis marriage and Jeffrey Campbell, characterizing his opinions as "the highest kind of idealism."[5]

The September 2 issue also contains a two-and-a-half-page response to van Schaick by John Murray Atwood, dean of Canton Theological School and son of Isaac Morgan Atwood (former general superintendent of the Universalist Church of America) entitled "Race Prejudice and Mixed Marriages." As Atwood's father had opposed van Schaick on the crucial 2–1 vote to keep the Suffolk Mission open thirty-six years earlier, Atwood now opposes van Schaick on the issue of mixed marriages in general and Francis Davis's marriage to Marguerite Campbell specifically. Atwood describes racial prejudice in American society and summarizes Van Schaick's argument by saying, "In the opinion of many, a colored skin is a kind of disgrace or misfortune."

Atwood continues, "Rather, I should say it is a tragedy where people continue to entertain and perpetuate, as they do, this idea and the resulting conduct of people. So long as we have this attitude and this ideology, so thoroughly un-Christian, we shall have all these discriminations, regulations, Jim Crow cars, separate schools, and other indignities imposed on a supposedly free people among us. We shall be doing our best, in spite of our protestations and useless professions, to breed in them a race inferiority complex. If I were of the colored race, I should resent the total implication with all my being."

Atwood also defends Jeffrey Campbell, though like van Schaick he never mentions him by name. He praises Campbell's three-year student ministry at the Universalist church in Winthrop, New

York: "The people of that parish, whom no one would accuse of being in any way radical, declare that he is the best preacher, pastor, and community worker they ever had, and if they had had the means they would have asked him to become their permanent minister."

Atwood had no illusions about his audience. Toward the end of his article he writes, "I suspect most Universalists in spite of their religious profession will be astonished at the views expressed here, and think, what a bunch of inexperienced, impractical, unrealistic young radicals they must have up there at St. Lawrence! Yes, we are undoubtedly in the minority, but we can take comfort in the assurance of the late [Universalist minister] Levi Powers, who was something of a social prophet, that the minority is usually right." And he concludes with this challenge to the Universalist faith community: "When we are able . . . to recognize and prize and honor true worth, disregarding physical distinctions of color or other kind . . . then we have the Christian attitude. Are we, or can we be, such Christians?"[6]

In the October 7 issue, Van Schaick called a halt to the publication of letters dealing with this subject. But this was not the end of the controversy.

Campbell's "Personality Not Pigmentation" essay in the February 24, 1940, issue of the *Leader* is preceded by an editorial by van Schaick entitled "Mr. Campbell's Article" (though Campbell was ordained and held dual fellowship, van Schaick did not give him the honorific of *Reverend*). Van Schaick's contempt for Campbell and his views permeates the editorial, and he is unapologetic about this. Yes, we should fight for equal rights, he writes, but "we can do all these things without training colored boys to be ministers of white churches, without approving of the action of a white boy in a school for our ministry taking a colored wife, and without endorsing marriages between the white and the colored."[7]

Campbell, writing from a small Welsh village where he was teaching, is clear about the purpose of "Personality Not Pigmentation"—a title which prefigured Martin Luther King Jr.'s anticipation of the day when people "will not be judged by the color of their skin but by the content of their character." Campbell writes, "My purpose is not to defend a Negro people whose American journey needs no defense. . . . The two young people whose wedding ceremony I was honored to perform have their thirteenth chapter of Corinthians. My worry is the Church in whose institutions I have been active for twenty years and the policy of segregation of minority races established in its editorial columns and tacitly accepted by its membership." One of the achievements of Campbell's essay is that he responds to the personal attacks on his parents, his sister and brother-in-law, and his call to ministry with an appeal for Universalism to live up to its oft-stated ideals.

Campbell describes his own identity, racial and cultural, in a way that today we would call multicultural: "My own background includes four generations of marriages between West African and Anglo-Saxon stock. These unions have taken place in England, Africa and America. They have occurred in slavery and out of it, in wedlock and out of it. Tribal chieftains, English gentlewomen, pre-Civil War governors of the South, mingle with seventeenth century colonizers of Massachusetts and generals of the American Revolution. In other words, I happen to be one of those products of intermarriage whose anticipation has been invoked for three centuries to smother the love people of differing stocks have felt for one another."

This "union of chromosomes" that grounds his identity makes Campbell the crucible for the conflict between the ideals of Universalism and the realities of racism. "It merely happens that in my case the smashing paradox between the ideal inescapably implied in the Universalist interpretation of theology and its woeful incapacity to implement that ideal is sharply illustrated." He saw this in his home congregation in Nashua, when they struggled over how to include him in the life of the congregation, sometimes failing and growing "bitter and unlovely" but "surprisingly often" triumphing over their fears and coming "closer to being what *they actually wanted to be* but hadn't had faith that they could." And he realized that applying to study for the ministry would extend the problem of how to cope with him "over a broader section of the denomination." Campbell says that in his college interview with Dean John Murray Atwood, "The problem presented to my ministry by the present development of American churchianity was put forward as strongly as I have ever heard it stated." Yet Atwood supported Campbell's admission and remained his steadfast supporter throughout the rest of Atwood's life. Campbell describes his six years at St. Lawrence as "the richest I have known."

It wasn't just Campbell's color that caused concern among denominational authorities. His politics were also suspect. He describes the interview with the Committee on Fellowship that preceded his ordination as "Thirty minutes on my theology and four hours on my political and racial attitudes." Referring to the state superintendent, he writes, "I can hear the thick rich baritone of my interrogator today: 'Now Jeffrey, about your politics . . . Are you a Communist?' 'No.' 'Urrrumph! Socialist?' 'Yes.' 'Urrumph! Well, what kind of a Socialist? Do you think Russia is a better place to live in than the U.S.A.?'"

But in the end, despite their prejudices, the committee voted for ordination, according to Campbell, because of a "far deeper fear. . . . They wanted their church to be the kind of institution which could unite its theory with its practice. Inwardly they knew that it was not, nor, within the limits of their imagination, could they see it becoming such. They feared lest that central weakness be demonstrated to the world. Through no connivance of my own I happened to be a walking demonstration of that weakness. Failure to ordain me would have been an even more flagrant confession of the same failure. In that dilemma they were caught and the whole denomination, not to mention liberal Christianity, with them."

Van Schaick had to preemptively attack Campbell's essay with an editorial in the same issue of the *Leader* because Campbell so adroitly destroys van Schaick's argument for racial separatism. Campbell points out that "My actual inheritance is a ratio of eleven-sixteenths to five, the preponderancy being on the Saxon side. Were I to assume the racial theory of the editor I would immediately proclaim myself a Saxon and proceed accordingly. This I will never do." Instead, Campbell asserts that he would continue to work against prejudice in the church and larger society. He writes, "Churches must create little oases in which persons from the widest possible variety of racial and cultural backgrounds can know each other as persons." This consciousness of humanity as one "must filter out into the shop, the dance hall, the school and the home. . . . For that reason I cannot submerge and do the comfortable thing which would morally weaken the spiritual stand which the Universalist Church must make or forfeit its reason for existence."[8]

John van Schaick's small-minded editorials had provided Jeffrey Campbell with the opportunity to highlight the challenges facing American Christianity in general and Universalism specifically in responding to the pervasive racism of American society.

Several subsequent issues of the *Leader* carry letters about the issue (the criticism of Campbell's essay centered mostly on his use of "big words") until van Schaick declares he won't print any more. But the April 4, 1942, issue includes a long letter from John Murray Atwood with the headline "Dean Atwood reopens the Davis case." Atwood notes that "the Universalist Church is notably short in its ministerial supply," yet Francis Davis, "one of the best equipped and qualified men we have ever sent forth," cannot find a congregation to serve because he is married to Marguerite Campbell. Atwood says he doesn't like to write so personally about the young couple (and there is blatant condescension when he says "Marguerite, whose skin by the way is as white as mine"), but has to acknowledge a problem in the church when such a qualified man, ordained and in fellowship, cannot find a congregation to serve.[9]

Atwood's plea had no effect. Following Francis's graduation from theological school in 1941, he and his wife returned to Nashua where Marguerite worked in a restaurant and Francis moved on to a career in social work. In early 1942, Atwood got wind that

Universalist Fellowship Committee was questioning Davis's fellowship, presumably on the grounds that they were convinced he would never serve a congregation. Atwood wrote to Universalist headquarters at 16 Beacon Street in Boston saying, "If they talk of disfellowshipping him (Davis) they can begin to disfellowship me." Denominational authorities quickly replied that they were only considering shifting Davis' fellowship from New York to New Hampshire.[10]

Davis never served a Universalist church but did go on to work for the Boston Urban League. He and Marguerite divorced, and in the mid-1950s Marguerite went to work at Universalist headquarters. She worked for the UCA and the UUA for more than thirty years, sometimes alongside men who had actively worked against her husband and brother's opportunities to serve a congregation.

Jeffrey Campbell returned from England in 1951 after spending almost twelve years teaching laborers as part of several English university programs, including the Oxford Extra-Mural program. In 1950, the *Leader*, now under a new editor, published his essay "How Britain Educates Her Workers." He started teaching English literature at the Putney School in Vermont in the Fall of 1951 and remained there until his retirement in 1980 at the age of seventy.

From 1967 to 1974 he served as part-time minister to the Unitarian Universalist congregation in Amherst, Massachusetts, commuting a hundred miles round trip several times a week, and later at the UU congregation in Brattleboro, Vermont, as an unpaid minister-on-call. At the 1969 General Assembly he delivered a sermon entitled "A Road for Everyman" at the Service of the Living Tradition at the Arlington Street Church in Boston. Jeffrey Campbell died on September 26, 1984, in Brattleboro. His obituary in the 1986 UUA Directory makes no mention of his racial identity (though it does refer to his "colorful ministry" at the Putney School), his early struggles to find a congregation to serve, or his "Personality Not Pigmentation" essay. Its author could not have known him very well.

The UUA archives contain documents and correspondence about and from Campbell starting in 1929 (when he began his studies at St. Lawrence) and ending in 1980. They reveal the inability of the Universalist, Unitarian, and Unitarian Universalist leaders to imagine a role for Campbell in their denominations. Universalist leaders opposed Campbell's entrance into St. Lawrence but Dean Atwood persuaded them to back down. When Campbell graduated in 1935, they said that he could not serve a white congregation because he was black, nor could he work among the poor African-Americans at the Suffolk Mission in Virginia because he had spent his entire life among whites.[11] At first, Atwood had hoped Campbell might go south to work but later confessed to him, "knowing you as I do now if I had the authority I wouldn't allow you."[12]

After Campbell was granted Unitarian fellowship in 1938, he would visit AUA headquarters at 25 Beacon Street but said that church leaders would turn around in the hallway and walk the other way when they saw him coming. AUA President Frederick May Eliot "would eye me sympathetically and say 'My dear boy, the world is as it is but we are trying. Be patient a little longer.'" Campbell said, "So far as official action is concerned I could still have been waiting in the anteroom for a quarter of a century."[13] In 1964 he writes about the denominational leadership, "At no time in these nearly thirty years has a single official recognition of my situation come to me."[14]

It is clear that leaders in both denominations wished he would go away, and in a way he did when he left for England to study in 1939.

When his part-time ministry in Amherst, Massachusetts, ended in 1974, Campbell wrote to the UUA, observing that no one ever contacted him to ask about his experiences as a black minister in a white denomination. A UUA administrator then invited Campbell to 25 Beacon Street for an after-lunch conversation. There was no further follow-up.

In one of the last letters from Campbell in the archives—a long polemic written to two UUA officials in November, 1979—Campbell harkens back more than forty years to a good friend who tried to persuade him "to get out of our ministry." "He did it for my good. I did not follow his advice. . . . Let me emphasize: I WOULD STILL UNDERTAKE THE CALL HAD I MY LIFE TO RELIVE."[15]

Universalism, Unitarianism, and Unitarian Universalism turned their backs on Jeffrey Worthington Campbell, never recognizing the gifts he could have brought to their ministry. And despite that failure of courage and imagination on the part of church leaders, Campbell never descended into bitterness and never regretted his call to the ministry. We are left to imagine what Unitarian Universalism would be today had Francis Davis, Marguerite Campbell Davis, and Jeffrey Campbell not been barred from the service they sought to give.

—John Hurley

Sources

Much of this essay relies on articles and editorials that appeared in the Christian Leader *between 1939 and 1942. Additional sources include letters written by John Murray Atwood, Roger Etz, and Jeffrey W. Campbell—now stored in the UUA Inactive Ministers File at Andover-Harvard Theological Library. An interview with Jeffrey W. Campbell by Mark D. Morrison-Reed in 1979 provides supplemental information.*

UNIVERSALISM'S THEOLOGICAL CONUNDRUM

African Americans could be counted among the founders of Universalist congregations in Gloucester in 1785 and Philadelphia in 1801. Given that Universalism's argument against slavery was based "on the assumption that [humanity] was 'one great family' which would ultimately 'share one common destiny . . . in the kingdom of immortal blessedness,'" it seems natural that they found such a religion appealing. Yet the Universalist declaration that all would be saved, and that black people are "your brethren and sisters, heirs of immortality"[1] did not attract many. Why, given its radically egalitarian message, didn't Universalism take root in the African-American community?

The Universalist itinerant George Rogers traversed North America from Upper Canada to the Deep South. His account, *Memoranda of the Experience, Labor and Travels of a Universalist Preacher*, was published in 1845. Rogers tells of meeting a "free colored man" and writes that

> his family are members of the Mt. Olympus [Alabama] society; the first Universalist person of color I had ever seen . . . [a man of] considerable intelligence; of industrious, prudent habits and much respected; he told me he was decidedly opposed to the measures of the abolitionists, and that he regarded the slavery of the African race in the light of a providential visitation upon them for their barbarous and unnatural conduct toward each other in the parent country; that, like all the divine dispensations, it will have a benevolent issue; at some future day

> they will be restored from their captivity, and carry home with them [to Africa] the lessons in religion, civilization, etc. which they have learned.[2]

From this black man's perspective, slavery and black suffering were divinely ordained, a repeat of the Babylonian captivity of the Jews. The plight of both were seen as God's retribution for the faithlessness of the Jews and sins of the Africans, in his eyes, God's way of transforming and redeeming black people. This points us toward what, for African Americans, is the central theological question: What is the meaning of our suffering? Universalism was never able to adequately answer.

William R. Jones, an African-American UU theologian, approaches this question from a different perspective. In the foreword to *Is God a White Racist? A Preamble to Black Theology*, he writes, "To raise the question of divine racism is actually to revive a perennial issue in black religion: what is the meaning, the cause and the 'why' of black suffering?"[3]

The "free colored man" that Rogers met offered one understanding; a slaveholder Rogers met offered another: "They all believe in endless misery, he said, "for reason, I suppose, that they want their masters damned, and think it would be hardly fair dealing to make them as happy as their Negroes in the next world."[4] It makes sense that the slaves would expect to be "happy in the next world," while their masters burned in hell. Indeed, when abolitionist Frederick Douglass—who frequented All Souls Church, Unitarian, when he lived in Washington DC—visited the Universalist Church in New Bedford, Massachusetts, he went especially to argue against the doctrine of universal salvation.

Why believe in eternal damnation? Because it provides the counterpoint to black suffering. The answer to the "why" of black suffering is that their suffering is evidence of God's favor—that as oppressed people, blacks are God's chosen. Jesus speaks to this: "But many that are first shall be last; and the last shall be first." "It is easier for a camel to go through the eye of a needle, than for a rich man to enter into the kingdom of God." In these New Testament passages, as in the Beatitudes, God's preference is clear. African Americans, as God's suffering servants, are redeemed by their unearned suffering and in the end will be raised up by God because they, like Job, remained faithful.

There is a third possibility, which Jones pointed toward: divine racism. God is not all good, nor just, nor loving. For those who came to this improbable conclusion, atheism would have offered a logical alternative.

The Universalists had to offer an answer to the conundrum of black suffering if they were to address the black experience.

The foremost Universalist of his era, Hosea Ballou argued that the wages of sin were immediate and personal. Equating sin with misery, he said that sinners suffered inner torment. The slave-holder, we can surmise, would suffer in this life. Not believing in punishment after death, Ballou wrote this about sin in *A Treatise on Atonement*: "There gnaws a worm that never dies, there burns the fire that is never quenched. A consciousness of guilt destroys all the expected comforts and pleasures."[5] One is hard-pressed to imagine a slave finding this convincing. The Restorationist position, which was the dominant one, put forward a logic with which a slave might more readily agree. Sinners first spent time in purgatory before ultimately being ushered into the glory of heaven. This is what E. H. Lake argued in *Key to Truth*, the book that led Joseph F. and Mary Jordan to Universalism.

Still, neither of these theological positions accounts for ethnic suffering, the suffering of African Americans as a people—degrading, institutionalized suffering visited upon them generation after generation; unearned suffering laid upon them not for having done something bad but simply for being. Since a righteous God would not do this, the "free colored man" in Mt. Olympus had to believe the suffering was retribution for black transgressions in Africa and that its purpose, being ultimately benevolent, would lead to the redemption of the mother country.

Approaching suffering from a Universalist perspective leads to a quandary. If, as the Universalists claim, all are ultimately saved, why have African Americans been singled out? In the Universalist context, their suffering had no special meaning, nor is it given particular justification. It is not necessary for one's salvation, yet it exists.

There is another possible conclusion, one implied by James Baldwin in *The Fire Next Time*: "But God—and I felt this even then, so long ago . . .—is white. And if his love was so great, and if he loved all His children, why were we, the blacks, cast down so far? Why?"[6] Baldwin invites the conclusion that God, in fact, does not love us all alike and that God is a white racist. Some, coming to this conclusion, became atheists; most did not.

What did Universalism have to say about what, by necessity, had to be the major religious question for African Americans? Why does God make us suffer so much? George Rogers, the itinerant preacher, reported that enslaved blacks were often "happier and more relaxed than the free whites."[7] His implied answer about why whites, who prosper from black suffering, should get into heaven is arrived at by minimizing black suffering and heightening that of whites. However, if one accepts the reality of black suffering, that is no answer at all, and beyond reasserting God's all-embracing love, Universalism had no explanation compelling enough to entice blacks to embrace a sort of double jeopardy—despised for their race and rejected for their faith.

Beyond offering what to African Americans is a theological non sequitur, there were other realities that impeded Universalism's ability to speak to African Americans. Historian Russell Miller touches on the attitude of the post-Civil War Universalists toward blacks: "The question was voiced occasionally of why so few Negroes were members of Universalist churches in either the North or South. Part of the blame for their absence seemed to lie in the lack of vigorous missionary programs such as those conducted by other denominations."[8] Instead, the Universalists decided to combine missionary work on behalf of Universalism with the establishment of educational opportunities for black people. One Universalist official described one of the efforts as "a partial discharge . . . of the obligation that our church, in common with all others, is under to aid in righting a great wrong."[9]

Beginning in the nineteenth century, some Universalists did dream of bringing their message to blacks, which is more than the Unitarians did. The efforts, however, were few. In the late 1850s, "an American Negro Universalist" B. Bowser, having settled in Cape Palmas, West Africa, "sought aid in establishing a religious mission." Receiving none, he turned to the Episcopal Church.[10] In 1879, a mission school for girls was started by a congregation in Chicago. The *Universalist Herald* mentions a Rev. Henry Holmes of Henderson, Tennessee, attending a Universalist ministers' meeting in 1896; ordained in 1894, he is listed in the *Universalist Register* from 1895 to 1900 and beyond. The itinerant Quillen Shinn visited a small church in Barstow, Georgia, established by "J.A. Murphy a Negro convert to Universalism"[11] in 1901, but opposition to Universalism from both blacks and whites was strong and that effort left to languish. In 1911, there were African Americans with Universalist sympathies in Rusk, Oklahoma. They asked the state superintendent, C.H. Rogers, to help them organize a church; Rogers, acquiescing to white demands, declined.

The Universalist undertaking in Norfolk and its nearby sister mission in Suffolk stand out but need to be seen in context. Universalism had spread rapidly and grown to have hundreds of thousands under its influence. But these free-thinking religious mavericks were innately anti-authoritarian, distrusting ecclesiastic or any other authority. This attitude made it difficult to create the institutional structures that could sustain such growth and aid the many small congregations that sprang up. By 1887, when the original mission in Norfolk was established by Joseph Jordan, Universalism was already contracting. Thomas E. Wise later extended the mission to Suffolk and Ocean View. Undermined by white Universalist officials, Wise left. Joseph Fletcher Jordan's efforts to revive Norfolk failed, as did another attempt made in 1913 when the Universalist Convention licensed Rev. Charles W. Jones, a former African Methodist Episcopal minister, to assist in pulling the old congregation together.

The Suffolk mission went on to succeed and positively impact that community. Its leadership was widely respected, the school a success, its Universalist-inspired spirit transmitted to many; and yet the religious mission did not flourish, not even among the young people whom Jordan believed would be more receptive than their elders. If Jordan had an answer to the conundrum of black suffering, we do not know what it was.

With Jordan's death in 1929, the church dissolved. The school, in time, because of improvements in public education and shifting denominational strategy, had change forced upon it. Renamed the Jordan Neighborhood House, it was given strong leadership by Annie B. Willis. The Universalists supported it through the General Sunday School Association and its American Friendship Program, the Young People's Christian Union, the Universalist Women's Association, and later the Universalist Service Committee. Yet in 1969, the newly formed UUSC cut the funding, and all traces of the old Universalist connection vanished at the moment when the UUA was, for the first time, trying to address the needs of the African-American community.

For most black folks, universal salvation was a theological absurdity. If the belief was true, knowledge of divine love would lead to the regeneration of the individual. Where was the proof? Why did the Southern Universalists argue for slavery's efficacy rather than free their slaves? Where was the justice in black people's extraordinary suffering in this world if black and white alike shared eternal bliss in the next? If, as Hosea Ballou said, "God saves men to purify them . . . and does not require men to be pure in order that he may save them,"[12] the ordeal of slavery loses its redemptive power. Slaves could not reconcile such an optimistic and forgiving message with their experience, nor could those living under Jim Crow laws and the ever-present threat of lynching. Universalism failed to speak to the African-American experience because it was unable to shed any light on the meaning of corporate black suffering, much less to proclaim its redemptive purpose.

By the time of the Great Migration, from 1910 to 1940, when millions of African Americans moved from the rural South to the Northeast and Midwest, Universalism had already been in decline for half a century. Following the trunk lines north, the migrants congregated in major urban areas; Universalism on the other hand was spread beyond these to smaller cities and towns across New England, North Carolina, Ohio, Pennsylvania, upstate New York, and Ontario.

Traveling from Canada to the Deep South, itinerant George Rogers met just one black Universalist family. In post-Civil War Waynesville, North Carolina, there was a small African-American community. A white family's oral family history says that these children attended Sunday school at the Universalist Inman Chapel, but the pictorial record does not confirm this. Following one of his fundraising tours, Joseph F. Jordan wrote, "In one city, I found a whole family on the church roll. In another, a young and intelligent girl is the pianist."[13] Jeff Campbell recounts that he and his sister, Marguerite, were the only African Americans in the congregations in Nashua, New Hampshire. When Marguerite's marriage to a white seminarian was attacked in the *Christian Leader*, not one of the many who responded, besides Jeff, identified themselves as being black. In Bristol, New York—a town south of Rochester that is not much more than a crossroads, a few houses, a general store, and a Universalist church—there were no African Americans; the same is true of Olinda, Ontario. Thomas Payne, an African American who ministered to the Universalists in Lyons, Ohio, does not write of having black parishioners. Even in a city like Rochester, the first black members did not join the Universalist church until after merger. Were there African-American Universalists beyond the handful that have come to light? Possibly, but proof has not emerged, and circumstantial evidence suggests not. Enforced both by law, social strictures, and clannishness, racial isolation was a dominant feature of American life that Universalism was unable to overcome. The modicum of Unitarian success can be attributed to two things: a metropolitan environment that provided a degree of anonymity and therefore freedom; and the degree to which the most politically progressive Unitarians were part of social circles where black and white middle-class intellectuals interacted.

When opportunities did arise in Barstow and Suffolk, the resistance to Universalism was ferocious. Today, it is hard for UUs to imagine, but during the nineteenth and first half of the twentieth centuries, Universalists were considered pariahs and decrying them the norm. "The devil was the first Universalist," proclaimed one evangelist.[14] This attitude has not completely passed, as Bishop Carlton Pearson, a Pentecostal African American, found in the late 1990s. After he preached the "Gospel of Inclusion," he was denounced and shunned and saw "his once 6,000-member megachurch dwindle to a few hundred before finally closing."[15] Beyond this anecdote is a statistical reality. Value surveys in *American Mainline Religion* locate traditional African-American denominations among the most conservative in the United States. The African-American soil that Universalist missionaries tried to cultivate was as rocky as it was ill-tended.

Racial prejudice and paternalism were another factor. The substantial difference in the subsidies given to Suffolk as opposed to the one provided for Japan, or the "quarter of a million dollars [for] Near East Relief,"[16] suggest this is so, as does the pedagogical dispute with Thomas E. Wise over the mission school's direction. The prejudice is unmistakable in regard to Jeffrey Campbell, who said that when he entered Canton Theological School to train for the ministry, the New York state superintendent "jumped all over Dean Atwood for wasting the denomination's money on a nigger."[17] The prejudice is virulent in the actions of John van Schaick, former editor of the *Christian Leader*. In 1903, van Schaick had been the most outspoken member of the Universalist commission that had undermined Wise's efforts. In 1911, when the denominational leadership endorsed Joseph F. Jordan's tour to raise funds to expand the school, van Schaick had been the lone dissenter. When he took over as editor in 1923, he turned what were once feature articles about the missions in Suffolk and Japan into brief updates buried further back. In 1939, when Marguerite Campbell and Francis Davis married, he used the journal to attack this young couple saying, "they are mistaken and from our standpoint they did wrong," while accusing Jeff of "despis[ing] his race" for wanting a white congregation.[18]

The story of John van Schaick and African-American involvement in Universalism ends with an ironic twist. From 1900 to 1918 and 1920 to 1922, John van Schaick, a man who Russell Miller said "exhibited more than a tinge of racism,"[19] was the minister of the Universalist National Memorial Church (then named Church of Our Father). Out of this congregation the last African-American minister from the Universalist tradition emerged. Thomas Eliron Payne grew up in Washington DC, within walking distance of Universalist National Memorial Church. He joined after being accused of heresy and cast out by the Baptist church in which he was raised. He went on to attend first Howard University and then its School of Religion. However, by the time Payne graduated in 1968 with a bachelor of divinity degree, Universalism and Unitarianism had merged.

The success of the mission in Suffolk notwithstanding, the reasons that Universalism as a religious option failed were manifold: theology, demographics, and prejudice each played a part. From the perspective of a black person, what would have been appealing about being part of a white denomination that offered inadequate support and made capricious decisions? Despite all of this, Joseph Jordan, Thomas Wise, Mary and Joseph F. Jordan, and Miss Annie were able to win the esteem of the African-American community. The religion itself, even among those who benefited from its school, did not.

To overcome this resistance, the message of Universalism would have had to have been compelling. It would have had to reconcile its proclamation of God's all-embracing love with the African-American experience—an experience that shaped a world view in which only 13.5 percent understand God to be a benevolent power, while the vast majority believe God's nature (like the God of the Old Testament) is authoritarian or critical.[20] Where is justice if white and black share the same destiny? If we are one human family and God loves us all alike, then "why we were cast down so far? Why?" The questions of suffering and justice are central, and for Universalism posed a theological conundrum that went unanswered. Or could it be that African Americans were looking for an answer in the wrong place? Rather than in heaven, might the meaning of black suffering be found in this too-often hellish world? Might it be found in the expansion of democracy beyond its initial embrace of white land-owning males, expanded by the Emancipation Proclamation and the Fourteenth and Fifteenth Amendments to the Constitution, expanded again in Selma, by Martin Luther King Jr. and the Voting Rights Act, and further still in the presidency of Barack Obama?

Four hundred years of grappling with the issue of race has—repeatedly—forced upon America the necessity of living up to its principles and, as James Baldwin wrote, "even when the worst has been said, it must also be added that the perpetual challenge posed by this problem was always, somehow perpetually met."[21] Met indeed, but having faith—whether in America or a loving God—while enduring unwarranted suffering and unmitigated misery requires the strength of Job; few have it, and that made Universalism a very hard sell.

—Mark D. Morrison-Reed

THE EMPOWERMENT SAGA

In 1963, early in the Universalists' and the Unitarians' new life together, a business resolution mandating nondiscrimination came before the General Assembly (GA) held in Chicago. What transpired underscores the complexity of and limits to the UUA's commitment to becoming a racially inclusive faith. The first document in this section is the resolution that, after much debate and modification, was passed. A year later at the UUA General Assembly in San Francisco, a new hymnal, *Hymns for the Celebration of Life*, was first used. Like the resolution adopted in 1963, the hymnal is indicative of that era's mindset regarding race.

Among the hymnbook compilers were Rev. Kenneth Patton, a white UU minister who made headlines in 1947 when he resigned from the white race; Rev. Arthur Foote, a member of the St. Paul Urban League and NAACP who, in 1952, had been on the Commission on Unitarian Intergroup Relations with Rev. Howard Thurman, a towering religious figure and prolific writer; and Rev. Christopher Moore, who in 1956, founded an interracial children's choir at the First Unitarian Society of Chicago that would evolve into the multicultural, multiracial Chicago Children's Choir. Because Patton was interested in world religions, the hymnal included Hindu readings from Rabindranath Tagore and others as well as Buddhist and Chinese readings. But the hymnbook included not one word or song written by an African American or reflective of that experience, despite these ministers' knowledge of black culture and their commitment to racial justice. As the brand new Unitarian Universalist Association was on the cusp of its first serious engagement with black culture, being an African-American UU implied entering into a cerebral UU religious milieu. This was not without appeal to those seeking a less emotive, more rational style of worship. The reality was that even within the congregations that succeeded in attracting African Americans, integration tended to mean assimilation.

That was about to change. Rev. William R. Jones's sermon, "The Negro's Image of White America: Its Influence on Integration Strategy," presaged what was about to take place. And Selma, Alabama, would play a major role.

During the twenty years following World War II, a broad consensus developed. Annually, in nine of the ten years leading up to Selma, one or more GA resolutions supporting desegregation, civil rights, integration, and African independence had passed. In 1963, over one thousand UUs, led by UUA president Dana McLean Greeley, participated in the March on Washington. In the meeting following the march, between President Kennedy and the civil rights leaders, the room was thick with UU connections. A. Philip Randolph, vice president of the AFL-CIO, would have known Ethelred Brown and many members of the Harlem Unitarian Church who were fellow Socialists. Roy Wilkins, executive director of the NAACP, had been first hired in 1931, when Mary White Ovington, a white Unitarian and its co-founder, was chair of the Board. Whitney M. Young Jr. was a Unitarian Universalist. Dr. Martin Luther King Jr. was close to Dr. Homer A. Jack, UUA director of social responsibility. The situation parallels that prior to the Civil War. A hundred years earlier, it had taken decades for Unitarians and Universalists to build an antislavery consensus; now, in the mid-twentieth century, liberal religionists, having forged a consensus, were part of a web of associations, personal relationships, common values, and commitments focused on racial justice. Thus, when King issued his call for "clergy of all faiths" to come to Selma after the savage beating of peaceful protesters, UUs were ready to respond. Indeed, they already had. On March 6, the day before Bloody Sunday, the Concerned White Citizens of Alabama had marched on the Selma courthouse, decrying white violence, and half of those seventy-two protesters were Unitarian Universalists from the congregations in Huntsville, Birmingham, and Tuscaloosa. Homer Jack wrote, "On Tuesday, March 9, forty-five of our ministers and at least fifteen of our laymen responded to Martin Luther King Jr.'s call to come to Selma."[1] "By mid-afternoon we marched, led by Dr. King, to the center of the Edmund Pettus Bridge."[2] Then, in response to Rev. James Reeb's murder, another wave of UUs, including the UUA Board of Trustees, arrived. Still more joined on the final day as the march from Selma entered Montgomery. Afterwards, a UUA program called "A Unitarian Universalist Presence in Selma," sponsored by its Department of Social Responsibility, was initiated. From April 1 to September 15, UU laity and ministers volunteered to spend fifteen days each in Selma.

African-American UU emotional involvement was high, but their presence was minimal. Henry Hampton, associate director of the UUA Office of Information, arrived from Boston on the same plane as Reeb. Dr. John L. Cashin Jr. and his wife, Joan, members of the Huntsville UU church, also marched. Cashin would go on to become the first chair of the National Democratic Party of Alabama and head a delegation to the 1968 Democratic National Convention that challenged the regular delegation. After Reeb's death, 71-year-old Lewis A. McGee came from California to attend the memorial service. Emerson Moseley from Barnstable, Massachusetts, and his daughter participated in the march from Selma to Montgomery. After the initial march ended and white UU Viola Liuzzo slain, Emerson Moseley's wife, Margaret, arrived. She came as a voting rights worker to support Selma residents in registering. An excerpt from her memoir, *Moving Mountains One Stone at a Time*, gives a sense of what those who went to Selma experienced. It was hopeful and harrowing.

While the beating of African-American citizens on the Edmund Pettus Bridge and the deaths of black Jimmie Lee Jackson and white UUs Reeb and Liuzzo galvanized Americans and led to congressional action, specifically in regard to Unitarian Universalism, Selma marked a sea change. Five hundred Unitarian Universalists participated, over 140 of them UU clergy[3]—representing 20 percent of the ministers in final fellowship. Meanwhile across the country, many other UUs were involved in protests and marches. The intensity of the experience transformed them. The consensus about racial justice sharpened. The level of commitment rose. While UUs had been promoting integration and equality of access since the 1940s, Selma signaled the seriousness of the UU concern for racial justice, a commitment reaffirmed when, in 1966, Martin Luther King Jr. delivered the Ware Lecture at the UUA General

Assembly. In spring 1967 the UUA "Report of the Committee on Goals" said that in a survey question about the involvement of liberal religion in education and action, 69.7 percent of respondents indicated that "racial integration" was "very important." That was the highest rating. Another 24.7 percent said it was "somewhat important." Six months later that commitment was challenged and the consensus crumbled.[4]

When discussing the controversy that erupted in the UUA over black empowerment, we leave the realm of the historical, and the implied distance that connotes, and enter what for me is personal and familial. The story told here, a product of both research and memory, warrants an explanation.

In the beginning, thinking that what had happened in the UUA between 1967 and 1970 had little to do with me, I ignored it. In October 1967, I was a freshman at Beloit College, when my mother, over my father's protest, flew to New York City to participate in the Emergency Conference on the UU Response to the Black Rebellion, held at the Biltmore Hotel. My mother was among those who withdrew from the planned agenda to form a black caucus. The meeting was inspiring and tumultuous. That seminal moment is explored in the article "Last Exit to Grosse Point." Written by Henry Hampton, it is a reflection on his experience that presages what was to come. Returning to Chicago energized, my mother, now one of seven members of the black caucus steering committee, threw herself into preparing for the first National Conference of Black Unitarian Universalists, which was to take place four months later.

At age eighteen, anything one's mother is involved in is suspect, particularly if, in her enthusiasm, she cajoles you into coming along. First, she dragged me up to Rev. Jesse Jackson, then into the plenary session. Listening to speeches was not on my agenda; I fled. A reminiscence written shortly afterward by Betty Reid Soskin succinctly captures the feel of that first-ever gathering. Other African-American UU voices then recount what happened in the ensuing months: a letter from child psychologist Kenneth Clark to Homer

Jack, a sermon following King's assassination, another letter sent in the build-up to the Cleveland General Assembly. These are followed by descriptions of the missions of the Black Affairs Council (BAC) and its counterpoint, Black and White Action (BAWA).

The foray with my mother ended my institutional interest in the UUA, until I decided to enter the ministry. In spring 1977, my meeting with the Ministerial Fellowship Committee was looming. To prepare, I participated in a mock interview. The only question I still remember is, "Would you have joined BAC in walking out of the 1969 Boston General Assembly?" I was eloquently mealy-mouthed and secretly glad I had not been there. Trapped is what I felt, would have felt, and continued to feel. During the fall of 1977, while I was serving as a ministerial intern in Bethesda, Maryland, I had a conversation with Paul Carnes, president of the UUA. When he asked about the empowerment controversy, I said it was another generation's fight, and we needed to get over it. A couple weeks later, Dalmas Taylor, an African-American UUA board member, called to report that Carnes, in making the point that we needed to move on, had quoted me. Dalmas advised, "You'd better be careful." Six months after that, I was reunited with Mwalimu Imara, an African-American UU minister who had been my youth group advisor in Chicago. Witnessing his outrage at what he saw as the UUA's retreat from black empowerment, I said to myself, "I'm not going near this," and decided to focus my D.Min. thesis on Ethelred Brown.

If only it had been so easy. In 1993, I led a history workshop at GA on Diversity Day in Charlotte, North Carolina. When I got to empowerment, a verbal fight erupted. While preparing the final essay of this section, I solicited the opinion of a respected colleague. He replied in support of the BAC, "It defined who I would be in relation to issues of race, in relation to institutional loyalties, in my understanding of to who and to what I am responsible. That is what places the controversy beyond reconciliation, and keeps it vibrant and vital in my life. . . . [w]hat is at stake . . . is nothing less than an unwillingness to compromise, apologize for, or explain away a deep and abiding commitment that set me on the path I have followed ever since." That moment in his life enabled him to define himself. Yes. Was it life transforming? Yes. But why should that make reconciliation impossible?

What is going on? Why has it been so difficult for the UUA to come to terms with what happened between 1967 and 1970? What is powering the ongoing acrimony? And why is reconciliation so difficult?

This section explores how the events set in motion in 1967 played out in three individual congregations. It includes a biography of Rev. David Eaton, who became the minister of All Souls Church, Unitarian, in Washington DC amid this upheaval; a sermon entitled "Blacks, Get Your Guns" that Mwalimu Imara delivered to his congregation in Urbana-Champaign, Illinois; and the story of the Black Humanist Fellowship of Liberation in Cleveland. What occured in these three very different congregations mirrors what was happening within the United States and the UUA. Imara's reminiscence aptly sums it up: "It was a wonderful time and the church was filled with wonderful people, but we, like the rest of the nation, were caught in a fantasy of brotherhood and the realities of our history and the times dealt severely with us."[5]

The final essay, "The Empowerment Paradox," endeavors to explain why these events played out as they did. But first, I will outline my point of view—my bias. Given my personal involvement, I owe this to the reader.

First, I will fail. Many will disagree with my explanation because there is little agreement on the facts. The facts depend upon one's feelings and the perspective from which one interprets the events; and there are, at least, two contradictory narratives. I speak only for myself and about what I have come to understand. I speak also out of disappointment and weariness, anger and amazement that we have allowed this to drag on for forty years.

Second, I assume that the participants were all good people, with noble intentions, doing what they thought best; people being loyal to their understanding of UU Principles; people committed to a vision of a better, fairer world. I assume that none of them were interested in a status quo that would leave African Americans second-class citizens.

Third, whenever I listen to people talk about that era, the underlying emotional charge is evident. The word *polemic* best describes the decade-old non-discussion. Those that speak out invariably lay claim to the moral high ground and, having few doubts, feel no contrition and seem unable—or unwilling—to listen attentively and respectfully to other points of view. The result has been an impasse.

Finally, I have come to believe that the only way to move forward is to look upon what transpired as a tragedy. What do I mean? These were honorable people responding to cultural circumstances not of their making while in the grip of emotional forces beyond their control. These circumstances compelled them to choose between dearly held values, and they brought to their decision making their humanness: lofty hopes and moral certitude, grim earnestness and inflamed passions, some self-delusion, lots of defensiveness, and as tragedy requires, hubris. Conceived of as tragedy, this drama does make sense. Such an interpretation emphasizes explaining over defending or blaming, and that is the tack this section takes in an effort to show why what happened had to happen.

"ADMISSION OF MEMBERS WITHOUT DISCRIMINATION" 1963

Two years after the merger of the Universalist Church of America (UCA) and the American Unitarian Association (AUA), the issue of racial inclusiveness was raised at the 1963 UUA General Assembly held in Chicago. Several changes to the UUA constitution were proposed, including an amendment to article III, section 4, regarding the requirements for Unitarian Universalist societies to maintain their voting rights within the association. The additional requirement stated that member congregations must "maintain a policy of admitting persons to membership without discrimination of race, color, or national origin."

The amendment was debated passionately and at length. The controversy centered on whether, if passed, the amendment would conflict with congregational polity—the absolute authority of the individual congregations to determine all matters concerning their governance. Duncan Howlett, the minister of All Souls Church, Unitarian, in Washington DC and longtime civil rights advocate, said, "The question before us is not integration—on that all of us are virtually agreed. The question is how we're going to achieve it in our kind of denomination. . . . In freedom we shall do it, not by legislation and not by constitutional amendment."[1] Rev. Kenneth T. MacLean queried, "Whenever the question of equal rights for Negroes comes up in whatever area of life, it is always in conflict with some other principle, sometimes an important principle—the principle of states' rights or neighborhood solidarity or, here, congregational polity. Are we going to say that every other principle comes first but that congregational polity can never be compromised? Human rights can be modified and can be compromised, but congregational polity, never!"[2]

A two-thirds affirmative vote was required to pass the amendment. The results of the vote were summarized in the 1964 UUA Directory: "The motion to adopt the amendment was defeated, the vote being 436 in favor and 379 against. On a motion to reconsider, the amendment was again defeated, 459 being in favor, 383 being against. By vote of the meeting, a resolution reminding churches and fellowships of their ethical responsibility to admit members without discrimination was laid on the table until other General Resolutions were in order."[3] *When this new resolution was introduced and debated later in the Assembly, it was adopted overwhelmingly, 583 voting in favor and 6 against.*

WHEREAS, the Unitarian and Universalist movements have historically affirmed the supreme worth of every human personality, the dignity of man, the use of the democratic method in human relationships, and the ideals of brotherhood, justice and peace; and

WHEREAS, refusal to welcome persons into membership in any of our churches or fellowship because of race, color, or national origin would contradict our historical testimony and the declared constitutional purpose of our Association;

THEREFORE BE IT RESOLVED, that all member congregations of the Unitarian Universalist Association be charged to declare and practice their faith in the dignity and worth of every person and that all member congregations of our denomination are hereby strongly urged to welcome into their membership and full participation persons without regard to race, color, or national origin; and

BE IT FURTHER RESOLVED, that to implement the declared constitutional purposes of our Association,

1. The President, with the concurrence of the Board of Trustees, be instructed to appoint a Commission on Religion and Race, composed of at least seven members, whose duty shall be to explore, develop, stimulate, and implement programs and actions to promote the complete integration of Negroes and other minority persons into our congregations, denominational life, ministry, and into the community;
2. This Commission be adequately financed within the budget of our Association; and
3. The report of the action and future program of the Commission be conveyed to the 1964 General Assembly.

AND BE IT FURTHER RESOLVED, that all groups applying for membership in the Association be informed by the Board of Trustees of the Unitarian Universalist Association before being accepted into membership of the Unitarian Universalist Association on the stated policy of the Association, which welcomes all qualified persons, regardless of race, color or places of national origin, into the membership of the churches, fellowships and organizations.

—*"Second General Assembly of the Unitarian Universalist Association,"* 1964 Unitarian Universalist Association Directory, *pp. 62–63.*

“THE NEGRO’S IMAGE OF WHITE AMERICA” 1964

Among the members of the AUA Fellowship Committee that interviewed William R. Jones during the spring of 1958 was Rev. Robert H. Schacht, the minister of the First Unitarian Church of Providence, Rhode Island. On earlier occasions the Rhode Island congregation had taken on new graduates as their assistant minister. The Fellowship Committee, understanding the precariousness of Jones’s and the AUA’s situation, encouraged Schacht to approach his congregation about hiring Jones. There was resistance. The Prudential Committee of the congregation held a special meeting in May 1958. In a letter to the congregation, the committee made clear “that this issue was not one we sought but one thrust upon us by forces beyond our control . . . [And] the special awareness of race relations problems in our country and across the world put us in the limelight whatever we do. . . . It should not invade our consciences, but it should sharpen our careful evaluations of the far-reaching results of what we do now. We are responsible to the Unitarian movement as a whole as well as to ourselves.”

It was reported after that meeting that “the majority of our parish desire Mr. Jones’s coming.” His tenure there lasted two years, during which he became “much beloved” and afterward remained active while a graduate student at Brown University. It was in that context and in reference to the events surrounding his selection that Jones delivered the sermon excerpted below on May 10, 1964.

The most fruitful way to describe the Negro's image of white America is to indicate what it was previously. Booker T. Washington used to argue: "The opportunity to exercise free political rights will not come in any large degree through outside or artificial forcing but will be given to the Negro by the southern white people themselves, and they will protect the Negro in the exercise of these rights." Washington believed it was only necessary to dramatize the undemocratic and immoral nature of discrimination, and equal opportunity and justice would gradually become a reality. In short, force was deemed neither necessary nor desirable.

Present civil rights tactics reveal the virtual abandonment of Washington's image of white America and the strategy derived therefrom; the past hundred years conclusively exhibits the spectacular inaccuracy of Washington's view. No matter what segment of the Negro community you focus upon, the view is the same: force is necessary. The burning question among Negroes today is no longer force or no force, but *how much* and *what kind* of force. The alleged rift among civil rights leaders is not a conflict over the desirability or necessity of force but a difference of opinion as regards what *types* of force are legitimate and *effective* expressions of *non-violent* coercion. . . .

It is an inescapable fact . . . that desegregation will not be to the immediate advantage of the white American in many instances; and who will voluntarily receive with favor what on its face value is detrimental to his own interests—unless compelled by a more threatening alternative? Desegregation for the American white can only mean a loss of economic and political *monopoly*, the elimination of time-honored social *privileges* and the status which he has construed as inalienable *rights*. . . .

I am alarmed that the image of white America in the Negro community is not substantially changed for the better. Progress in the direction of desegregation by the white majority is being interpreted primarily as an unavoidable concession to stay on top. . . .

I am concerned . . . lest present tactics pass beyond the coercive rehabilitation of the white American from his racism to a form of violent retribution for his practice of the latter; lest the conclusion be reached—as the Black Muslims argue—that racism is so deeply ingrained in the majority of white Americans that they are irreformable. . . .

I am fearful, too, because there is a deep reservoir of animosity, if not hatred, towards whites for their callous indifference and unjust treatment. I know it is there, because it surges within me. I recall . . . when I took special note of it. I remember my thoughts when the question of the advisability of an assistant minister who was a Negro became an issue here. I was shocked at first; my image of fair New England and liberal Unitarianism had simply been different. My feeling, then, was not outright hate, for there was a tinge of pity; I could only wonder how people got this way.

—William R. Jones, from "The Negro's Image of White America; Its Influence on Integration Strategy," sermon delivered May 10, 1964, the First Unitarian Church of Providence, Rhode Island.

“MOVING MOUNTAINS ONE STONE AT A TIME” 1965

Born in 1901, Margaret Moseley was raised in Dorchester, Massachusetts, in a family of mixed African, Indian, European, and Mexican heritage. A lifelong activist, she was involved in the Women's International League for Peace and Freedom (WILPF) and served as president of its national board. She was also the president of the Community Church of Boston, founded by Universalist Clarence Skinner, and later chair of the board of the Unitarian Church of Barnstable.

At the time of the March on Washington for Jobs and Freedom in 1963, my daughter and my husband both went and marched. In 1965 they participated in the fifty-mile march from Selma to Montgomery. . . .

I could not do that because I could not walk that distance due to arthritic conditions. (I was sixty-three years old at the time.) My walking was limited so I had to try to find other ways to feel that I was making some kind of a contribution.

It was only a few days after the march from Selma that a group of women—six of us from WILPF—went to Selma to work on voter registration education and to work on helping to feed the people who had been put out of work because of voting rights efforts. . . .

I was very happy to be accepted as one of the persons who went. I happened to be the only person of color in the group. . . . Even though almost the entire contingent was white, we were very warmly received by the people in Selma. Their homes were open to us. As poor as they were, they shared what they had with hospitality. . . . They gave us the warmest kind of friendships. They never tired of saying they were grateful to those who were extending the hand of friendship because they felt the need for support. Psychological support was as important to them as the material practical things we could do.

I had the experience of working principally on the voter registration education end of it. . . . [One] particular day, a man had been following me in a car. Every house I went in, he would sit in the car and wait for me to come out, and lean out his car window and make gestures and so forth at me. I think he thought eventually I would give up. But I was persistent until I went up on a little porch and, instead of sitting in his car, he got out and went onto the porch next door. The houses were very close together. . . . He leaned over and made gestures and faces at me. I rang the bell, no answer. I rang again and didn't get an immediate answer. I just took my courage in my hand. Instead of going down the steps and walking up the street, which I was fearful of doing, I turned the knob, opened the door, and walked in. . . .

The door opened into a living room. A woman was just coming to the door. She smiled at me, didn't seem angry that a stranger was standing there. I introduced myself, and she said, "Are you with the people who have come to help us?" I said, "Yes." She said, "Pardon my being slow to answer the door." She was still barefooted. When she got home from work after standing in salt brine all day long, her feet were so swollen and so sore she had to bathe them in a tub of water before putting on fresh stocking and shoes. She said it was very difficult to even walk after getting home. So she soaked her feet while we talked.

There were so few jobs they could get and she had to accept a job like that because at least it paid something. Wages were disgracefully low.

Then I told her why I opened the door and walked in. She said, "You did the right thing. I shudder to think what might have happened if you hadn't done that. You should not be on the street alone. They hate white people. They hate light-skinned black people. They hate anybody who comes to give us courage to demand our just rights. We are so grateful to those of you who come to suffer with us and to share, to give us the benefit of your knowledge. Our doors are open to you any time. You shouldn't even have rung the second time, you should have come in the first time."

She had tried to register many times but was always given excuses about why she was not qualified. A college professor was told he didn't qualify. She was discouraged, didn't know if she would ever try again. Blacks attempting to register to vote were given tests which were never given to whites.

I promised the woman that I would stand at the bottom of the courthouse stairs and offer protection to anyone who came to register on a certain day.

When I got there that morning, those coming to register had to walk up a long flight to go into the courthouse to register. I stood at the banister at the foot of the steps. Opposite was that awful creature you read about in the news—Bull Connor—standing at the opposite post. . . . He glared at me and I glared at him. We looked each other right in the eye. He thought he could look me down and I would finally give up. But I just stood there and looked at him, and he was the one who first gave up. As people came, I would give them a pat on the back and push to start them up the stairs while I kept on looking at that man as much as to say, "I dare you to try to stop them from going in!"

When it was all over and I was safely back in the place where I was staying, I shook like a leaf because the tension was broken.

I felt very sorry for the white members who were working with us because, even though they were wholeheartedly into what they were doing, the hatred toward them was more pronounced than towards me. And I feared for them sometimes even more than for myself.

There was one woman from Concord, Irene Hoagland, a very good friend. We both were afraid that we might not make it. The day we were going to the airport to return home—they knew every move we made, they had spies watching us the whole time—there were about three cars organized to push us off the road into the ditch, the way they did Viola Liuzzo. . . . Because she had a car, she was making trips carrying people from the state capital back to their homes in Selma. The people who had marched had no money, no transportation; they marched to the capital but needed a way to return home. . . .

On one of her trips to go back and pick up another load, members of the Ku Klux Klan drove up—a car in front of her, a car in back and a car beside her. They were pushing her farther and farther toward the ditch. There were deep ditches in that area. . . . She was shot and her car was forced into the ditch and she died.

And so, when we were in a like predicament on the way to the airport, the cars were pushing us further and further toward the ditch, the driver of the van said. . . "I'm going to try to make it to the airport. I'm going to speed. Don't be afraid. IF I do make it to the airport, (and it was the 'if' that scared the life out of me), if I make it to the airport, the moment I stop the van, don't wait for your bags, run as fast as you can into the terminal. But if they catch us before we get to the airport, there's no telling whether you will get home or not."

And so we just sat there holding on, as tense as could be. The moment he drove on to the parking lot, he opened the door and said, "Now run."

We saw the cars coming onto the airport terminal parking lot. We both ran. . . .

—*Margaret Moseley, from* Moving Mountains One Stone at a Time: Memoirs of Margaret Moseley, as told to Berry Shea, *edited by Judith Barnet, Unitarian Church of Barnstable, Massachusetts, 1993, pp. 21–27.*

"LAST EXIT TO GROSSE POINT"
1967

On August 6, 1965, President Lyndon B. Johnson signed the Voting Rights Act into law. Five days later, there was a massive riot in Watts, a neighborhood of Los Angeles. Civil rights protests continued and so did urban upheaval. During the summer of 1967, there were seventy-five major riots in cities across the United States, resulting in eighty-three deaths. That October, in an effort to be proactive, the UUA Commission on Race and Religion convened the Emergency Conference on the UU Response to the Black Rebellion, at the Biltmore Hotel in New York City. UUA Director of Information Henry Hampton attended. He had held the position since 1963, and in that position, he had gone to Selma in 1965. In so doing, he observed the power of the media to influence public opinion. Subsequently, in 1968, he founded Blackside, Inc., and went on to earn acclaim as the filmmaker who directed the award-winning documentary series about the civil rights era, Eyes on the Prize.

Hampton was one of the thirty-four African Americans who withdrew from the Emergency Conference agenda to form a black caucus. Looking back on his experience from the vantage point of twenty years, he said,

> *I was raised in a good, black, middle-class family in St. Louis, and we were all raised to believe in the equality of the races and in a sense of excellence about ourselves. . . . And the idea of being in an all-black meeting was just incomprehensible to me. . . . It was simply not part of my experience to walk into a room where*

> *the only reason you could be there is because you are black. And it upset me. I had to really think about whether I was going to stay or not. But I went to the Caucus meeting. It took awhile, but very quickly it simply became clear that what could happen in a meeting of all black people is that the agenda could become very clear and that it was a very useful and provocative setting . . . where I had talked about and learned things that I hadn't thought about in years—indeed, I never knew. Just hearing other black people talking about themselves and about the turmoil and pain and isolation sometimes of being black. Especially those of us who had grown up in predominantly white institutions.*[1]

The following is from an article he wrote following that October 1967 gathering, which captures the mood of that moment.

It was as if I had never been black.

It was as if the reality of my Black and Unitarian beings had never existed.

It was as if I had come alive.

To have been black and a member of the Black Caucus at the Unitarian Universalist Emergency Conference on the Black Rebellion was to undergo a basic and passionate change. For the first time I was a Unitarian Universalist and at one with my fellow liberals.

To have been white at the same conference must have seemed like a new low for modern liberalism.

To have been black and unable to participate in the Black Caucus must have been hell. . . .

Most of our lives are so delicately turned that we rarely look at ourselves except in the most controlled of circumstances and always by our own will. But, rarely, if ever, do we move or allow ourselves to move into circumstances which we cannot control.

And there is no reason entering the lobby of the Biltmore for one to suspect that here could be a place where one could lose control. At the Friday evening session beginning the meeting, a tall, young, sophisticated UU said to no one particular, "I have the uneasy feeling that it just isn't going to be enough to simply be here unprejudiced."

And it wasn't.

—*Henry Hampton, "Last Exit to Grosse Point,"* Respond, *Fall 1967, UU Laymen's League.*

"RACISM FOR THE UUA?"
1967

Kenneth B. Clark, PhD, noted African-American child psychologist, served with his wife, Mamie, also a psychologist, as an expert witness in Briggs v. Elliot *that rolled into the 1954* Brown v. the Board of Education of Topeka, *in which the U.S. Supreme Court ruled segregated schools illegal. The first African-American president of the American Psychological Association, Clark wrote, among other books,* Prejudice and Your Child, *which was published by Beacon Press, and* Dark Ghetto.

Clark was also a member of the Community Church of New York, a congregation that by 1967 had been integrated for over fifty years. Its long history of involvement in civil rights dated back to John Haynes Holmes, who had been a founder of the NAACP in 1909 and minister to white Unitarian Mary White Ovington, one of its principle founders and mainstay.

Following the Emergency Conference that had taken place on October 8, 1967, Rev. Homer Jack, the UUA director of social responsibility, must have communicated with Clark. By November 2—in the lead-up to the November 12 meeting between the UUA Board of Trustees and the Black Unitarian Universalist Caucus (BUUC)—Clark had sent a letter to Jack, outlining his position on Black Power. When the Board balked at meeting the BUUC's demands, the BUUC and its white allies expressed great dismay.

The following is an excerpt from Clark's letter to Jack. It later appeared as an article in the Register Leader *in May 1968.*

It has been argued that one should be more attentive and responsive to the racist demands of the Black Power movement because this is necessary to build a racial pride and dignity which must precede serious racial justice in America. I do not accept this for a number of reasons. First, a similar argument could be offered in support of the racism of white segregationists. One could accept even the most cruel and flagrant manifestation of white supremacy as essential to building the dignity and pride of otherwise deprived and insecure whites. Second, I do not believe that any genuine pride in race or nationality can be built upon the realities of racial desegregation, the realities of economic deprivations, the realities of criminally inferior and racially segregated education, the realities of the total pattern of pathology inherent in racially segregated housing. Genuine pride and dignity for whites and Negroes can come only when an affluent society such as ours makes available the necessary financial and intellectual resources to bring about the massive social and economic changes essential for social justice. We have the resources; so far we have lacked only the commitment. And third, I personally question the validity of pride based on color of skin, whether it be white or black. Such a pride seems to me at best tenuous and at worst destructive to the potential of a human being to develop a more fundamental basis for pride and dignity.

While I can understand the depth of frustration out of which the Black Power movement comes, and understand also the fact that the masses of Negro people justifiably are revolted by verbal civil rights "victories," tokenism, and the pervasive moral hypocrisy which perpetuated dehumanizing American racism, I am personally convinced that the Black Power and Black Caucus method of reacting to these realities is self-defeating in that it tends to intensify rather than to remedy this violent disease of American racism.

I cannot accept with equanimity a call for racial separatism coming from human beings with dark skin any more than I can tolerate such calls coming from human beings with lighter skin. Both groups of human beings to me reflect the pathos, the despair, the anguish of unfulfilled lives. It is no more just to acquiesce to the demands of the one more than those of the other—particularly when they are the same in effect. Justice can be served only by remaking our society so that it realistically fulfills the requirements for dignity for all human beings. This demands that Negroes, whites, and all others join forces, speak together, work together, argue with one another, and fight the formidable forces of irrationality and immorality as allies.

—*Kenneth B. Clark, "Racism for the UUA?"* Register Leader, *May 1968, pp. 11–12.*

"ALL OF THE PEOPLE THAT I AM"
1968

During the Emergency Conference on the UU Response to the Black Rebellion in October 1967, the Black Unitarian Universalist Caucus (BUUC) was formed. When they rejoined the conference after meeting separately, they presented a list of nonnegotiable demands. One of these was the establishment of a Black Affairs Council (BAC), whose membership would be chosen by BUUC and would be funded by the UUA for four years at $250,000 a year. After a heated debate, the conference endorsed the demands unamended and forwarded them to the UUA Board of Trustees. The other plan that emerged from the caucus was to hold a National Conference of Black UUs on February 23–25, 1968. That first-ever gathering was held in Chicago and drew 207 of the approximately 600 African-American UUs. Its agenda included electing the membership of the BAC, comprised of six black and three white members.

Among those in attendance was Betty Reid Soskin. A long-time member of the Mount Diablo Unitarian Universalist Church in Walnut Creek, California, she is a cultural anthropologist, writer, and community activist who, in 1995, was named Woman of the Year by the California State Legislature. Currently a park ranger with the National Park Service, she is involved in civic engagement and community outreach.

In the following letter, written soon afterward, she reflected upon what the National Conference of Black UUs had been like for her.

It has something to do with all of the people that I am. My black. My woman. My mother. My person. I arrived in Chicago pretty well integrated within my being. Now: My black wants to fight! I can feel the weight of the brick in my black hand and black muscles straining to throw it. My woman, to love, and to somehow bring about manhood through my womanhood. My mother, to pick up my children and leave the country to protect my young. My person, my human, to bring all those I love (black and non-black) together and tell them that my me, behind my eyes, the real me, and the you, behind yours, are placing too much emphasis upon the housing we are encased in; black ones and white ones. That we're falling into the trap which man has constructed for his own destruction. Perhaps my fear has a great deal to do with this inner revolution which is perhaps where the real battles are fought, the outer revolution being only the physical manifestation of this.

I shall not forget Rennie Gaines (later changed to Mwalimu Imara) and the "Requiem to a Black Prince." Val Gray Ward and letting myself get lost in her beauty in "What Shall I Tell My Children?" . . . The "Happening" of Gospel Singing for well over an hour on Sunday morning which started timidly and swelled in meaning until we were weeping with the power of the old songs. I shall not forget.

My perception, which is keen, saw people bursting from the womb, still wet and shining . . . and BLACK! What an awesome sight!

Night found me exhausted, unable to sleep, crying with the sadness of the days which must follow and the joy of witnessing the new birth of blackness . . . for the sadness of the white liberal, whose work in past years has allowed the first stages of our blackness to occur . . . and the rejection of them now and the puzzlement, the fear, yes and the pride they feel at our release. I cry for them.

—Betty Reid Soskin, "Letter to Hayward Henry," February 1968, BAC/BAWA file, Morrison-Reed Collection, Sankofa Archive, Meadville Lombard Theological School Library, Chicago.

“MARTIN LUTHER KING JR.”
1968

On February 29, four days after the National Conference of Black UUs ended, the Report of the National Advisory Commission on Civil Disorders was released. It found that the riots across the United States were a result of black frustration over the lack of economic opportunities, and it warned that “Our nation is moving toward two societies, one black, one white—separate and unequal.” Confirming what many intuitively knew, it added to the sense of urgency.

Gearing up for the UUA General Assembly to be held in Cleveland, the white support group FULLBAC (Full Recognition and Funding for the Black Affairs Council) gathered on April 4 for its first meeting. Held in Philadelphia, the meeting included representatives of the BUUC and the BAC; they organized in the face of what was seen as resistance and half-measures from the UUA Board. However, when Martin Luther King Jr.'s assassination was announced, the group automatically separated along racial lines, as African and Euro-Americans went off to grieve. In Chicago, a member of the church youth group, not knowing where to turn or what to do, was drawn to church. Blinded by tears, he walked into the sanctuary and then into the bell room. He took hold of the rope and tolled the bell. He tolled and wept until drained, he stopped. Returning to the sanctuary, he found it packed with people weeping, singing, and holding one another. Richard Gilbert, the UU minister in Ithaca, New York, cried “unashamedly” as he and his colleagues talked of how to keep “the dream alive” while they planned a memorial service for Cornell University. Sunday came three days later. At the First Universal-

ist Church of Rochester, New York, its minister John Brigham spoke about King but also about the shooting of Medgar Evers, the NAACP Mississippi field director; the slaying of civil rights workers James Chaney, Andrew Goodman, and Michael Schwerner in Philadelphia, Mississippi; the killing of James Reeb; and also the shooting of his UU colleague, Donald Thompson, in Jackson, Mississippi. Across the country, ministers addressed King's death; among them was Rev. Lewis A. McGee. The eulogy he delivered follows.

Lewis Allen McGee was an army chaplain, social worker, and minister; his wife, Marcella, was a librarian, who was elected to the UU Women's Federation Board in 1960. Both were universally loved. McGee had first been attracted to Unitarianism during the early 1920s, but when he approached a Unitarian minister in 1927, he had been advised, "you'll have to bring your own church." While he was attending Meadville Lombard Theological School between 1946 and 1947, he and Marcella were among the organizers of the Free Religious Fellowship, a predominantly African-American congregation on Chicago's South Side. He then became its first minister. In 1958, after having served for five years as the field secretary for the American Humanist Association, he was called to serve as Stephen Fritchman's associate minister at the First Unitarian Church of Los Angeles. In 1961 Rev. Richard Boeke was serving as a circuit-riding minister between Chico, California, and Reno, Nevada, when three of the strongest financial supporters of the Chico congregation asked him to resign so that they could hire Lewis McGee.[1] Boeke agreed. When the Unitarian Fellowship of Chico hired McGee he became the first African American since Clarence Bertrand Thompson to serve as senior minister of a white Unitarian congregation. In 1965, while pastor of the Humboldt Unitarian Fellowship in Bayside, California, he had gone to Selma following James Reeb's death and was the only African-American UU minister there.

I'm proud to share with you this hour of tribute to Dr. Martin Luther King, leader of the Southern Christian Leadership Conference. In his assassination all of us suffer the loss of a true friend. And when I say all, I mean all. My daughter, Mrs. Joan Harris, told me yesterday [that] one of her Caucasian friends called her to offer condolences as she grieved over the tragedy—as if only Negro people are the losers in the death of Dr. King. Of course they are the losers, but I venture to say that in this century the white people of this country had no better friend than Martin Luther King. There is no racial or national boundary to the feeling of loss, as evidenced by the universal outpouring of sympathy and testimony to Dr. King's contribution to [a] non-violent solution of our problem.

As much as any modern person, perhaps more than most, he combined the compassionate good-will of Jesus with the flaming indignation against social injustice of the Old Testament prophets. His voice gave expression to the best that is in the Negro church.

I feel a special kinship with him, having come out of the Negro church myself. That warm eloquence of the Negro preacher, at once so consoling and so commanding to righteousness, which Dr. King personified, is the thing that brought me into the ministry. Just over three years ago I heard, as many of you did, King's call from Selma, Alabama, asking his brother ministers from all over the country to come to Selma to help destroy the racial barriers of the black belt of the South.

It was at that time and place our Unitarian minister, James Reeb, lost his life and Dr. King, a Baptist minister, delivered the eulogy at a memorial service for Rev. Reeb, a Unitarian minister, in the local A.M.E. Church. There was not the slightest feeling of denominational or racial difference.

And now we are engaged in a memorial service for Dr. King himself. I can only say, he, being dead, yet speaketh. The last months of his life were devoted to assaults upon the evils of racism in the North, where those evils are more subtle, more hidden, more evasive, and therefore more difficult to combat. In addition, he took upon his shoulders the weight of the enlightened American conscience as he spoke out against the war in Vietnam. His final encounter with the established power in Memphis was on behalf of the poor garbage and trash collectors, 95 percent of them Negro.

Today, King's spirit calls to every one of us, calls to every citizen of this country, black and white, in North, South, East, West, to unite in loyalty to the American dream—King's dream—of equality and justice and opportunity for all our citizens and for a whole wide world of peace and brotherhood, inclusive of all mankind. I find it significant that this call coincides with the publication of the recommendations of the President's Commission on Civil Disorder that this be a matter of number one priority.

If we respond as we should and as he would wish, we shall overcome, and find some adequate meaning for his untimely joining the great cloud of witnesses, the prophets and martyrs of the human race. May the memory of his character and his work find a home in the minds of men everywhere.

May the spirit that was in Jesus, and Mahatma Gandhi, and in Martin Luther King be in us all, enabling us to think and feel and act in promoting justice and equality of opportunity for all, and for the construction of a warless world for all the home of man.

—Lewis Allen McGee, "Martin Luther King Jr.," McGee file, Morrison-Reed Collection, Sankofa Archive, Meadville Lombard Theological School Library, Chicago.

"I CANNOT APPROVE"

1968

The Honorable Wade H. McCree Jr. was an attorney, the first African-American judge in the Sixth Circuit Court of Appeals, and the second African American to serve as the United States Solicitor General. Having returned to Detroit in 1948 after graduating from Harvard Law School, he and his wife, Dores, at whose wedding Tracy Pullman, minister of Church of Our Father (later known as First Unitarian Universalist Church) had officiated in 1945, joined the congregation. In 1950, Eugene Sparrow, who Wade had known since childhood, was put forward as a candidate to become the congregation's assistant minister. Wade was away the weekend of Sparrow's candidacy, and his reaction to the rejection of Sparrow is unknown. Dores's feelings, however, were tinged with a sense of relief. At that time there was, perhaps, one other black family in the congregation, and in her honest estimation, the church was simply not ready. By 1955, the Detroit congregation's African-American membership had grown to around fifteen, and it was one of only a dozen Unitarian congregations that had five or more black members.

Prior to 1950, calling an African American was something only Community Church of New York had done. Having begun to integrate thirty years earlier, in 1948 it called Rev. Maurice A. Dawkins as its minister of education. Not until 1958—when Lewis A. McGee became the associate minister in Los Angeles and William R. Jones the assistant minister in Providence, Rhode Island—were black men again called to predominantly white congregations.

In 1965, Wade McCree, who by then had served on the church board and proudly taught in the church school even after being called to the federal bench, became the first African American be to elected to the UUA Board. As its vice moderator, he sat on the executive committee and was a member of the UUA Commission on Race and Religion as well.

He understood the impetus behind what the Black Affairs Council (BAC) was demanding and wrote in a Register-Leader *article titled "Earnest but Mistaken":*

> *Why do the middle-class Negro young men and women who are members of our church so fervently believe a Black Affairs Council is necessary? The answer lies in the discovery by black Americans of the underlying reason for their plight. With the elimination of all legal barriers to acceptance as an equal citizen and human being, the Negro had found revealed to him at last the underlying reason for his submerged condition: the fundamental racist attitude of America's whites, or most of them. He has learned that the overwhelming majority of white Americans, deep down in their psyches, are motivated by a racial arrogance which influences their every reaction to nonwhites.*

He continued, "I am not altogether sorry that the Black Affairs crisis confronts us. It has stimulated some of the most honest dialogue in our denomination that I have ever witnessed." He concluded, "their proposal affords us the opportunity to re-examine ourselves and our innermost feelings. And if we do, we will convince our earnest, if mistaken, young black Unitarian Universalists that we, as a church, can show the larger society the way to racial peace, justice and amity. If we can't, who can?"[1]

Hopeful words, but it was not to be. Soon after this article appeared, McCree sent the following letter to UUA president Dana Greeley in response to a letter from Greeley about a meeting Greeley had with the BAC and FULLBAC (Full Recognition and Funding for the Black Affairs Council).

May 17, 1968
Dr. Dana McLean Greeley
25 Beacon Street
Boston, Massachusetts 02108

Dear Dana,

I have your letter about the meeting with representatives of the BAC and FULLBAC and I, too, regret that I could not be with you.

As sympathetic as I am and as much as I am identified with the expressed goal of the BAC representatives to eradicate racism from our Association and the great society of which it is a part, I cannot approve their vehicle of a racially exclusive body within our institutional framework. It seems fundamental and self-evident that corrective measures must be undertaken by whites and Negroes working together in a common effort of mutual self-respect and equivalent dedication.

I feel so deeply about this that I am seriously considering resignation as I would feel obliged to in the event of action by the board to establish a White Affairs Council.

I will be grateful if you will have this letter reproduced and sent to the moderator, officers and trustees of the UUA.

Sincerely yours,
Wade H. McCree Jr.

—Letter from Wade H. McCree to Dana McLean Greeley, May 17, 1968, Wade H. McCree Jr. Collection, Walter P. Reuther Library of Labor and Urban Affairs, Wayne State University, Detroit.

THE BLACK AFFAIRS COUNCIL AND UNITARIAN UNIVERSALISTS FOR BLACK AND WHITE ACTION

1970

A divided UUA Board had declined to fund the Black Affairs Council (BAC). Instead, the board invited it to apply for affiliate status within the UUA while also creating the UU Fund for Racial Justice. The fund, with a budget of $300,000 per year, would be administered by a reconstituted Commission on Race and Religion that was later renamed Commission for Action on Race.

In May 1968, a group of Afro- and Euro-Americans calling itself the Black and White Alternative, later changed to Black and White Action (BAWA), organized in New York City. It sought support for projects promoting blacks and whites working together to eliminate racism.

In June, the UUA General Assembly (GA) met in Cleveland. Carl B. Stokes, its newly elected African-American mayor, delivered the Ware Lecture. In the business meeting, the BAC funding proposal was placed on the agenda, and in an atmosphere of extraordinary emotional tension, the proponents of BAWA and the BAC competed and struggled for the support of the delegates. On the third day of the assembly, the delegates voted 836 to 327 to fund the BAC at $250,000 a year for four years. The delegates also voted to give $50,000 to BAWA, over the protest of the BAC.

Following the GA, the UUA Board of Trustees voted to give the BAC $250,000 for that year but not subsequent ones. It also learned that all its discretionary reserves had been depleted. The follow-

ing spring, the administration recommended that the sum given to the BAC not be reduced. The board supported that position but also another, not put forward by the Greeley administration, to give $50,000 to BAWA. The BAC objected both to returning to GA annually for a reaffirmation of the commitment made in Cleveland and to the funding of BAWA.

At the 1969 GA in Boston, the Black Unitarian Universalist Caucus (BUUC) commandeered the microphones and demanded that the agenda as planned be rescinded by vote of the delegates and replaced by a new one that put the BAC funding first. After an unusually bitter debate, assembly delegates refused to accept this change. In response, many BUUC members left. Subsequently, those who supported them also left and regrouped at the nearby Arlington Street Church. A denominational schism seemed possible, but mediation was successful and the delegates came together again. Then, in a vote of 798 to 737, the delegates voted to support the BAC but not BAWA.

Following the 1969 GA, under the new presidency of Rev. Robert West, the administration discovered the full extent of the financial situation. In an effort to balance the budget, the board cut one million dollars, which eliminated all funding to UUA districts. It also adjusted the BAC appropriation from $250,000 per year over four years to $200,000 over five years. Later, it reconsidered but voted not to restore the original schedule. In 1970, the BUUC voted to disaffiliate the BAC from the UUA and launch its own funding campaign selling BAC bonds. The BAC was then dropped from the UUA budget. At the General Assembly held in Seattle in 1970, a motion to restore full funding was defeated, whereas a motion to protest the use of church facilities as private schools to avoid desegregation passed.

Below are the preamble to the constitution and bylaws of the BAC, and also the description of BAWA that appeared in the 1970 UUA Directory. They give a sense of the organizations' understanding of their missions and the differences between them.

BLACK AFFAIRS COUNCIL

The Unitarian Universalist Black Affairs Council is a programmatic affiliate of the Unitarian Universalist Association designed to execute programs which lead to the empowerment and self-determination of that Community and seek to establish a greater denominational relevance to that Community and its problems, and to promote the full participation of all persons, both within and without the Unitarian Universalist Association without regard to race, color, sex or national origin in carrying out this work.

With reference to the term "Black Community," it is an inclusive term which extends to both Black persons and to persons of other ethnic origins located in those geographical areas generally so categorized, and contemplates the elevation of all persons so located in areas both in the United States of America and Canada whose needs require the attention of our program.

To a great extent the program of BAC (which is a nine-member interracial council) will be achieved through the Black Unitarian Universalist Caucuses across the country. One should think of these Caucuses as a kind of field staff for the Council which will be highly dependent upon them for the channeling of information relative to the Black concerns of various locales.

UNITARIAN UNIVERSALISTS FOR BLACK AND WHITE ACTION

We oppose any attempts to separate and divide one human being from another by race, color, class, or other arbitrary distinctions. We are organized to bring people together in the Unitarian Universalists' belief in the brotherhood of man, undivided by nation, race, or creed.

Our vision is a society in which all citizens, black or white, rich or poor, young or old, participate fully in the opportunities and responsibilities of American life. Our vision is a society in which no man is judged, whether for good or bad, by the color of his skin. Our vision is a world in which no man need feel uncomfortable in the presence of another because we will all recognize our common humanity.

Our goal is to assist Unitarian Universalist churches and fellowships to share experiences, to know and appreciate all the cultural and ethnic diversity in their communities, to appreciate as well the uniqueness of each individual, and to recognize that as human beings we share a common destiny that requires our joint effort to achieve a just society.

Our method is to communicate with our UUA constituency through our Project Papers and Newsletters, to make expert counsel and technical assistance available to churches and fellowships and to offer financial assistance to those projects that are consistent with our vision of the future.

—*"Affiliate Members,"* 1970 Unitarian Universalist Association Directory, *pp. 165–66.*

DAVID HILLIARD EATON
1932–1992

I am neither an integrationist nor a separatist. I am simply a black man first, an individual second, citizen without a country third, and I reside in the United States of North America.

—David H. Eaton

The swirling currents of the 1960s bore a haunting resemblance to the period of Reconstruction a century earlier. American participation in the civil war in Vietnam produced divisions in American society not seen since its own between North and South. The civil rights legislation and demonstrations of the 1960s resumed the aborted efforts begun a century earlier with the Fourteenth and Fifteenth Amendments. The conservative backlash led to Martin Luther King Jr.'s assassination. His assassination and that of the Kennedys produced societal trauma comparable to that following Abraham Lincoln's. An area of Washington DC, just blocks from All Souls Church, Unitarian, was burned to the ground in the riots following King's slaying. The Vietnam War showed that American twentieth-century Cold War interests were inextricably linked with international developments. In Africa, one country after another attained independence. For progressives, the liberation of oppressed peoples around the world became a concern as abolition had been at the time that All Souls had been a stop on the Underground Railroad. As had happened a hundred years earlier, women's rights emerged as an issue, and hard upon that, attention turned to those discriminated against because of their sexual orientation. This was the context within which All Souls Church found itself as the congregation searched for a new senior minister. The ideal new leader would be someone who could help All Souls remain true to its heritage in such a contentious time.

The 1968 Committee to Nominate a Minister adopted the motto, "Maximum feasible congregational participation." The profile they produced from the congregation's descriptions of the kind of minister it wanted inspired this verse:

> Our profile's composed now, amidst autumn breezes,
> Our standard's so high, we've disqualified Jesus.[1]

After a year, the committee recommended Rev. David Hilliard Eaton of Washington DC. A special congregational meeting on June 15, 1969, approved him by a vote of 276 to 32, with 4 abstentions. Calling a black minister was a direction the congregation had been moving in for years. It had hired Bernice Bell Just, an African-American woman, as its director of religious education in 1957. In 1964, a black man, Harold B. Jordan, had become chair of its board of trustees. When Just left in 1966, another African-American woman, Margaret Williams, replaced her. Having African Americans in positions of leadership was not new for All Souls.

Eaton, who at the time held standing with the Methodist Church, accepted the call. Was this, indeed, the match that All Souls had sought? His predecessor, Rev. Duncan Howlett had created a stir when he suggested that the church consider black candidates for senior minister. All Souls was one of the few, even in this very liberal denomination, bold enough to try.

Bold, indeed. In the interview, the search committee asked Eaton, during a discussion about black power, "How do you see your ministry?" He responded, "I am first a black man, and second, an individual."[2]

Next the committee asked, "How can you then call yourself a humanist and say you can minister to all the people?" Eaton responded, "I believe with every sinew of my being that the first society that builds its priorities on the disinherited will be the first universal society. When our agenda is tailor-made for the Black, the Chicano, the American Indian, the poor White, the poor of our land, then we'll understand that the last can be first. Then we'll understand that when we do it for the least of our brothers, we do it for ourselves."[3]

Reflecting on this years later, Eaton wrote, "I wish in every sermon I preach I could heal the sores, could help you slip through life as smoothly as possible. I certainly would be popular. I would run less risk of being misunderstood. But if I understand the traditions of the prophets, if I am to use my insight, if I am to struggle with you so we can develop our insight together and come to a new perception, it will be a bumpy road for us, and it will start with our fears and our depression. It will start with the oppressed among us and in us, and will go a bump at a time, to a new heaven and a new earth. It's a bumpy road, but it's the only one I can see that will get us there."[4]

A bumpy road it would be.

Although he was born almost in the shadow of All Souls in 1932, it could not have been apparent that Eaton's path would eventually lead there. His mother was a clerk for the IRS, and his father had parlayed a chauffeur's job into his own moving and real estate business. Educated in DC public schools and graduating from the esteemed Dunbar High School in 1950, David went to Howard University and majored in philosophy. Receiving his BA in 1954, he was commissioned as a second lieutenant in the U.S. Army. After serving in Germany, he continued his studies at Boston University School of Theology (BUST) and earned an MDiv. In 1964, he would spend five months studying the philosophy of theology at Oxford University and in 1972 was awarded a DMin from BUST.

While attending divinity school, Eaton became president of the young people's group of about 140 people at Second Church (Unitarian). He also served as temporary assistant minister in several

Unitarian churches in Massachusetts. Attracted by what he said was "the opportunity to explore my own spiritual depth without having to pay heed to the restrictions of creeds and dogma," he approached the AUA president about the possibility of serving a congregation. Dana Greeley told him, "Personally, I'd love to have you but I'm afraid we couldn't settle you."[5] Upon his graduation in 1959, Eaton moved to Pacoima, California, where he became the founder and first pastor of a Methodist church. Returning to Washington DC, he assumed a series of posts in higher education, first at Howard University and later at Federal City College (now the University of the District of Columbia), where he was serving as dean of student services and associate professor of education when called to All Souls.

With his broad smile and easy manner, Eaton was equally at home among black radicals and white intellectuals. An imposing figure, standing well over six feet tall, he had lively, penetrating eyes and long, expressive hands that at times in sermons could be as accusatory as a fire and brimstone preacher.

Assuming his duties at All Souls on September 1, 1969, he wasted no time demonstrating that his commitment to community involvement and activism would continue. On Sunday, October 12, a man who said he represented the Black United Front, which Eaton had helped to found, interrupted the service and asked to be heard by this overwhelmingly white congregation.[6] Eaton invited him into the pulpit. The man said, "My people know today their kids are hungry, they need food, better jobs, yes and better places to live. They no longer listen to that religious current of 'pie in the sky.' . . . What's wrong with them living now? . . . Many of our people lived and died that this nation can exist as it is today. How can you sit there and ask us to wait until tomorrow while you are enjoying the full fruits of their labors today?" He then requested $250,000 for his cause. Eaton responded, "regardless of how churches in America may fear demands coming to them from outside, we should welcome these demands in order to set our own house in order. We should fear no earthly power. We should fear only ourselves, if we negate our responsibility. . . . The day has come, the hour has come. I feel secure just with the few people that I have met in this church, old and young alike, that we have already started working in the area of economic development."[7]

So it was to be.

Meanwhile, within the UUA, what became known as the Empowerment Controversy raged. New to the denomination, Eaton had watched the tumult from the sideline, but when the Black Unitarian Universalist Caucus (BUUC) disaffiliated the Black Affairs Council (BAC) from the UUA in order to pursue independent funding, Eaton acted. In June 1970, he exhorted the members of All Souls to purchase $200,000 in bonds from the BAC, the proceeds from which would be available to DC's black community. The proposal was voted upon and approved by a ratio of three to one.

In another expression of his intention to rebuild the community, Eaton joined in the church's effort to revive an earlier project to gain Federal Housing Administration support to provide low-cost housing in the surrounding neighborhood, which had been side-tracked by the 1968 riots. In February 1970, All Souls agreed to cooperate with other churches in the area to raise funds, making available $10,000 of the church endowment, while church members contributed another $8,000 of seed money. Six years later, a groundbreaking ceremony was held for Columbia Heights Village, the first federally assisted housing project in the area.

The housing project is one of many substantial, if relatively inconspicuous, contributions All Souls made toward rebuilding the community under Eaton's visionary, empowering, go-do-it leadership—inconspicuous because few viewing this development knew about the Church's role. By contrast, the minister himself in the 1970s appeared frequently in the public eye as a firebrand for social, political, and economic justice.

The most striking episode occurred on May 3, 1970, in the sermon "Take the Blindfold Off the Lady." Denouncing the pending District of Columbia Omnibus Crime Bill—which condoned preventive detention, wiretapping, and "no-knock" searches of private residences—he advised concerning the latter provision, "I suggest to you and I instruct myself that, because of the oppression that is growing in this country, any time a person breaks into your home without a warrant, shoot him." He went on to reject "any concept of law and order that does not first deal with the concept of justice. Where there is no justice there can never be real law and order. No order of the spirit. No law of reciprocal decency."[8]

Eaton's stand provoked considerable controversy. A *Washington Post* editorial questioned his morality.[9] The All Souls Board of Trustees responded with a letter strongly supporting their minister, but nonetheless dozens of members resigned. Eaton, however, was vindicated when Congress dropped the bill's "no-knock" provision.

Some in the media recognized that this new All Souls minister was acting very much in the tradition of a church that had not so long before harbored Rev. A. Powell Davies—who had launched a successful campaign to desegregate Washington DC restaurants and had been one of the strongest voices against rampant McCarthyism.

Eaton's reputation grew. He served as co-chair of the Task Force on Race and Minority Group Relations of the 1971 White House Conference on Youth, and conducted hearings nationwide with minority youth. At the same time, he served as chair of the DC Human Relations Committee. *The Washingtonian* magazine listed him as one of the top ten leaders in the area, describing him as "tough, practical and likes to work behind the scenes, but . . . willing to take chances, too."[10] Eaton's activities provided him with more direct access to the media. The audience for his WOL-radio call-in show, "Speak Up—You Are on the Air," grew. In late 1970, he launched the "David Eaton Show" on Channel 4 TV, which, in two years of running, garnered successive awards from the Capital Press Club and the National Academy of Television Arts & Sciences. He used these forums to highlight issues such as reparations for blacks, home rule for DC, and opposition to the Vietnam War.

Such high visibility brought recognition for Eaton, All Souls, and Unitarian Universalism; it also made him a target. During this period, the government's response to the activities of the minister of All Souls and the church led Eaton to join with eight others who had been under scrutiny to file for damages for violation of their constitutional rights by the DC police and the FBI. In 1986, after repeated appeals by the government, the *Hobson v. Wilson* case was settled in the plaintiffs' favor.

All Souls' ministry with David Eaton engaged the social concerns of the period. In February 1973, Eaton spoke out against the practice of brain surgery when its sole aim was behavior modification. He was a member of the Study Panel for an Energy Policy of the National Council of Churches. He joined other members of the church in pressing for a moratorium on nuclear power. Between 1976 and 1977, Elizabeth Johnson, a senior member of the church, collaborated with Eaton in making the church a stockholder in Pepco, the local power company, and in national corporations, including Honeywell. Johnson and others spoke out at the Honeywell stockholders meeting. Eaton led the church's support of the Wilmington Ten, civil rights activists who had been wrongly convicted of arson and conspiracy in North Carolina.

For Eaton, there was no separation between ministry in the church and ministry in the community. He said politics and ethics were both about how people live together. His engagement with social issues in the city was a bridge between the church, the African-American community, and other socially conscious people. Eaton worked among the city's leaders, and at one point, Marion Barry, the city's second elected mayor, and three city councilors were members of All Souls. The church grew more diverse and continued to attract members who also held positions in government or on boards and commissions, people engaged in DC and its issues.

Eaton said that when he

> came to All Souls in 1969 the church was 90–95 percent Euro-American. Around 1970, working with the Board of Trustees,

> [a mission was set] to make it an all-inclusive congregation. We purposefully attempted to make this a multi-racial . . . pluralistic congregation. We worked at it. We had to deal with both whites and blacks in the church over the question of the black power movement. We lost a significant amount of members . . . [who] found it difficult to deal with some of the problems that came with being a multi-racial congregation. It wasn't something that was easily done. Now it appears to be very comfortable, but it's only comfortable because a lot of hard work was put in to it, because people thought it was a mission well worth obtaining.[11]

The early years did not witness simply an unbroken string of successes, nor did all of the previous membership accept the new leader and his style. Membership had numbered over one thousand when Eaton was called and gradually shrank to half the size over the next two decades. The ability of members to choose to attend a number of nearby Unitarian Universalist churches provided a safety valve that contributed to the longevity of David Eaton's ministry. Those who stayed at All Souls were those who wanted to be part of the cultural change.

Music helped to transform the sanctuary on Sunday mornings. The All Souls Jubilee Singers, founded in 1977 by Ysaye Barnwell, became the third formal music group. The multiracial singers specialized in a rich heritage of black musical selections. Along with the All Souls choir and Madrigal Singers, a wide range of music supported racial and religious pluralism in the church. When respected minister of music and organist Karl Halvorson departed for health reasons, he was succeeded by Samuel Bonds as director of music and Marvin Mills as organist. For the first time, the music program, except for the Madrigal Singers, was under the leadership of black artists. These changes might have been expected, given the city's demographics and a church attempting to become integrated. Nevertheless, such an unsettling process must have tested the comfort threshold of even the most loyal church members.

In the final analysis, throughout Eaton's ministry, the enthusiasm of his supporters outweighed the reservations of his critics, and the church continued pursuing its leadership role in the community. An early dramatic vote of confidence for the new minister came in 1973, from Dr. Earl R. Beckner and his wife, Dr. Meta S. Beckner, when they made an initially anonymous gift of nearly $1 million to the church. The investment income from the gift was to be used for projects that would enhance the influence of All Souls church and help make the immediate community more cohesive, attractive, and forward-looking.

By the beginning of the 1980s, David Eaton had truly become a pillar of his community and a recognized leader in the Unitarian Universalist denomination. Elected twice to the DC Board of Education, he served an unprecedented three consecutive terms as the board president from 1982 to 1985. In 1985, he was elected to the UUA Nominating Committee. He received numerous awards, among them the Clarence Skinner Award in 1985, an honorary doctorate from Starr King School for the Ministry in 1986, and the Man of the Year award from the YMCA of Metropolitan Washington in 1990.

The 1980s also brought challenging issues within the church. Perhaps the most volatile concerned performing same-sex unitement ceremonies (what we now typically call services of union). The openly gay minister of education and senior programs, Rev. Frank Robertson, had performed over a dozen unitement ceremonies at the church since 1974. However, the issue first became widely discussed when a May 1980 article in *Jet* magazine carried the headline "Church 'Unitement' Ceremony Joins Two Women, 500 Attend" and included pictures of two women, one dressed in a wedding gown and the other in a tuxedo.

While All Souls, an urban church struggling to maintain its membership, held conflicting views about homosexuality, the UUA position on the issue left no doubt about the importance of the principles involved, or its affirmative stance. Reflecting on the matter in his sermon, "A Direction for the 1980s," David Eaton called the issue one of the most difficult experiences of his ministry at All Souls. He explained that he had in fact eight years earlier verbally agreed that Robertson could perform such ceremonies. Now, after all the publicity surrounding the *Jet* article and many hours of discussion in the church, he attempted to find middle ground. At the January 1981 Board meeting, he recommended a new policy in which unitement services could be held in his study as part of a private counseling session, with no certificate issued. This offended constituents, who said the change represented inferior treatment. After a heated controversy, the congregation approved use of the sanctuary, establishing a policy requiring that any such service be held under the guidance of the senior minister, not as a public ceremony but as the culmination of a counseling process. Later, indicating the depth of the controversy, the Board refused to reappoint Robertson to a new term. Members who supported him protested this decision but the Board refused to reconsider and Robertson left. After Eaton's death, however, when the church was transitioning between ministers in 1993, a new resolution was passed, affirming the church's support for gay and lesbian rights.[12]

"Activist Pastor at All Souls Leaving Pulpit" read the headline in the March 30, 1992, *Washington Post*.[13] Seriously ill with hepatitis B, Eaton ended his twenty-three-year ministry on Easter Sunday that year, and the following September, he passed away. David Hilliard Eaton's ministry forever changed All Souls Church, left a lingering mark on Washington DC, and modeled the meaning of inclusiveness for the Unitarian Universalist Association. He took his ministry to the community and brought the multiracial community into the church. He preached a gospel of love and justice, and he empowered people to act.

At Eaton's memorial service, UUA president Bill Schulz opined that David Eaton had accomplished something in twenty years that all of Unitarian Universalism had not accomplished in two hundred.

—Paula Cole Jones and Mark D. Morrison-Reed

Sources

This essay relied heavily on the unpublished biography "A Leader for the Second Reconstruction: David Hilliard Eaton," written in 1998 by Allison Blakely. The authors also had access to Eaton's papers, archived at All Souls Church (Unitarian); an additional unpublished biography entitled "Social Justice from the Pulpit and the Pews: Reverend David Eaton (1969–1997) and All Souls Church, Unitarian," written by Sean Sanford; articles from the Washington Post *and* Jet*; and an 1985 interview of Eaton by Carol Dornbrand. Eaton was Paula Cole Jones's minister and Mark Morrison-Reed's colleague and mentor.*

"BLACKS, GET YOUR GUNS"
1969

Renford Gaines, an Afro-Canadian who now goes by the name Mwalimu Imara, found out about American-style racism when, as a young man, he was spit upon and cursed in upstate New York. Imara was the first black seminarian to attend Meadville Lombard Theological School since Lewis A. McGee in 1947. In his final year of school, he attended both the Emergency Conference and the National Conference of Black UUs. Graduating in June 1968, he was called to the UU Church of Urbana-Champaign in Illinois. During his first year, he participated in a radio broadcast series. In his program, "The Psychopathology of Racism," he described racists as showing all the earmarks of a disturbed mind. After the third program, the backlash began. In the mail, at church, and at home, he received cards showing the back of his head in crosshairs. He walked into a garage to ask for help, and a guy yelled, "You're that son-of-a-bitch" and threw a tire iron at him. He went to the sheriff and asked for protection; his request was dismissed out of hand. He got a message saying, "We are going to bomb your home with your kids in it." The police still did nothing. He knew a group called the White Hats was behind it. One day, while he and the president of the congregation were in the church office, Imara called the president to the window and pointed at a White Hat's car parked, as usual, in front of the church. The white, middle-class congregation, found his reports of being harassed impossible to believe. In this context, Imara delivered the following sermon to the congregation. In 1970, he left to become the senior minister of Arlington Street Church in Boston.

My closing words in last week's sermon should not have created misunderstanding by anyone living in this country in this year of 1969. But it did. Blacks are often misunderstood when they announce or confirm their right as human beings to defend themselves from unlawful vicious attack by clansmen, white citizens' councils, minute men groups or illegal police action.

Black people live with the reality of a police state every day. It is hard, difficult, perhaps impossible for white people in America to understand that blacks do not have the same protection of the law and from the illegal law coercion that white people enjoy. It matters little whether we live in a suburb or a ghetto. The white man with a badge on his chest and a gun on his hip has unlimited license to kill blacks. In a situation where we are without protection, should I recommend that the flower of tomorrow's black manhood allow themselves to be passively butchered? If you found the "benediction" upsetting, a soothing therapy would be an effective involvement on your part in bringing about citizen's review committees for Champaign County, or in some other way insure justice for blacks here. Two black men died "mysteriously" this year in county jail. We forget so quickly.

There has been some criticism this year of the amount of blackness in our services. Some members have threatened to withdraw their money and/or their membership. Always, the decision to remain in full, participating membership in our churches is a matter of personal decision. But please before you act; examine the facts. Last year there were only five Sundays devoted, in whole or part, to Black themes.

There were times when my soul cried out to communicate an episode, event or idea connected to black life in America but I would hesitate because I knew many would be offended. ALL THAT IS OVER.

Middle class blacks have been too silent while young black people have been dying to bring humanity and justice to black people in this country. I have played the "button-lip game" along with the rest. I am through with that. From here forward our communication about race will be issued in person, from the pulpit and my pen, as I feel they should. I notice that ministers who advocate black moderation and black non-existence in our movement do not reserve their opinions exclusively for discussion groups, but use their pulpits and their newsletters to promulgate their racism.

The black minister in the white church—how will the experiment run? For the past sixteen months I have ministered to this community, white and black. You have not hesitated to call on me, nor I to respond when your marriage, your children, or your friends needed what I, as a minister, had to offer.

I believe that various tasks of ministry in this church have been conducted in fairness without racial bias or exclusion. As long as I am minister, this policy will continue. However, let us understand each other on this point. I, as a black man, live in two worlds. If you wish to retain me as minister you will have to share as much of both my worlds with me as I share your intimate life with you. When the black shoe pinches on a universal corn I will speak to the hurt with power. If you feel that you cannot or would rather not have this relationship, please let me know.

I am not the only middle-class black in the community eye speaking a "get-your-gun-when-attacked" benediction. Listen to your NAACP and Urban League chapters. All we as blacks affirm is our right to life. Whites negatively respond to this often because it threatens their comfort and peace of mind.

Time is running out for all black people. We are about the business of survival, not parliamentary debating points of romantic escapism.

—Renford Gaines, "Blacks, Get Your Guns," sermon delivered November 1969, Universalist Church of Urbana-Champaign, IL, Mwalimu Imara file, Morrison-Reed Collection, Sankofa Archive, Meadville Lombard Theological School Library, Chicago.

THE BLACK HUMANIST FELLOWSHIP OF LIBERATION

The winds of fate are fickle and blow where they may, our lives and communities buffeted by large, sometimes overwhelming, forces. So it was with the Black Humanist Fellowship of Liberation, an experimental African-American Unitarian Universalist congregation in Cleveland that existed from 1969 to 1979. Its story serves as a reminder of just how little control people have over their lives and institutions. The birth, life, and dissolution of the fellowship had as much to do with outside forces as they did with decisions made by the congregation's members.

The story of the Black Humanist Fellowship of Liberation begins with the birth of the Unitarian Universalist Society of Cleveland. In 1951, the First Unitarian Church of Cleveland decided to move from its building at the corner of Eighty-second and Euclid to Shaker Heights. This decision was prompted in large part by economic and cultural realities. The Hough neighborhood, where the church was located, was experiencing white flight as it became predominantly African American—and with that a slow but steady economic decline. When the church was built in 1904, the neighborhood had been one of the wealthiest in the entire country. However, by 1951, much of Cleveland's middle and upper class was moving to the suburbs, and the congregation's minister, Robert Killiam, wanted the church to follow. In a close vote, the majority of the First Unitarian Church decided to relocate.

At the time, the First Unitarian Church had a membership of close to 1,200. About 300 members did not favor the move to

Shaker Heights. According to an early congregational history, the founders of the society wanted "a Unitarian Church that will attract persons of various cultural, economic, and racial backgrounds—in short a truly cosmopolitan membership."[1] With this vision, they bought the church building from First Church and organized the Unitarian Society of Cleveland.

The new society called Jesse Cavileer as its first minister. Cavileer served until 1956, and during his ministry, the congregation emphasized social justice work and engaged in intentional outreach towards African Americans. Cavileer's tenure was followed by that of Emerson Schwenk, from 1957 to 1962, and Dennis Kuby, from 1962 to 1968. Both continued the emphasis on social justice and the effort to become racially integrated. By the time the congregation called Farley Wheelwright as its fourth minister in 1968, it had a reputation of working for civil rights, speaking out against the Vietnam War and advocating for social justice. It was also integrated, with about 10 percent of its membership African American.

The church's location and mission were a source of strain in congregational life. The society was located a half mile from the corner where the 1966 Hough riots had started, in which four people were killed and parts of the neighborhood burned. By the time Wheelwright arrived, tensions between the church and the neighborhood had developed. In 1968, the congregation had purchased a house nearby, with the intention of opening a community center to foster better relations between the congregation and the surrounding neighborhood. Arsonists burned down the house in the spring of 1969. A short while later, in a letter addressed to Dr. Joseph Barth, the head of the Unitarian Universalist Association Department of Ministry, dated May 21, 1969, and copied to the society's board of trustees, Wheelwright described the situation of the congregation this way: "The problem is the neighborhood and our almost total lack of relationship to it. In the past year we have had robberies, muggings, gun hold-ups, threatened rape. . . . One never knows as he drives to work or to worship what he will find—or more appropriately what he will not find! The building we acquired for the parking lot was set afire. Last Monday I was pelted with empty coke bottles and told 'get out of the neighborhood!' I got."[2]

In the same letter, Wheelwright ruminated on a possible solution to the society's problem. He wrote, "After this long build-up at last comes my idea how to get out of the bind I see us in. I think it might be possible for us to relate to this community by staffing the Unitarian Society with a Black Minister to the Community. He would be charged with building a black liberal religious constituency and ministering to the neighborhood."[3]

Barth received this letter in the wake of the 1967 Emergency Conference on the UU Response to the Black Rebellion, the formation of the Black Unitarian Universalist Caucus (BUUC), and a vote at the subsequent 1968 UUA General Assembly in Cleveland to direct one million dollars to black concerns. At that moment, the association was considering what they called an "Experimental Ghetto Ministry." And in September 1969, the Division of Ministry, Churchmanship, and Extension contracted with John Frazier to "develop a meaningful, relevant and empowering religious community in the ghetto."[4] Frazier came to Cleveland shortly afterward.

Wheelwright was fifty years old in 1968. He had been active in the civil rights struggle and gone to Selma, and now was involved in the antiwar movement and the counterculture. He knew Martin Luther King Jr. and was familiar with other nationally known civil rights leaders. Indeed, before his assassination, King had been scheduled to preach Wheelwright's installation sermon. Wheelwright had come to Cleveland because he was interested in serving an inner-city church with a social justice ministry.

Frazier was just twenty-eight when he moved to Cleveland. Fresh out of school, he had never served a Unitarian Universalist congregation as its settled minister. However, he had known Wheelwright for several years. The two had met when Wheelwright was in Mississippi. Frazier was active in the civil rights movement there and had been impressed by the commitment to the struggle for racial equality the Unitarians of Jackson, Mississippi, had shown. He joined that church and, after finishing his undergraduate degree, enrolled in Crane Theological School. While Frazier was in seminary, Wheelwright, serving a nearby congregation, became one of his benefactors and mentors. After graduation, Wheelwright raised money so that Frazier could spend a year studying at Manchester College, the Unitarian seminary that is part of Oxford University.[5]

Prior to coming to Cleveland, Frazier was considered for pulpits in Philadelphia and Chicago Heights, Illinois. Correspondence between Frazier and one of the search committees indicates that racism on the part of church members had at least something to do with why he was not called to either of those congregations.

Shortly after he arrived in Cleveland, Frazier organized the Black Humanist Fellowship of Liberation. The fellowship began as a congregation within a congregation. It was initially made up primarily of members of the Black Unitarian Universalist Caucus (BUUC), a group of African-American Unitarian Universalists from the society and other area Unitarian Universalist congregations. Formed only a few months earlier, the BUUC was the local chapter of the national organization of the same name. Both were committed to the philosophy of black nationalism.

Hayward Henry, the national chairman of the BUUC, described black nationalism this way in his essay, "Position Paper on BUUC Ideology: From Black Power to Black Nationalism": "Black nationalism . . . holds that Africans in America are a colonized people in a fundamentally racist society that is incapable of self-initiated change. . . . our only recourse is to come together in order to overthrow white oppression by whatever means are appropriate and to proceed . . . with a total restructuring of society. Such a society would be institutionally restructured around . . . the Black experience rather than the white Western experience." A goal of the BUUC was to take control of and redirect resources from the white community to the black community.[6]

Over the summer of 1969, the relationship between the society and the Hough neighborhood had deteriorated further. Two women had been attacked in the church parking lot in June. Members of the congregation were afraid to visit the church at any time other than Sunday morning. The church secretary had threatened to quit unless the security conditions improved. People, particularly families with children, were resigning from the congregation's membership and attendance was dwindling.

Shortly before Frazier arrived in Cleveland and organized the fellowship, Wheelwright had drafted a confidential memo for the society's board. He laid out several possible options for the board and the congregation's membership to consider. The last one was to "Turn the 82nd Street Unitarian Society of Cleveland over lock, stock and barrel to a Black Unitarian movement, with the initial leadership coming from BUUC."[7]

Wheelwright's memo sparked a controversy that over the next months consumed the congregation, bringing it to national attention and ultimately resulting in the gift of the Eighty-second Street and Euclid property along with significant other assets to the BUUC and the fellowship. The controversy took place against the backdrop of Carl Stokes's election in the autumn of 1968 as mayor of Cleveland, becoming, along with Gary Hatcher in Gary, Indiana, one of the first African-American mayors of a major U.S. city, and the wider conflict over black power within the Unitarian Universalist Association. Wheelwright's memo was followed by a letter from the president of the Board of Trustees, James Huston, "calling a congregational meeting for Sunday morning, November 2 . . . to consider the future of our church." In his letter, Huston also announced "a series of speakers . . . [to] address the subject of Unitarianism, Black, White and integrated."[8]

The series was balanced between those who favored Wheelwright's proposal and those who opposed it. Advocates included David Eaton, the African-American senior minister of All Souls Church, Unitarian, in Washington DC, Hayward Henry, and Wheelwright himself. Those opposing the transfer of assets included John Hayward, director of religious studies at the University of Southern Illinois and Glover Barnes, co-chair of Black and White Action (BAWA), a national Unitarian Universalist group that opposed the black nationalism of the BUUC and advocated integration. Donald Harrington, senior minister of the historical integrated Community Church of New York, was also scheduled to participate but had to cancel.

Not all of the sermon texts from the series have survived. The existing texts indicate that the two camps fell roughly along the lines of supporters of black nationalism and supporters of integration. Henry preached "a case for blackness" and challenged the congregation to be "one of the few white institutions that has peacefully turned over power to Black people."[9] Speaking the next week, Barnes called the philosophy of black nationalism "garbage" and suggested that to give the property away was to "join the counter revolution." He urged the congregation to try "true integration" instead and to struggle for "their rights and integrity" across the boundaries of race.[10] During his sermon, members of the BUUC walked out.

This walkout was meant to mirror a similar action at the General Assembly of the Unitarian Universalist Association, where a few months earlier, supporters of the Black Affairs Council (BAC) had walked out of the assembly to protest the agenda and proposal to fund BAWA. Wheelwright, a supporter of the General Assembly walkout, was not impressed when the same strategy was used in his congregation, writing in the society's newsletter, "Walking out on discussion kills discussion." The action caused him to wonder if "What I interpreted to be a cutting-edge experiment, a new dimension in race relations [has] suddenly . . . [been] revealed as a power play with either ill-advised or inept power-players."[11]

The passionate debate over the congregation's future did not take place only on Sunday morning or from the pulpit. The society's president, James Huston, moderated at least two weekday evening congregational conversations, and George T. Johnson, a minister from San Francisco, led a discussion, "Unitarians in a Black Community." Meanwhile, members of the congregation made their views known through a flurry of mimeographed letters published by the society under the heading "Viewpoint." Authors of the majority of existing documents opposed the gift of property. Their reasons varied greatly. One opposed the gift on moral grounds, claiming that the gift represented "a course of separatism . . . [that would do] a severe injustice to our children."[12] Another opposed the gift because of "the financial burden [it placed] upon the Unitarian Society compared to other largely white Unitarian congregations."[13] A community member unaffiliated with the congregation accused those considering the gift of "running away."[14] Yet there were also those who felt that it was time for the congregation to leave Eighty-second and Euclid because the "hope [for the congregation] had not been realized"[15] or because the society's resources were "no longer sufficient to prolong our physical existence at 82nd and Euclid."[16]

The November 2, 1969, congregational meeting attracted wide attention. Two television stations requested permission to broadcast the proceedings but were denied. Print journalists attended in abundance, seeking an exciting story. The members of the congregation did not disappoint. In a series of four votes, they voted once against moving and twice by wide margins (22 to 108) against turning over the congregation's property and assets to the BUUC. A fourth vote—held, according to congregational lore, after many members had left to attend the Cleveland Browns football game—netted the desired result. By a margin of 60 to 31, the congregation passed a motion reading:

1. That the Unitarian Society turn over the total property at 8143 Euclid Avenue, Cleveland, Ohio, to the BUUC who, in cooperation with other institutions, intend to establish a black community-controlled institution.
2. That the Unitarian Society grant to the BUUC enough assets to begin the establishment of its operations.
3. That the Unitarian Society will be permitted to continue its

operation at 8143 Euclid Avenue, Cleveland, Ohio, for as long as the Society wishes.[17]

Shortly after the meeting, a petition signed by twenty-nine members was circulated, calling for a second congregational meeting to affirm the decision of the November 2, 1969, meeting. That meeting took place on December 14, 1969, but before it did, members dissatisfied with the outcome of the initial meeting, led by African-American member William Mack, began litigation against the society's board. An injunction temporarily preventing the transfer of assets was ordered, and the second congregational meeting took place under court supervision. Opponents to the transfer of society assets to the BUUC were disappointed when the congregation reaffirmed its previous decision by 84 to 60.

As the drama around the second congregational meeting unfolded, a group of members opposed to the transfer sought counsel from Donald Harrington. Harrington, honorary co-chair of BAWA, was actively opposed to the national BUUC. At the time, the congregation Harrington served claimed a membership of 1,700 and boasted that more than 25 percent of the congregation were people of color. Both prior to and following the second congregational meeting, Harrington spoke with members of the society via telephone. His participation outraged Wheelwright, who, on January 4, 1970, delivered a sermon addressed to Harrington, entitled "An Open Letter to a Colleague." He accused Harrington of interfering "in the affairs of another [minister] without invitation from the minister himself, or . . . from his Board of Trustees."[18] Wheelwright then listed five ways in which Harrington had interfered with the events at the Unitarian Society of Cleveland. Perhaps the two most damning accusations were that Harrington helped finance Mack's lawsuit and strategized with the UUA president, Robert West, to prevent the transfer of congregational assets to the BUUC. Harrington replied in his own open letter. He did not deny his involvement and even admitted to raising money for the court case. He did, however, challenge Wheelwright's assumption that his involvement in the society's affairs were without Wheelwright's permission (and thus a major breach of ministerial protocol), claiming instead that it was Wheelwright himself who gave the society members in question Harrington's phone number and suggested to them that Harrington might help them "organize the integrationist members more effectively."[19]

Shortly after the exchange between Harrington and Wheelwright, Mack lost his case against the society's board. During a worship service to which Mayor Stokes and Robert West sent greetings, on March 1, 1970, the deed was transferred between the society and the BUUC. At the same time, the society transferred $35,000 "for seed money and building repairs for a two-year span" to the BUUC, representing about 20 percent of the congregation's cash assets.[20]

Meanwhile, the BUUC filed articles of incorporation with the Ohio secretary of state, declaring that "The purpose of the Cleveland Black Unitarian Universalist Caucus is to cultivate in its particular situation in the Cleveland area the means and methods of developing a meaningful, relevant, and empowering community, and to advance the principles of Unitarian Universalism as they relate to Black people."[21]

After taking control of the building, the BUUC and the fellowship received significant financial support from the Unitarian Universalist Association and a number of other granting agencies. Its efforts were also met with enthusiasm. The fellowship's first annual congregational meeting on November 29, 1970, recorded a membership of ninety-six and a youth program with about thirty participants. At that time, the congregation's stated purpose was:

1. To be a summing point for community involvement; and
2. To create through the people, a seven (7) day a week religious model.[22]

What that meant for the fellowship was never entirely clear. While the congregation was initially able to generate a lot of enthusiasm, it was not able to develop a focus. Within the first year, a theater; a drug addiction clinic; a store for African art, clothes, and literature; an educational program; and a counseling center were planned, and funding for most of these programs was secured. The National Endowment for the Arts supported the theater program. The Unitarian Universalist Association paid for the minister and administrator's salaries. The fellowship staff quickly grew to six.

No plan was ever developed to raise the funds necessary to keep the fellowship operating from year to year or to make its programs sustainable. Grant money was constantly sought, but members of the congregation were not required to make substantive financial contributions. Pledging goals were set, for example, at 1 percent of members' monthly incomes. Several fund-raising efforts were held—Lionel Hampton did a benefit concert—but none of these generated significant enough funds to pay for the congregation's operating budget, maintain the building, or support its staff. The financial situation deteriorated quickly, and by the end of 1971, only about twenty months after the fellowship took possession of the building, they actively tried to sell parts of it. Pictures of the church's four Tiffany windows were sent to auction houses and museums across the country. A plan was formulated to sell the pews and chancel. With the congregation unable to generate cash, its staff began to resign.

At the same time, the fellowship was hemorrhaging members. The 1971 annual congregational meeting minutes report a membership of thirty-six, only fourteen of whom were present. Instead of adjusting the fellowship's plans to its changing circumstances and resources, the projected budget ballooned. The planned budget for 1973 was over $130,000. The most serious problem was probably that it never developed a deep religious life. The worship services, when they happened, varied greatly, and more often than not consisted of theater performances, drumming, and lectures by outside speakers. Alcohol was frequently served after the services. Throughout the minutes of the fellowship's board meetings are frequent references to poor service attendance.

The fellowship folded not long after outside funding ran out. Frazier left the area in 1974, and the Unitarian Universalist Association's last record of the fellowship is from 1979, when it had only seventeen members.

Attendance at the society's services continued to dwindle, and by early 1971, a decision was made to move the congregation to the Coventry neighborhood of Cleveland Heights, one of the centers of the Cleveland area's bohemian community. After the move, the society's membership plummeted, and by 1972, it was no longer able to retain a full-time minister. Wheelwright left, and not until 1976 could the society replace him with the very part-time Violet Kochendoerfer. During the same time, the African-American membership at the society shrank to almost nothing.

It is hard to imagine how things could have turned out differently for either the society or the fellowship. Outside forces exerted enormous pressure. In the late 1960s, the Unitarian Universalist Association had been looking for a place to start an experimental ministry, and Cleveland seemed like a logical match. Black nationalism was on the rise throughout the country and within the religious association. Cleveland had elected its first black mayor. The congregation's neighborhood was rapidly changing. These forces shaped the decisions of the members of the congregation.

Also, by 1970, the UUA faced a severe budget crisis and, with its own membership numbers declining, had to retreat from earlier commitments. Outside funding ceased to be available in 1972 to pay for Frazier's salary or support the activities of the fellowship. The national mood shifted as well. Political radicalism and the left, in general, were in decline. The association-wide conflicts within the UUA over racial issues and black power had left some African Americans disheartened with Unitarian Universalism and uninterested in liberal religion. The national BUUC had withdrawn from the activities of the association and was in the process of collapse.

The fellowship's demise was neither the first nor last time an effort of our liberal, dual faith tradition to engage an African-American community would fail. Nevertheless, that the society survived, even when the fellowship did not, is a testament to those who stuck with it, believed in it, nurtured it, and fought for it after its near collapse, no matter which way the winds of fate blew.

—Colin Bossen

Sources

The major source for materials on the Black Humanist Fellowship of Liberation are the Humanist Fellowship of Liberation and John Frazier papers at the Western Reserve Historical Society. Other sources that I drew upon for this essay are the archives of the Unitarian Universalist Society of Cleveland and the Farley Wheelwright papers at Andover-Harvard Theological Library.

THE EMPOWERMENT PARADOX

"I was involved in the Black Affairs Council from the beginning. In fact, I was involved before the beginning," said Benjamin F. Scott, in an address delivered ten years after the 1968 Unitarian Universalist Association General Assembly voted to fund the Black Affairs Council (BAC). Scott continued,

> The occasion was a hot night in Boston in the summer of 1967. A group met in the apartment of Homer Jack and made the decision to hold a conference about the "Black Rebellion." I was against it because I had no confidence that any assemblage of white liberals would really do anything but rationalize and maybe pass a resolution of support. I had become increasingly radicalized by events since 1954. . . . I was angry and disgusted at what this country was, and I felt that a large part of the reason for the state of the country was to be laid at the feet of people like those who gathered that night and that included me.
>
> So I was really ready for the Black Caucus which Lou Gothard formed at [the Biltmore] conference. I had no idea what would come of it but it was at least different from what we had been doing. Well what came of it was BAC and a total immersion of the people of the UUA in the fury and the glory of the Black Movement.[1]

What forces were at work between 1967 and 1970 to bring about the events that immersed the UUA in this "fury" and "glory"?

Following World War II, the nation and our congregations were on the move. Not only had the population midpoint shifted from east of Baltimore in 1790 to just east of St. Louis in 1960, but the latter half of the twentieth century also saw a migration from city to suburb. After a period of contraction during the first half of the century, our faith was growing, a third of that due to the Fellowship Movement, as Holley Ulrich outlines in *The Fellowship Movement: A Growth Strategy and Its Legacy*. Many of these fellowships, drawing from soldiers using the GI Bill to further their education, sprang up in college towns. In Washington DC and Detroit, established congregations helped seed new ones in the suburbs. Established congregations in Cleveland and Rochester relocated there themselves. Unitarian Universalism systematically exited the areas with large concentrations of African Americans and moved to regions where there were few. In the South, the reality of Jim Crow kept the races apart and, with the exception of the Sun Belt, was not an area that saw much UU growth. In general, the denominational growth strategy did not contemplate attracting African Americans. Where that happened can be traced to specific, activist ministers and committed congregations in exclusively metropolitan settings that had a significant African-American middle class: John Haynes Holmes in New York City, Leslie Pennington in Chicago, Duncan Howlett in DC, Rudy Gelsey in Philadelphia, Stephen Fritchman in Los Angeles, Jack Mendelsohn in Boston.

Although the history of both Universalism and Unitarianism went back to the eighteenth century, in 1967 the UUA was only six years old as an organization. Its theology of necessity was a cobbled-together compromise rather than a compelling faith statement—something that would emerge only as the next generation lived out what it meant to be Unitarian Universalist. An institutional infant, it was still working through a difficult merger of theologies, cultures, and administrative styles, as was evident in the Unitarian Universalist Service Committee decision in 1967 to withdraw funding from Jordan Neighborhood House. These tensions, while difficult to pinpoint, also had a bearing on what transpired. In addition, the president of the UUA, Dana McLean Greeley, was approaching the end of his term. As these events began to unfold, an election approached, and a new leader and new direction not yet in place.

Greeley had served since 1958, first as president of the American Unitarian Association (AUA), then of the UUA. However, at this moment of crisis, unknown to most, his ambitious agenda and vision had financially drained all the UUA's nonrestricted funds and created a sizable deficit. Then again, money was always in short supply. UUs give less to their congregations and denomination than any other American faith, and this chronic stinginess forced the institution to focus on survival rather than outreach.

The impact of the Fellowship Movement also affected the UUA's ability to respond to the times. Fellowships were inclined to be supportive of social and racial justice. Yet, their members, largely come-outers, had little sense of UU history and tended to be anticlerical, anti-institutional, distrustful of power, and protective of congregational autonomy. Ulbrich writes, "Resistance to authority often extends to distrust of denominational leadership. . . . Fellowship members express a mixture of disdain, ignorance, and indifference to the [UUA]."[2] That, too, would play out when it came time to act.

Regarding race, our religious tradition's attitude during the first half of the twentieth century shifted with the nation's—as its attitude liberalized, so did ours. We were engaged in, but not at the forefront of, a movement calling for racial justice. With the exception of the support the Universalists gave its mission in Suffolk, Virginia, both denominations had been largely indifferent, when not hostile, to promoting liberal religion in the African-American community. Not until the administration of Frederick May Eliot did the AUA make any effort. Then, in 1942, a general resolution was passed condemning racial prejudice; in 1952, the Commission on Unitarian Intergroup Relations was established; in 1956, Rev. Howard Thurman delivered the Ware Lecture. Nonetheless, there has never been an aggressive, sustained effort to propagate liberal religion in the black community. Throughout the 1950s, half-hearted efforts to settle African-American ministers largely failed, and good, qualified ministers discerning this failure went elsewhere. In 1963, the GA rejected a resolution that would have required congregations to drop racially discriminatory restrictions from their bylaws. In doing so, the annual meeting chose to reaffirm what must be considered a bedrock UU principle: congregational polity over freedom of access. Subsequently, the same assembly overwhelmingly supported a resolution encouraging congregations to practice nondiscrimination, requiring it of new congregations and creating the Commission on Race and Religion. The ten-member commission included five African Americans and one Latino: Howard Harris, Wade H. McCree, Cornelius McDougald, Howard Thurman, Whitney M. Young Jr. and Gonzalo Molina. Two years later, Martin Luther King Jr. issued his call for people of faith to join him in Selma. This event produced two UU martyrs: one lay, one minister; one female, one male; both white. A large number of ministers and laity participated. Many later described the march as a high point in their careers. It was the UUA's most serious commitment to civil rights, and although for some it reaffirmed UU commitment to an integrated struggle for justice, the majority of the ministers who went to Selma were radicalized and would later become supporters of the BAC.[3] Then, in 1966, King delivered the Ware Lecture. When 1967 arrived, these memories were fresh and powerful. In 1967, the question was how, not if, the UUA would respond to the "rebellion" in black communities, the radicalization of black consciousness, and the further fracturing of a civil rights movement that had never been monolithic.

Riots were only the most obvious manifestation; campuses, churches, and other organizations were also swept up in the cultural turbulence. That year, the Congress on Racial Equality, an organization of which UU minister Homer Jack had been a founding member in 1941, and whose primary principle was "interracial direct nonviolent action,"[4] did an about-face, became militant, and embraced black nationalism. In 1968, at the annual meeting of the African Studies Association, an organization controlled by white

American and English academics, its black scholars presented a list of demands. When a year later, the deadline passed and these self-professed white liberals had made only minimal accommodations, the black scholars formed the African Heritage Studies Association. In May 1969, James Foreman, a leader of the Student Non-Violent Coordinating Committee, interrupted a service at predominantly white Riverside Church in New York City to deliver the "Black Manifesto," which, among other things, demanded reparations for slavery. In response to the urban upheaval and the rise of black consciousness, the overwhelmingly white Reformed Church in America designated a seat on its governing body to be filled by an African American. Rev. Norman Vincent Peale vacated his seat to make this possible. And for a brief moment in 1967 and 1968, UUs were on the leading edge of the response. However, for the reasons mentioned above—lack of leadership, inadequate resources, institutional immaturity, a contentious relationship to denominational authority, and an absence of significant roots in the black community—they were not able to sustain the commitment.

Some ask why African Americans have not joined liberal religious congregations in larger numbers. Go back as far as you like—to Gloster Dalton in 1785, one of the eighty-five signatories of the Charter of Compact of the Gloucester Universalist Society; to Amy Scott in 1801, one of the incorporators of the First Universalist Society organized in Philadelphia; or to Lewis Latimer, one of the founders of the Unitarian Church of Flushing, New York, in 1908—and you will find African Americans. However, they were often unsought and unwelcomed, scattered in time and place, and with a few exceptions, never formed a critical mass within a Unitarian or Universalist congregation.

The answer is that neither the Universalist Church of America (UCA) nor the AUA ever gave sustained backing to African-American congregations. The Universalists had opportunities in Barstow, Georgia, and Rusk, Oklahoma. The Unitarians had opportunities in New Bedford, Massachusetts; Cincinnati; Harlem; and Chicago. In 1903 the AUA formed the Committee on New Americans that did mission work with immigrants but never backed African-American ministers who might have formed African-American congregations, such as Rev. William Jackson in 1860, Lewis A. McGee in 1927, Harry V. Richardson in 1930,[5] Alvin Neeley Cannon in 1945, Eugene Sparrow in 1949, or David H. Eaton in 1958. Furthermore, prior to 1969, only two African Americans held significant positions of power within the denomination: AUA board member Errold D. Collymore and UUA board member Wade McCree. African Americans who were part of the UCA or AUA functioned in isolation, often without knowledge of one another or of the depth of their history within these two faith communities. Ethelred Brown's church in Harlem was largely West Indian rather than African American. The Universalist mission in Suffolk, Virginia, was allowed to die. Therefore, Unitarian Universalism never developed forms of worship, liturgy, writings, music, or theology reflective of African-American experience. Unitarian Universalism had almost no black churches nor presence in black communities. Black folks came to UU congregations, not the other way around. Therefore, when 1967 arrived, there was nothing around which to build a specifically African-American UU identity and no natural interface with the African-American community. After one hundred years of squandered opportunities, the consequences came home to roost. The chaos that followed was the result of this self-created void.

Who were the stalwart African Americans who nonetheless became Unitarian Universalists? Educationally and professionally, they were similar to Euro-American UUs: professionals with college educations. Like most Unitarian Universalists, they had left the religion of their birth because they were seekers who cherished religious freedom. Also, their ties with the African-American community were either loose or unassailable enough that they would not have been shunned for joining a white, non-Christian religion. Many worked in white institutions and probably thought of themselves as being in the vanguard of integration. In 1967, based on the denomination-wide response to Selma, they could not help but have elevated expectations.

What was their experience? My father tells a story about how frustrated he felt having to deal with naive Euro-American incredulity that echoes Mwalimu Imara's experience in Urbana-Champaign, Illinois. Dad was participating in a church meeting at which blacks and whites were discussing race. What he heard annoyed him so much that he stood up. "Listen!" he said, "You white folks can all walk out of here and you can do whatever you want. We walk out of here and we are still black. You can do whatever you want but we can't." Later, he said, "I'll never forget how cavalier their attitude was. Like it was no big deal and somehow the Civil Rights Act had changed everything. It hadn't, and I was amazed because a lot of them weren't aware of all the subtle ways bigotry plays a role in determining black people's whole lives. That every aspect of our lives are controlled by people who are unsympathetic and not about to treat people of a different color in an equitable way." In the mid-1960s, the language with which to name white privilege did not exist, nor did white liberals understand that their own attitudes were part of the problem. So the crisis mounted.

As rioting engulfed city after city, it became clear that legislation had not addressed African-American poverty or frustration. That was the context in which, in October 1967, the Emergency Conference on the Unitarian Universalist Response to the Black Rebellion gathered at the Biltmore Hotel in New York. Thirty-seven of the 150 attendees were African Americans. They made up 25 percent of a gathering in a denomination of which they comprised only 1 percent, hailing from the urban churches in a faith community that was becoming more and more suburban.

Soon after the conference began, thirty-three of the African Americans[6] withdrew from the planned agenda to hold their own meeting. Seminarian Thom Payne, an imposing presence, was posted at the door to shoo white interlopers away, and there were a few. This Black Caucus met through the evening and late into the night. As they talked, they tapped into the raw emotion hidden behind middle-class reasonableness. They searched for an identity more authentic than the futile attempt to be carbon copies of white people. They saw white liberalism's emphasis on integration as a one-way street that elevated white and debased black. Civil rights had changed the law but had proven ineffective at remedying black poverty; liberal religion had failed to address the experience of blackness or to settle an African American in a major pulpit. The group called for a new agenda, and by the time they emerged, the Black Unitarian Universalist Caucus (BUUC) Steering Committee had been formed. They insisted that their agenda be voted up or down without debate, and that included a resolution that one million dollars (12 percent of the UUA budget) be directed toward the black community over a period of four years.

What happened at the Biltmore Hotel makes sense. Most of these African Americans would have been used to functioning, both professionally and religiously, in a Euro-American environment. They would also have felt that they had given up pieces of themselves in order to do that. What they needed at that moment was an exclusively African-American space in which to explore and consolidate a new identity and agenda. Whites could not help them with the question of identity. Jack Mendelsohn laid it out soon afterward in his sermon, "Black Power and the Liberal Church":

> I don't care how devotedly integrationist and equality-minded whites may be, they cannot bestow upon Black people a sense of their own identity. Whatever else Black Power may be or may come to be, however constructively, destructively, or stagnantly it may develop, its soul is a revolutionary attempt by Black People to define at last for themselves who they are, what they are worth, and what they want. It is more than a militant revulsion against the hollow promises and moral betrayals of affluent white America. At its heart it is an unprecedented, trailblazing quest for Black self-acceptance, Black assertiveness, Black accomplishment, and Black pride.[7]

Likewise, the agenda would have been formulated differently if whites had been part of the discussion. Blacks also knew the conference would want to debate their recommendations to death, drawing the process out when they felt the needs of the African-American community were urgent, and whites had already proven they did not have remedies. Yet, although the all-or-nothing tactic worked with this particular group of socially committed Euro-Americans, over the long haul it was doomed to fail—because ultimately UUs are wedded to individualism and reflexively distrust and resist authority, whatever the cause.

The conference sent shock waves through the UUA. Ben Scott, who was there, recalled, "It was also traumatic. I am not the only UU who was irreversibly shaped by it. Thousands were born again. They came to better understanding of the whole world through the BAC. They came to a thrilling sense of the awesome potential of human society. In our little UU corner of the world, lifelong friendships crumbled, marriages dissolved, careers were ended . . . and congregations factionalized."[8] Scott's words only hint at the intensity of the feelings. For many, what happened during the ensuing years would be nothing less than life defining.

A paradigm shift away from integration and toward black self-determination was taking place, a change for which the UUA was ill-prepared. Some depict this as a failure of vision. Jack Mendelsohn predicted that "familiar denominational racial routines" would prevail.[9] The paralysis, however, is understandable. How does one decide whether to support black demands for empowerment and justice, or to respect the democratic process with its vagaries and delays? John Wolf, white minister of All Souls Unitarian Church of Tulsa, laid it out in his sermon "Black Power Comes to Unitarianism." He said, "I am forced to choose between two rights . . . democratic procedure . . . [or] the redress of grievances of an oppressed minority." He then concludes that "it is not a question of right against wrong or of right against right, the issue is wrong against wrong."[10]

Wolf came down on the side of the BAC; others did not. Among those who didn't were three powerful black Unitarian Universalists: Judge Wade McCree, the vice moderator of the UUA board from 1965 to 1968; Cornelius McDougald, chair of the UUA Commission on Race and Religion that convened the Emergency Conference on the Black Rebellion, a lawyer and former board chair of the Community Church of New York—the UUA's most successfully integrated congregation at the time; and another Community Church member, Kenneth Clark, the foremost African-American child psychologist in America. Clark, with whom the UUA Board consulted, wrote that he questioned the validity of pride based on skin color: "Such pride seems to me at best tenuous and at worst destructive."[11] A fourth African American, Whitney M. Young Jr., a member of the Unitarian Universalist congregation in White Plains, New York, and of the UUA Commission on Race and Religion, did not seem to have been involved in UU politics. Nonetheless, he saw in the response of whites who supported such demands at a new left political conference earlier that year a new kind of racism. "The white radicals," he wrote, "fell over themselves trying to comply with the ridiculous demands of the blacks. They gave them half the votes in the convention, approved insulting resolutions, and listened to wild talk that debased the purpose for which they assembled. In doing this they exhibited a subtle kind of racism themselves, for their implicit assumption was that blacks had to be humored and pacified."[12]

The UUA board meetings following the Emergency Conference were contentious. A decade earlier, a drawn-out process of listening to all points of view and consensus building had led to the merger of the AUA and UCA. Now, as cities burned, there was no time to mediate differences of opinion. What else could be expected in an era of urban upheaval and Vietnam War protest, when demonstrations and distrust of authority were the norm? Feeling trapped and not really understanding what was fueling the new situation, the UUA Board proposed restructuring and renaming the Commission of Race and Religion. From the BAC's perspective, their overture completely missed the point.

The first National Conference of Black Unitarian Universalists gathered in Chicago in February 1968, with 207 attending.

On April 4, Dr. King was slain, and in June, the General Assembly met in Cleveland. African Americans and their white supporters were there. In the aftermath of Dr. King's death, what white person, given the guilt they felt, was going to vote against a resolution coming out of the BAC? Not surprisingly, the proposal to fund the BAC passed by a wide margin, 836 to 327.

It makes sense that the vote at the 1968 Cleveland GA did not resolve the issue. There was a vote but no consensus; starkly different worldviews still prevailed. The cauldron from which that vote emerged included: a sense of urgency versus a commitment to the ponderousness of the democratic process; a person's relationship—or in the case of most white UUs, lack of relationship—to the African-American community, compounded by a guilt-ridden sense of responsibility; indifference toward, impatience with, or loyalty to the UUA; a sense of betrayal and anger on all sides; and how to prioritize institutional necessities, such as the presidential campaign versus the needs of the black community. Add to this a lame-duck president, Dana McLean Greeley, whose finest hour had been at Selma but who, as he watched his legacy collapsing around him, was not in a position to offer leadership. The depth of the ongoing division and confusion can be seen in the closeness of the votes a year later at the Boston GA on whether to reconsider the agenda—and later in that meeting, the decision to fund the BAC but not BAWA.

The BAC won again and, in that moment, lost. That too makes sense. Good leadership knows about institutional inertia and that conflict is both inevitable and necessary to trigger change. But change is time-consuming, and without leadership, it is almost impossible. Nor can a group move ahead when half is moving one way and the other half another, because force only begets resistance, and when relationships are abrogated, change cannot succeed.

Six months later, under a new president, Robert N. West, the UUA Board had to face the magnitude of the deficit and, understandably, reconsidered the association's budget, priorities, and commitments. A million dollars—40 percent of the budget—was cut, eliminating all twenty-one district executives and their offices, while the Office of Social Responsibility was combined with Religious Education to become the Department of Education and Social Concerns. The Board focused more on survival than justice. What reductions were possible? Which programs to eliminate? Hard choices had to be made. Bearing responsibility for the institution's viability, the Board decided to spread the million-dollar commitment to the BAC over five years instead of four, which makes sense. The BUUC's response, to disaffiliate from the UUA, could not have been about the money alone.

It was natural, following Dr. King's assassination, for African Americans to be swept up in a cascade of emotion. Full of rage and grief, and in reaction rather than by choice, many held white people collectively accountable for his death. Alongside that anger and despair was a renewed sense of urgency and impatience with white foot-dragging. African Americans had to lead in the struggle for black self-determination and identity; anything else would have been patronizing and futile.

In addition, middle-class, Unitarian Universalist African Americans probably became suddenly (and painfully) aware of how disconnected and isolated they were from the black community. Some probably felt a sense of guilt and needed to reestablish that connection. Proving that their UU community could be relevant was one way. Other African Americans felt the need to distance themselves from whites and white institutions. My mother felt this way and left her post at the University of Chicago to teach at predominantly black Kennedy-King Community College. My sister cut off all her Euro-American friends. My brother, who a little more than a year earlier had returned from attending a Swiss boarding school, chose to attend Morehouse College. I joined VISTA to work in the black community. Mwalimu Imara, a proponent of the creation of the Black Humanist Fellowship, left the parish ministry to become minister-at-large for the Benevolent Fraternity of UU Congregations, then left Unitarian Universalism to return to the Episcopal Church and work as a chaplain at Morehouse Medical

School. Future UUA Board member Norma Poinsett stayed, Alex Poinsett (chair of the Chicago BAC) left, BAC leader Ben Scott stayed, Richard (later Mjenzi) Traylor and Rev. Harold Wilson disappeared. Thom Payne, who chose not to be "a part of the UU Black Empowerment camp," stayed, while future UUA President Bill Sinkford left. Some left in anger. Some left broken-hearted.

Some blame the UUA funding decision for the decline in African-American membership, but that argument ignores the fact that funds were available from other sources and oversimplifies African-American attitudes. In 1972, two years after the BAC disaffiliated itself from the UUA, the Veatch program, through the UUA Racial Justice Fund, earmarked $180,000 for the BAC, so money was available. As to African-American attitudes, they were not monolithic. Some people stayed; others stormed off. Some told their ministers, "Sorry. I feel torn, but right now I have to put my time into the black community." Many silently drifted away. For some, anger may have provided a cover for guilt as they did what they needed to do—distance themselves from their white friends. Black UUs sought ways to reconnect to the African-American community. The balance shifted. Affirming black identity became more important than nurturing liberal religious identity. People left for various reasons. Some must have felt that the energy required to transform the UU community would divert energy from the pressing needs of the African-American community. For others, integration had lost its sheen. Perhaps the radicals made the moderates feel like Uncle Toms. How many needed comforting rather than more turmoil? Or maybe their reasons were the same as those of the Euro-Americans who were departing, as overall UU membership declined.

Finally, it makes sense that after forty years, many wish for, but few are ready to seek, reconciliation. Why has there been so little movement toward reconciliation? Because they were all the good guys. They all stood on principle. They all claim the moral high ground. They are all still seeking vindication. Each side spins a narrative in which they defended the good cause and suffered for it. Having constructed a sense of integrity out of righteous hubris, they recite the ancient justifications whenever they feel defensive. Contrition is for the guilty, and they are not.

All sides feel victimized, betrayed, and misunderstood; they defended principles while others betrayed them. Integrationists felt they were being asked to repudiate their earlier actions and long-term commitment to equality. Also, they were shocked that there was no longer room to hold a different opinion and follow another path, and still be in fellowship. Institutionalists felt they were staving off ruin and preserving the democratic process. The BAC and its supporters felt as though whites were unwilling to put justice first or to trust African Americans with power. For blacks, the "familiar denominational racial routines" echoed the empty promise of forty acres and a mule made to the freed slaves. The result and further tragedy is this: No one who was involved feels understood or appreciated, much less honored.

It is time to honor the passion, fervor, and commitment to principle of all who were involved—and to thank them for caring so deeply. Portraying the empowerment controversy as an institutional failure is short-sighted and misleading. The UUA stumbled, and had to, but it also set the scene for women, lesbian and gay people, the disabled, Hispanics, and other marginalized groups in the UUA to speak out, claim their space, and make demands. These identity groups also experienced resistance, but the outcry was neither as prolonged nor as intense. Who today would challenge an oppressed group's right to gather together to explore its identity, formulate a strategy, and take a stance? Never again since 1969 has the UUA Board of Trustees, Nominating Committee, or Commission on Appraisal been without significant African-American representation.[13] Never again would we produce a hymnal or religious education materials without reference to African-American experience.[14] The events set in motion by the black rebellion traumatized but also transformed some and educated us all. As Ben Scott said, "The tragedy would have been if successive generations had had to continue to struggle the way they did."[15]

Unitarian Universalists never stopped trying. Reticently, clumsily, episodically, UUs continue to lurch along. Euro-Americans have come to see that it is their own racism and cultural illiteracy they are called to address. This is what always needed to happen, but reparation—the giving of one million dollars to black concerns—however noble, was not meant to address that. In fact, money's power to assuage guilt may have delayed this white awakening as much as the ensuing trepidation did.

Jean Ott aptly called these events "the white controversy over black empowerment."[16] In a denomination that was 99 percent white, what else could it be? It happened because of the bigotry and mistakes of earlier generations of religious liberals, because society was forcing change upon religious liberals and change is difficult, because middle-class black UUs needed to redirect their priorities—and this meant, for some, leaving. These were all good people torn by competing loyalties and conflicting values, some of which ran counter to their deepest traditions of polity and individualism. It happened because of institutional immaturity, fear, and hubris. It happened because it had to happen.

—Mark D. Morrison-Reed

STILL SEEKING A WAY

In 1980, UUA Executive Vice President William F. Schultz wrote that "with the decision in 1970 to end UUA funding of the Black Affairs Council, all effective UUA attention to racial justice ended too. Our relief translated itself into inaction. Like children with hot stoves, we shunned the burner. For us, indeed, 'no fire next time.'"[1] The association turned its attention away as other events overtook the empowerment quagmire. In fall 1971, it published *About Your Sexuality*. The candid and graphic curriculum set off not only a storm of criticism but a legal skirmish as well. Hard upon that controversy, an even larger tempest arose when Beacon Press published *The Pentagon Papers*. Meanwhile, a schism developed within the Black Unitarian Universalist Caucus (BUUC). After one faction of the BUUC orchestrated a breakaway from the Unitarian Universalist Association (UUA), other BUUC members took them to court. By the time the case was resolved in 1976, the UU cause célèbre was feminism, and the association's energies were directed toward passing and then implementing the 1977 "Women and Religion Resolution."

After the racial institutional upheaval of the 1960s, the 1970s proved to be more a hiatus from hyperbole than a time of inaction. In August 1970, Margaret Williams, who had been the director of religious education at All Souls Church, Unitarian, in Washington DC, joined the UUA staff as an educational consultant. By 1971, African Americans had been elected to the UUA Nominating Committee and the Commission on Appraisal, and two were sitting on the Board of Trustees. In 1973, the UUA General Assembly mandated that each year, the UUA report "its efforts to provide equal employment opportunities to women and racial minorities at all levels of its staff." By the time Robert West left office in 1977, the number of people of color on the UUA staff had climbed to 17 percent. In 1974, the UUA became a member of Project Equality, which "promotes equal opportunity in employment, use of ventures and purchasing." In 1975, the UUA joined with other organizations in calling for school desegregation in general, and specifically supported integration through court-ordered busing in Boston. Elected as president in 1977, Paul Carnes attempted to re-approach the issue of racial justice, but those efforts were cut short by his illness and death.

Following Carnes's death in 1979, O. Eugene Pickett became president of the UUA. Moving rapidly to make racial justice a priority, he hired Dr. Loretta Williams, an African American and UUA Board member, as director of the section on social responsibility. In the fall of 1979, he invited all of the African-American UU ministers to Boston for a consultation. Jeff Campbell, David Eaton, Marshall Grigsby, Thomas Payne, John Frazier, Graylan Hagler, Ron White, and Mark Morrison-Reed attended. Pickett, a member of the National Urban League board, and Schulz met with Vernon Jordan, then the executive director of the Urban League, to explore ways the league and the UUA might work together. Pickett also met with Marion Barry, then mayor of Washington DC. Early in 1980, there was an all-day racial awareness training for the Department of Ministerial and Congregational Services. The UUA imprint, Skinner House Books, published *Black Pioneers in a White Denomination*. The UUA Board voted to proceed with an institutional racism audit.

Other significant policy developments ensued. The Committee on Urban Concerns and Ministry, chaired by Jack Mendelsohn, proposed that the UUA allow dual fellowship. The committee went to the Ministerial Fellowship Committee (MFC) with this argument: The UUA is having difficulty settling African-American ministers but, despite that, when transfers comes to us, we demand that they relinquish their accreditation in their current denomination before we will consider them. The MFC agreed that the policy unfairly shifted the UUA's problem to the African-American ministers they were trying to attract. The Urban Concern and Ministry Committee then went to the Unitarian Universalist Ministers Association (UUMA) Executive Board. Board members were reluctant, but the argument was compelling, and after a debate during the UUMA annual meeting at the 1983 GA in Philadelphia, they endorsed the proposal, which was subsequently approved by the UUA Board that October. This decision opened the door for

Mel Hoover, Dan Aldridge, Chester McCall, and Tim Malone to enter the UU ministry.

As the 1980s progressed, the number of African-American Unitarian Universalists serving as religious professionals throughout Unitarian Universalism and on its governing bodies increased, as did awareness of how deeply racism was embedded in its institutional practices. In 1988, minorities comprised 18 percent of all UUA employees. More significant was the increase in the proportion of that 18 percent who were professional staff—it had risen from 51 percent in 1977 to 61 percent. One member of the Nominating Committee was an African American, as were two members of the Commission on Appraisal and two of the UUA Board, while a year earlier there had been four on the Board.

Among the most articulate and respected of the African-American leaders within the UUA was theologian William R. Jones. This section begins with his biography. Ordained in 1958, just before the merger, he links us to pre-consolidation Unitarianism. His analysis of the nature of oppression, his advocacy of black humanism, and his critique of contemporary Unitarian Universalism made his voice particularly important during the latter decades of the twentieth century. His story is followed by Yvonne Seon's autobiography. The first African-American woman to be ordained as a UU minister, Seon recounts how and why she became the founding minister of the intentionally diverse Sojourner Truth Congregation in southeast Washington DC. Considered together, these two essays exemplify the breadth of the African-American UU religious perspective.

As the 1980s came to an end, liturgical and organizational changes in the UUA were evident. Three documents highlight these changes. The first is the sermon "Affirming Beauty in Darkness," by Jacqui James, an African American who was the staff liaison to the UUA Hymnbook Resources Commission. Preached in March 1988, it addressed why the commission felt that it was important to pay attention to language and imagery when developing a new hymnal. The second is the agenda for the first meeting in 1988 of what would become African American UU Ministries. The third is the press release announcing its formation.

Ordained in 1986, Michelle Bentley was the third female African-American Unitarian Universalist minister. A newspaper article written in 2000 describes Bentley's ministry at the Third Unitarian Church of Chicago—which chose to remain in what had become a working-class African-American neighborhood—and Third's efforts to be involved in meeting the needs of that distressed community.

Fifteen-year-old Thomas Payne started attending National Memorial Universalist Church in 1957. By 1967, his last year in seminary, he was part of the black caucus that formed during the Emergency Conference at the Biltmore Hotel. His ministry went on to span the 1970s, 1980s, and 1990s. The essay on Payne shows how many of the changes Unitarian Universalism went through in the latter half of the twentieth century enabled him to minister in later years in ways denied him in the beginning.

Two pieces—a newsletter column, "Why Change? Why Now?" and an essay, "Reconciliation with the Carter Family"—recount the efforts of two congregations to come to terms with the past. In celebrating the lives of Don Speed Smith Goodloe and William H. G. Carter, these congregations set an example that brings us full circle. Both congregations made a commitment not to forget by holding up and celebrating the role African Americans played in the UU liberal religious tradition. The latter essay also critiques Unitarian Universalists' overweening need for control and reveals how that compulsion undermines our efforts at dialog, reconciliation, and healing.

The story of the First Unitarian Church of Cincinnati demonstrates that we cannot engage in authentic conversation about race and at the same time be in control. William Sinkford's memoir, "The First," begins at that same congregation; it is where, as a teen, he became a UU. It culminates with his experience serving as the first African-American president of the Unitarian Universalist Association and his reflections on the challenges that await us.

An afterword explores why, despite its best intentions, becoming more racially and culturally diverse has proven difficult for the UUA, and how, nonetheless, hope lies in remaining faithful to its foundational principles.

WILLIAM ROLAND JONES
1933–2012

> *I went around announcing that we were living in the last days, that Armageddon was upon us, all the while dragging in alleged absolutes to justify the what, why and when of my moral decisions. I finally had to admit that I was cheating. I had to confess that I was using a subjective principle, that—whether gleaned from the Bible or nature or computer by reason or science—I had not discovered, as I claimed, an infallible and omni competent guide.*
>
> —William Roland Jones

Born in 1933 in Louisville, Kentucky, William R. Jones was marked for church ministry. He worked to frame this calling in ways consistent with the theology and pulpit presentation of evangelist Billy Graham. It would not be long before, following in the steps of Henry Wise Jones Sr., his grandfather and the pastor of Green Street Baptist Church, he was licensed to preach within the Baptist tradition.

Jones unpacked the scriptures and preached accordingly. On his way to a noteworthy career within the venerated African-American tradition of ministry, his work tied him to the practices of his family and the leadership patterns of his community. The path, however, was far from smooth. "I found myself wrestling," Jones reflects, "with these agonizing choices: Should I hold fast to those Christian truths that my family upbringing imprinted on my being as absolute, infallible, and divinely ordained? Or should I incarnate the verities I was unearthing in . . . humanist existentialism?"[1] His response was to leave the tradition of his upbringing —to reject religion as an oppressive force—and embrace "the apostate credo of black humanism."[2] By doing so, Jones embraced an alternate perspective on soteriology (the doctrine of salvation), in which the highest good does not require conformity to an ultimate reality but rather anticipates the triumph of nonconformity.

During the years of his initial break with the African-American Christian tradition, Jones saw religion as problematic and rejected it as fundamentally flawed. "I reached," Jones would later write, "the erroneous conclusion that to get rid of oppression you had to put religion out of business."[3] However, drawing in large measure from the work of Carter G. Woodson, Benjamin E. Mays, and others, he recognized that religion came in a variety of forms, not all of which demanded a theistic posture, and turned his attention to the distinctions between modalities of religion that buttressed oppression and those forms that supported human progress. He realized that it was unnecessary to leave religion in total; rather, he need only find a religious orientation supportive of his practices and consistent with his beliefs—religious humanism.

Jones's humanism marked a new orientation for him. It did not grow out of the Enlightenment but was rather in line with French existentialism and sensitive to the condition of African Americans within the framework of modernity. In developing this position, Jones made and continues to make a distinction between theoretical atheism and theism, and practical atheism and theism. The former position is held by atheists who assume that one cannot demonstrate the existence of God and theists who argue that one can. The other option is practical atheism and theism. Here Jones differentiates between belief and action—that is, atheists acting in the world in ways that express atheist mentality, and theists behaving in ways that express theistic mentality. Jones's humanism moves beyond an agnostic stance to action expressive of an atheist mentality. This does not, according to Jones, involve a destructive posture toward the black churches. Rather, he acknowledges his debt to the black church and its past achievements and "respectfully declines to further its theistic claims" in favor of "functional ultimacy"—the rejection of an undocumented absolute.[4] From his perspective, every decision begins and ends with human intentionality.

In a country marked by an aggressive rhetoric of theism, Jones's stance can be seen as noble. But nonetheless, coming out of the African-American Church tradition, Jones resisted the radical individualism in which one works through humanist sensibilities in isolation. He wanted community, but a community that would allow him to maintain the integrity of his practical atheism, his black humanism, which sought "its constituency from this large unchurched group, this secular 'congregation' that appears to be multiplying rapidly."[5] For Jones, a humanist interested in religion and seeking community, there were few places where these two postures could be held in creative tension; it seemed the Unitarian Church would allow him to practice his outlook.

After graduating from Howard University in 1955, Jones received a Rockefeller Grant for graduate training and decided to attend Harvard Divinity School. There he encountered a giant of humanist thought and practice—James Luther Adams. Yet it was not Adams who motivated his move into the Unitarian community. Instead, while traveling with a fellow student—a Unitarian—to a Rockefeller Grant conference at Yale University, they stopped at the Unitarian church in Wellesley Hills, Massachusetts, where his schoolmate was student minister. Subsequently, this church asked if Jones would like to teach Sunday school. This invitation, offered during the era of segregation within society at large and within religious institutions in particular, was a significant gesture—one that caught Jones's attention. It appeared, based on this invitation, that the Unitarian churches did not suffer from an intense practice of race-based discrimination. And what is more, the Unitarian Church had no problem with his theology. So he became involved.

He completed the master of divinity degree in 1958, at the age of twenty, and was ordained shortly thereafter, with James

Luther Adams preaching his ordination service. Discovering—as did another Howard graduate, David Eaton—that there were "no ministerial slots for Negro ministers,"[6] Jones accepted the position of assistant minister and director of religious education at the First Unitarian church of Providence, Rhode Island. Subsequently, in 1969, he received a PhD from Brown University and took a position at Yale Divinity School. After Yale, he moved to Florida State University, from which he eventually retired but where he remains an active and significant presence.

Jones's early work in theology and philosophy, as presented in *Is God a White Racist?*, extended the reasoning behind his early embrace of humanism and challenged the assumptions and methodologies of African-American religious studies, particularly black theology, as they related to the eradication of oppression. Within the traditional black religious orientations, scholars and religious practitioners alike were not prepared for this question and its philosophical and ethical implications. Whereas liberal religious organizations such as the Unitarian Church fell short on issues related to the nature and substance of racism, black churches considered themselves the true arbiters of racial justice. Met with less than an embrace—and with charges of being outside the black community and of a questionable epistemological blackness—Jones pushed against the assumptions of ultimate reality and developed new ways to assess and counter racism. What Jones promoted was an alternative methodology, an alternate approach to evaluating and addressing oppression that moved beyond Christocentric and Afrocentric postures.

Although colleagues were often troubled by his arguments, and at times dismissive, his mentoring of students and his overall presence at Florida State University and in higher education continues to be noteworthy. Named in his honor are the William R. Jones Outstanding Mentor Award and the William R. Jones Enhancement Fund (for research, which was established by students and colleagues in 1991). In 1992, Jones received the State of Florida Ida S. Baker Black Distinguished Educator Recognition Award.

His professional commitments continue and include the directorship of the Policy Institute for Conflict, Oppression, and Terrorism Studies at Tallahassee Community College. Teaching, researching, and lecturing, nationally and internationally, on his theoretical model of oppression and conflict formed a significant component of what we might label his ministry. The benefits of his work for humanism, in particular, have been recognized in a variety of ways, including by the bestowal of the American Humanist Association Humanist Pioneer of the Year Award in 1992.

Within Unitarian Universalism, Jones has held a variety of positions, including serving as a member of its Ministerial Fellowship Committee and the UU Service Committee Board, and as a UUA trustee-at-large. His contributions made over the course of more than four decades were recognized in 2001, when he was awarded the highest honor given by the association, the Award for Distinguished Service to the Cause of Unitarian Universalism, bestowed on him because, as Margaret Sanders noted, he is "one of our movement's foremost religious thinkers and social critics."[7]

Sanders refers to Jones's ongoing commitment to a systematic interrogation of the structures of racism in the society at large as well as within the UUA. With regard to the latter, Jones has pulled no punches, calling into question a variety of UU assumptions. UU humanists lack, he argues, a proper phenomenology of humanism but instead hold to a form of "reasonism" not akin to the scientific methodology as claimed. As a result, they impose an undocumented absolutism. Furthermore, he raised questions concerning the theological significance of the association's Principles. Jones maintains that they are "a statement of our espoused theory, not our theory in use . . . based upon a person's theological position on what they practice, not what they preach. So that's not our first principle in practice." He continues, "We preach equality, but we practice oppression."[8]

Considering Jones's relationship to and work within the UUA, we cannot forget that his unwavering critique stands alongside his steadfast commitment. Jones first entered the association because of its foundational norm. Over the years, his ministry has been that of a gadfly, provoking and challenging the UUA to not only speak its best but to match that rhetoric with concrete and sustained deeds. "The permanent [norm] in Unitarian Universalism that I advance as the preferred therapy returns to the birth of our movement and its raison d'être," writes Jones, "as a protest against oppression—a protest based on a doctrine of pluralism and its affirmation of individuals and groups as coequal centers of freedom, authority, and power." It was this protest, as represented in the offer for him to teach Sunday school, that initially caught his attention. "However," he continues, "when our birth norm of pluralism is used to assess our faith community today, I find a radical abandonment of this permanent (pluralism) in favor of its opposite, the transient (assimilation)."[9]

The race-based challenges facing the UUA are exemplified by those African Americans uncomfortable with the theological orientation of traditional black churches but likewise frustrated by the strands and frameworks of racialization present within the liberal domain of the UUA. Jones brought to these discussions his sharp mind and his commitment to action as ministry. He provides diagnostic tools for exposing and assessing "neo-racism" within the UUA, whereby theories in use and deeds are interrogated.[10] His goal, from 1958 to the present as a minister and scholar, has involved the resurrection of the best of the association's tradition, resistance to oppression, and revolution/rebellion against nonproductive strategies and practices. Through this process and by means of enriched exchange during which we, as Jones says, "cuss and discuss,"[11] we are able to generate activities marked by a commitment to integration and pluralism. As Jones's work and thought suggest, hard work done by human hands is all we have, all we can count on.

—Anthony B. Pinn

Sources

In addition to William R. Jones's principal work, Is God a White Racist? Preamble to Black Theology, *this essay is based on multiple interviews and conversations with Dr. Jones. Other sources include "The Case for Black Humanism," in* Black Theology II: Essays on the Formation and Outreach of Contemporary Black Theology *(1978), "The New Three R's," in* The Transient and Permanent in Liberal Religion: Reflections from the UUMA Convocation on Ministry *(1995), "Moral Decision-Making in the Post-Modern World: Implications for Unitarian-Universalist Religious Education," in* Unitarian Universalism 1985: Selected Essays, *and articles from the* UU World.

THE SOJOURNER TRUTH CONGREGATION

Sojourner Truth Congregation of Unitarian Universalists was an experiment in diversity that grew from both the success and the failure of the Unitarian Universalist Assocation's antiracism campaign. The congregation started as a response of a number of people to the presence in the Unitarian Universalist ministry of the first African-American woman, and their vision for her ministry—my ministry. That vision was driven by the disparity between the UUA goal of African-American inclusion and my experience seeking settlement. The congregation's story cannot be separated from my personal journey toward ministry as it intersected the association's encounter with the struggle for civil rights in America.

I grew up during the Great Depression and experienced the privation that went along with World War II. All my cousins spent time being cared for by my grandmother, and we went with her on Sundays to the charismatic Christian church three doors away. She lived in a black neighborhood in Washington DC. The church, a converted row house in the Shaw area, was filled on Sundays with the sounds of clapping, shouting, and jumping to the accompaniment of tambourines and a well-worn upright piano. Walking in the front door, one entered a large room with rows of chairs on either side of the aisle. At the front, an archway marked the edge of a raised area where the bishop, his deacons, and the choir sat—all dressed in various kinds of robes. On the arched wall, in large gilded letters, was printed, "God is Love."

This was my first lesson in theology, and it embraced all I needed to know. Nevertheless, I soon found that the chaotic sights and sounds of church were a distraction from religious thought and behavior. As children, my cousins and I imitated the bishop's preaching style and laughed; we pretended to be various members of the congregation; we mocked their "amens" and "uh-hums," their faints and their swoons. But we got another view of religion and church at Grandma's house as she evolved in her own spirituality and ministry.

I witnessed my grandmother's religious evolution close up when I went to live with her while my mother was working in Baltimore as campaign manager for a candidate for the U.S. Congress. Mom risked her life running John Camphor's Progressive Party headquarters near the docks, knowing I was safe with her mother. Meanwhile, Grandma told of visions of impending world events. She fed the hungry. She shared resources with those in need, saving several small community businesses with a gift or loan at a critical juncture. She prayed for the sick.

In her spiritual life, my grandmother drew from religious traditions of the world. She burned incense in a seated figure of the Buddha. She fasted in sympathy with Mahatma Gandhi as he protested British rule over India. She designated an upper room as her "prayer garden," where she worshiped and laid hands on the sick and infirm. She placed a rack of votive candles and a prayer rug in front of the one window in the room, which faced east. She asked a talented artist of the church to paint a picture of Jesus in the Garden of Gethsemane on the north wall. (She insisted that Jesus be facing to the actual East in the painting.) A framed representation of Black Jesus and several hymnals were remnants from her time in New York, following Marcus Garvey. Everyone who entered her home was welcomed with "Salaam alykum," the Islamic greeting of peace.

When my mother's baby sister reached high school age, she got permission to walk from Grandma's house to St. Luke's Episcopal Church. I had been baptized there as an infant, and begged her to take me along. I was six and able to read well enough to follow the liturgy in the *Book of Common Prayer*. I soon knew the creeds and many prayers by heart. I appreciated the simple chants and the quiet, structured worship of this black congregation that practiced "high church."

When I was eight years old, my parents separated, and later divorced. In order to spend more time with my father, I started attending with him the Baptist church in which he grew up. One day, at age twelve, I found myself at the front of the church, asking to be baptized. My father, who was blind, went up with me and rejoined the church. We were both baptized a few weeks later. By the time I reached high school, Sunday morning church with Dad was an increasingly rare activity. But I was getting old enough to travel to church with my peers. I discovered that several friends were going to a small Episcopal church close enough for me to walk; I returned to the church tradition of my mother's side of the family.

In college, I began to question religion but never God. I questioned the concept of the trinity, the divinity of Jesus, and the ritual of Holy Communion. During my senior year at Allegheny College, I took a required course on religious traditions and Christian practices. The instructor was a Quaker who helped us explore the philosophy of nonviolence and taught us to share in silence! We generally came out of silence trying to find justification for violence. Were there no exceptions to nonviolence?

During that semester, the subject of religion dominated conversations with my closest friends. As I expressed my views, someone said, "You sound like a Unitarian!" and suggested I visit the First Unitarian Church of Meadville, Pennsylvania. One Sunday, I went there alone in search of church community, a place where my personal beliefs were not out of place. That Sunday is one I will never forget. The minister spoke to my deepest beliefs about God and religion. I got up at the end of the service feeling full, wanting to share. But the members, all white, peeled off in every direction, speaking to one another. I was left standing alone in the middle of a pew near the center of the church. There were no hellos, no handshakes, and no words of welcome. It was as though I were invisible. Nevertheless, I walked back toward the entrance to greet the minister.

As I stood at the back of the line, I saw an African-American woman coming up from the basement, carrying a tray of muffins for the coffee table. I moved out of line to greet her, but she quickly turned her back and returned downstairs without responding to my smile. Was there no church community there that could include African Americans, I wondered?

This initial encounter with Unitarian Universalism was in 1958, just as the civil rights movement was starting in earnest. Although I knew of All Souls Church, Unitarian, in my home town of Washington DC, I had never been there. All the churches I had attended to that point were filled with black worshipers. I was aware, however, that All Souls Church was perhaps the only place in town where an interracial couple could worship together. I was also aware that the church had sponsored Dr. W.E.B. DuBois as a speaker the February after he had been shunned as a liberal and a Communist, and his reputation tarnished by the House Committee on Un-American Activities.

When my black and white friends at Allegheny heard about my experience at the First Unitarian Church of Meadville, they were confused. Neither the Unitarians nor the Universalists had ever excluded African Americans. I would later learn that Allegheny, the oldest liberal arts college west of the Allegheny Mountains, had in 1906 awarded a degree to one of the earliest African Americans to train for Unitarian ministry at the seminary in Meadville. Although he never pursued ministry, Don Speed Smith Goodloe went on to become the first principal of what became Bowie State University in Maryland.

My reintroduction to Unitarian Universalism would come much later. I had graduated from Allegheny College, traveled to Peru, and used a Woodrow Wilson Fellowship to complete an MA degree at the American University in Washington DC. I had traveled to Kinshasa to work for the government of the country that would become Zaire, the Democratic Republic of the Congo. As executive director of the Inga Dam Project in the Congo, I had traveled to several other countries in Africa and in Europe. Everywhere

I went, I searched for a spirituality that made sense to me. I would first try the prevailing Christian worship tradition. Sometimes this was Catholicism. Often, it was the regional Protestant church. In some of the cities, there was a Church of England, where I found the comfort of a familiar ritual in the language of my native land. So I continued to think of myself as Episcopalian and part of the church in which I had been baptized as an infant.

After returning home to Washington DC in May 1963, I ran into an old friend, who turned out to be a neighbor down the street. In October of 1966, we were married in a local Episcopal church, where we sang together in the choir. The following fall, we moved to Yellow Springs, Ohio, where I found work with Wilberforce University. Affiliated with the African Methodist Episcopal Church, Wilberforce was the first college in America founded by and for African Americans. There I began formal research on African and African-American history and culture, including African traditional religions. I had stopped attending church but was discovering spiritual perspectives from African cultures that rang true for me.

Meanwhile, Wilberforce gave me two assignments that nudged me towards UU ministry. First, I was asked by the president of the university to serve as one of two representatives on the Consortium for Higher Education Religion Studies. In that capacity, I worked closely with the administration of Payne Theological Seminary, once part of Wilberforce. I was also invited to participate in a year-long symposium on African religions organized by Professor Newell Booth of Miami University of Ohio. Second, my primary assignment at the university was shifted to coordinator for Student Life Programs. In this latter capacity, I was visited by Professor Gene Reeves, chair of the philosophy department and a Unitarian Universalist minister.

It was my job to schedule speakers for the cultural development course, and Dr. Reeves suggested I consider inviting Rev. David Eaton, newly appointed senior minister of All Souls Church in Washington DC. Dr. Reeves, one of several white instructors at this traditionally black campus in southern Ohio, had had a role in linking Eaton, his classmate and friend at Boston University School of Theology, to the UUA. The well-respected Eaton was the first African American called to a major urban UU church. I agreed to invite him to Wilberforce.

Thus began a conversation with Gene Reeves about Unitarian Universalism, its stand on civil rights, its record in social justice, and more. When Rev. Eaton arrived, Dr. Reeves was his host. My family came to dinner. David Eaton spoke of his vision for black participation in the UUA and invited my husband and me to come to All Souls whenever we returned to DC. For the first time, I saw Unitarian Universalism in a favorable light. When we returned to the DC area in 1973, I began attending with my children.

At All Souls, I felt community among Unitarian Universalists. I was excited about the excellent gospel choir, which was my entry point into participation. I attended my first General Assembly singing with the Jubilee Singers in Philadelphia. Soon thereafter, I was invited to participate in a seminar on the history and philosophy of the UU movement and to sign the membership roll. Having learned that King's Chapel in Boston had become the first Unitarian church in America when the minister removed all references to the Trinity from the *Book of Common Prayer*, I was sure I was in the right place.

One Sunday, Rev. Eaton asked me to speak for a summer service, suggesting a topic related to my expertise in Africa as a possible subject matter. This was an important step on my path to UU ministry. I chose to speak on Mozambique's proximate achievement of African self-determination. Speaking that Sunday, it felt as though I belonged in the pulpit.

The actual call to ministry came in March 1979, as my grandmother lay dying in the group home where she had been cared for over many years. I rushed to be at her side. As I crossed the threshold to her room, I saw my grandmother open her eyes. She expired as she saw me walking to her bedside, giving me her last breath as a legacy. I took this as a sign that I was being called to continue her ministry of compassion and healing. Closing her eyes, I silently committed to the call.

Meanwhile, the minister who funeralized my grandmother introduced me to Rev. Dr. Leon Edward Wright. Dr. Wright was a New Testament scholar and mystic who helped me move forward with this "call," recognizing me as a "channel for the flow-through of the love of God." I also talked it over with my minister, Rev. Eaton. He asked me, "Do you want to be a minister?" I replied, "It's not something that one 'wants.' I don't have a choice; it's a calling." Rev. Eaton agreed to support my application to Howard University Divinity School. He warned, however, that I would be challenged both as black and as female within the UUA. Women were generally consigned to ministry as religious educators, and at that point, as far as we knew, there were no African-American women trained in ministry or moving towards parish ministry. He also spoke of the suspicion many UUs would have of my nonrational spirituality. That fall, I entered Howard University's Divinity School as a single parent supporting three offspring.

While in divinity school, I was invited to a spiritual retreat led by Dr. Wright. He talked about the healing ministry of Jesus, and we were encouraged to "follow" rather than to "imitate" Jesus. He taught us to meditate daily as part of the process of staying attuned to God's will for our lives. I was reminded to re-read Ralph Waldo Emerson's "Divinity School Address" and study the Transcendentalist movement. On the last day, I mentioned to Dr. Wright a car accident following which my peripheral vision had gradually diminished to the point that I had less than 10 percent sight. He assured me that I would need my eyesight for the work ahead. He invited me to sit near him at lunch to discuss intercessory prayer in ministry. At the table, he spoke of the energy that comes from attunement to God, and suggested that Jesus used the overflow of this energy to heal. Impulsively, he asked if he could lay hands on my eyes to target them for the overflow of energy he was feeling. I agreed. He reached across the table, and when he removed his hands, I could see again. This experience and the message of the retreat became the core of my own ministry.

Meanwhile, at All Souls, I did not feel free to talk about a contemporary healing ministry. Then, some unfavorable publicity in a nationally known black magazine again challenged my relationship to Unitarian Universalism. *Jet* magazine published an article and a picture of the civil union of a black lesbian couple. Shortly thereafter, the magazine featured an article about the denomination that was considering removing "God" from its statement of Principles and Purposes. Suddenly, I found myself being called upon by classmates to explain this religion that allowed all sorts of behaviors and beliefs—including atheism.

Not familiar with the concept of gay marriage, I decided to ask the minister involved to help me understand what had happened. Rev. Frank Robertson explained that the church had quietly allowed him to perform services of civil union for gay and lesbian couples. Usually, they occurred in his office, witnessed by a few close family members and/or friends. On this occasion, a black lesbian couple wanted a large gathering in the main auditorium; they wanted pictures, and they wanted to dress in an elaborate gown for the "bride" and a tuxedo for the "groom." He had agreed. The photographer turned out to be someone who had spent over thirty years as photographer for the African-American newspapers and for Johnson Publishing Company. Rev. Robertson's approval left the church and senior minister open to national condemnation without furthering the cause he was advocating. I felt that blacks in the church had been used to make a point for gay rights that was not an issue for most African Americans. The incident took the focus away from the rationale for civil union and commitment in the gay community, and made the issue more about homophobia among blacks. I considered this a serious misrepresentation of fact and a setback for African-American inclusion in the UU movement.

Soon after I entered Howard University Divinity School, family and friends began to call on me to minister to them. They encouraged me to start a church. I asked at school for permission to use the old chapel on the main campus of Howard for a weekly

Wednesday afternoon service. Generally, twelve to twenty people attended regularly. They began planning for fundraising, a regular meeting place, and an organizational structure. An attorney worked on incorporation papers for the Garden of Gethsemane. A dentist whose wife was a friend of my mother volunteered to serve as chair of the board. We asked to use the chapel of the divinity school for a formal opening in the spring of my senior year. I graduated a few weeks later, in May 1981.

In fall 1981, I was ordained by All Souls; a few weeks after, I presented myself to the Ministerial Fellowship Committee. The committee gave me conditional approval. I worked with Rev. Eaton to satisfy the conditions to prepare for the event. On November 23, 1981, over two hundred clergy and laypersons gathered at All Souls Church to affirm and support my call to ministry. Two months later, Adele Smith-Penniman became the second black woman minister to be ordained. I began to communicate with the UU Office of Ministry in Boston and to prepare a packet to use in the settlement process.

Because the UUA was being challenged to be intentional about diversity, my name was included as a candidate for several searches. I was kept busy preparing packets. But search committees generally wasted no time explaining to me why I was not a match. Meanwhile I continued to minister to the members of the Garden of Gethsemane. UU colleagues invited me to join the Greater Washington Area Religious UU Professionals. I received invitations to speak at UU congregations and fellowships in the region. Honoraria for these sermons ranged from $100 to $250 each. My income varied from $200 to $400 a month. My estranged husband was unemployed and not contributing to support the children except when they were with him in Ohio. With three to feed, clothe, and shelter in addition to myself, I had to find a settlement or another job very soon. I went to Rev. Eaton for help.

Eaton suggested that I apply for a grant from the All Souls Beckner Fund to support me in UU campus ministry at Howard University. The award was enough to support me for about six months. I attended weekly meetings with the other chaplains and Dr. Evans Crawford, the Dean of Chapel. When the Lenten season arrived, I realized that the planned program would exclude all who were not Christian. I proposed to Dean Crawford that each chaplain make a presentation regarding his faith tradition under the umbrella of "Seasons of Spiritual Renewal." The dean asked me to coordinate the program. As the chaplaincy neared an end, David Eaton called me in to suggest full-time work with the District of Columbia Public Schools. I applied and was hired. I continued to pastor the Garden of Gethsemane and to submit packets when asked by the Office of Ministry.

Soon after my ordination, Elois Hamilton, an African-American UU, and Werner Mattersdorf, both members of Davies Memorial Church, began to pay close attention to my path within the UUA. Elois, then president of the Prince George's County Chapter of the Southern Christian Leadership Conference (SCLC), was known throughout the county as an effective change agent. Werner was active on the board of the SCLC chapter and a member of the board of Davies Church. As part of their vision for a more inclusive UUA, both Elois and Werner had a vested interest in seeing me settled as a UU minister.

Werner began to visit area churches and district conferences when he knew I would be speaking at them. The first time Cedar Lane Church in Bethesda, Maryland, invited me as guest speaker in 1982, Werner came to hear me. After that, whenever he learned of settlement options that seemed a possible fit for me, he would tell me about them and encourage me to seek to get my name on the list. Still, no congregation was ready to invite my candidacy. Werner was convinced that race and gender were factors. He began to take action on my behalf without my knowing it. Soon thereafter, Werner brought his wife, Anna, to visit the Garden of Gethsemane, and they came regularly to be spiritually fed. He began getting information that he hoped might lead to the Garden of Gethsemane becoming a UU congregation so that I might be settled there. Two things had occurred by then to convince him that, where my ministry was concerned, the UUA was neither open to or prepared to include the diversity that I represented.

First, Davies Memorial was looking for a minister. The search committee was having trouble agreeing on someone. While I was never told this directly, I later suspected that my name had come up and that the committee was not willing to consider my candidacy. Werner apparently spoke to some of the other board members about having me serve in an interim capacity to give the search committee more time to complete its work. He may have also wanted to give the congregation an opportunity to experience my ministry as a way of confronting their concerns. At any rate, I received a call from the chair of the board outlining the terms of a proposed contract to start the following Sunday. My first day in the pulpit, the search committee chairperson unexpectedly came up to make an announcement. She announced that the committee had agreed on the new minister to be recommended and gave her name. I was convinced that the committee had rushed to make a selection before the congregation had any opportunity to find out whether their fears about an African American were warranted. That same day, I was asked to be present to a husband whose wife had just died. I helped rally the congregation around the family and worked with the husband on funeral arrangements. From that time until my contract ended, members treated me as their "real" minister. A bonding occurred, and we parted without malice.

The second wake-up call occurred when I asked to be considered for the UU United Nations Office. I knew that I was a strong candidate because of my background in political science and international affairs, and because of my fluency in French. I was invited to interview. During our conversation, the interviewers intimated that they were concerned that I would not remain for five years. I had not been aware that this was a criterion. Moreover, it was not clear that others would be asked for a five-year commitment. Sure enough, the search committee selected the other finalist—or finalists: a couple who would both work in the job for the price of one!

Werner saw this selection as unfair competition. He was incensed and wanted to sue the UUA. I was tired, and still needed a job. I asked Werner not to sue so that instead I would have time to focus on finding a way to support my offspring. I had now been in the search process for nearly eight years. It was then that Werner suggested we launch a campaign to make my existing ministry at the Garden of Gethsemane an official settlement. I contacted David Eaton, who suggested we talk to Sid Peterman, our district representative. Sid came to DC to brainstorm strategies for getting me settled. He, Werner, and David agreed that it was time for the UUA to take some responsibility. It was the fall of 1987. Werner agreed to work with a committee of the Garden of Gethsemane to affiliate with the UUA. Peterman agreed to look for funding possibilities for a "new start" congregation. He also agreed to consult with Tom Chulak and Lucy Hitchcock, who were working with urban UU ministries.

By the General Assembly of 1989, the Southeast Congregation of Unitarian Universalists was voted into UUA affiliation. Some of the members had created a banner for the opening parade at GA. The group had a regular meeting place for Sunday morning worship. We had hired someone to help open the auditorium we used on Sundays. About twenty-eight members signed the roll. Initially, the membership was truly diverse, a mixture of black and white, male and female, young people and seniors, gay and straight. We found space for a small office in the basement of a community center at Ninth Street and Pennsylvania Avenue, southeast. Later, we rented a large room on the first floor so that office space and worship space were in the same place. The UUA organized meetings and retreat sessions during which we articulated our mission as "an intentionally diverse religious community," agreed on a covenant, developed an advertising campaign, and discussed ways to raise money and increase visibility. Around this time, the suggestion was made that we find a more suitable name. The name Sojourner Truth Congregation of Unitarian Universalists was put forward. Another member agreed to bring in information about

Sojourner Truth's life so that the membership could make an informed decision. Members volunteered for various tasks related to the organizing, training, and performing of a drama group for youth. The proposed new name made it a natural to call them the Youth of Truth. The vote the following Sunday was unanimous in favor of the new name.

The congregation grew slowly but steadily. The UU church of Arlington, Virginia, committed to a buddy relationship. Several people came in specifically to work with the drama group. One worked on scheduling performances of the group's first play, an anti-drug drama called "Undercover Bird." Elois Hamilton organized pizza parties for the group and allowed them to meet in space rented by the Prince George's County SCLC. A professional actor and director of black theater agreed to coach the group in dramatic technique. The congregation was so proud of the achievements of the youth that they agreed to send them to perform at General Assembly in Hartford, Connecticut. Funds were found to send four youth to GA: William and David Chappelle, Masavia Greer, and Rachel Walker. Their performance called attention to drug-related crime and youth homicide rates that had reached epidemic levels in DC. "Is it more important to save the whales or save black males?" their presentation asked in a humorous sketch. A near-capacity audience received the group with resounding applause.

The following year, members of the congregation began to spend more time in disagreements over the means of achieving what should have been common goals. Church politics overshadowed the spiritual grounding of the group. Board meetings became gripe sessions, with one faction trying to score points over another and everyone thinking they knew better than the minister. In addition, UUA funding for the new start was being scaled back to encourage greater self-reliance. Some members were convinced that priorities would have shifted and that this was a time for downsizing rather than growth. Some questioned whether they could afford a minister. I wondered whether they could afford not to have a minister.

There came a point when it appeared that black, straight members were in battle with white, gay members for control. When a black jazz musician joined the congregation, the white pianist had trouble cooperating with him to share responsibility for the music and to create more diversity of musical styles. The black jazz musician stopped coming to church. A white woman who lived in the neighborhood was attracted to the message of hope in my sermons. However, she wrote me explaining that she could not sign the book because of an unpleasant personal encounter with members outside of the worship service. A gay member of the church began to advertise the congregation in the *Blade* newspaper. He did this without the knowledge or consent of either the minister or the board of directors. The ads seemed to promise services or special outreach that were too much for the young congregation to deliver. Moreover, it seemed that this member of the church was looking to consciously create a predominantly gay congregation, using the thirst within the denomination for true racial diversity to promote his hidden agenda. This felt like a betrayal for members truly seeking to come together, embracing our diversity as a way to grow and flourish. I began to feel burned out as I tried to negotiate these conflicts while maintaining my own spiritual center and nurturing the spirituality of the congregation.

In the end, the money for the new start ran out. But before that happened, the members of the congregation who had the initial vision began to slip away, one by one. Some moved to begin new lives in new places. Some became too ill to continue the struggle. Some, like me, were burning out. Those who were left were too much alike to spark creative tension. However, the vision that created Sojourner Truth Congregation of Unitarian Universalists had been made manifest within the UU movement. Another step had been taken and the denomination would never again be the same.

—Yvonne Seon

"AFFIRMING BEAUTY IN DARKNESS"

1988

Established in 1986, the UUA Hymnbook Resources Commission was chaired by Rev. Mark Belletini and included Rev. Ellen Johnson-Fay, Helen Pickett, Mark Slegers, Barbara Wagner, Rev. Fred Wooden, and originally Fred Wilson, an African American who was later replaced by T. J. Anderson, another African American. The UUA staff liaison, Jacqui James, was also an African American. Instructed by the UUA Board to develop an "inclusive" hymnal, the commission knew it would need to address the issues of degenderization, sexist language, patriarchal imagery, and gender balance, but it went beyond that. This was before the UUA began using an "anti-racist, anti-oppression, multi-cultural" frame of reference; nonetheless, at its first gathering, the commission came to a consensus that the hymnbook would be multicultural. This meant breaking with an unwritten, and largely unconscious, rule about singing only "good" music, "good" being code for classical European music.

Mark Belletini brought forward another concern. Having grown up in Detroit and been exposed to the Black Madonna and Motown's black music and culture, he was concerned about the use of white/black, light/dark imagery in UU hymnology. Fred Wilson agreed and pressed the commission to examine UU hymnology in relation to race. Subsequently, in separate conversations with the chairs of the United Methodist and Mennonite hymnal commissions, Belletini learned that they had wrestled with similar concerns over imagery and cultural inclusivity.

Commission member Fred Wooden was assigned the task of composing a position paper on behalf of the commission and wrote "Is There No Beauty in Darkness?" Some colleagues complained that the commission was making a mountain out of a molehill, others criticized it as an exercise in political correctness, while a few responded in a way Belletini describes as "outright ghastly." On March 8, 1988, in response to the commission's discussions, Jacqui James delivered a sermon on the topic, "Affirming Beauty in Darkness." An excerpt follows.

Among the new hymnal's primary resources were the fifty-three recast hymns from Hymns for the Celebration of Life *that appeared in* Hymns in New Form for Common Worship *and the hymnbook* How Can We Keep from Singing! *Published in 1976 by the First Unitarian Church of Los Angeles, a congregation with a long history of activism,* How Can We Keep from Singing! *was developed starting in 1952 during the ministry of Stephen Fritchman, considered among the most radical of Unitarian ministers. The initial instigators of the Black Unitarian Universalist Caucus were members of the Los Angeles congregation, and one of them, Jules Ramey, wrote the song "I Can't Wait Another Hundred Years," which appeared in* How Can. *That hymnbook—by including the black national anthem "Lift Every Voice and Sing," and songs such as "We Shall Overcome," "I'm on My Way," "Oh, Freedom," and "De Colores"—presaged the direction* Singing the Living Tradition *(SLT) would follow. The commission also delved into new hymnbooks from denominations that included more African Americans in their numbers to find which spirituals they were using. Released in 1993, SLT offered a wide range of musical styles that included folk, spirituals, and jazz as well as readings by African-American Unitarian Universalists, several taken from the meditation manual* Been in the Storm So Long, *edited by James and Mark D. Morrison-Reed in 1991.*

Before coming to Boston to work in the UUA Department of Ministry, James served for eleven years as director of religious education at the First Unitarian Church of Pittsburgh. She was a key player in the anti-oppression effort that transformed the UUA during the 1980s and 1990s. In addition to her work as director of worship resources, she co-authored with Judith Frediani the Weaving the Fabric of Diversity *curriculum, coordinated the Beyond Categorical Thinking program, and is recognized as the mother of African-American Unitarian Universalist Ministries and the driving force that set Diverse and Revolutionary Unitarian Universalist Multicultural Ministries on its way. She also served as the UUA's affirmative action officer.*

My mother and I have been discussing grandparents and great-grandparents a lot lately. Remembering her grandmother, she writes me, "I am certain that Grandma never considered herself prejudiced, but consider: I was the darkest of the grandchildren, the youngest and her favorite, whether because I spent so much time with her or because she pities me, I don't know. But she called me her 'Brown Sugar' and often said, 'Poor, Brown Sugar Child, all your mother did for you was to give you a nose and a little hair.'" My own beloved grandmother, whom I never thought had a prejudiced bone in her body, when faced with the stillbirth of her only son's child said, "It's all for the best." I thought she meant because my aunt and uncle were both nearing forty and the marriage seemed in trouble. My mother tells me, no, she was afraid the child would be dark like my uncle's wife. I don't think either of these foremothers of mine was operating out of prejudice, but rather out of the knowledge that in this culture, white is perceived as good and black is not!

What does all this have to do with religion and UUism in particular? Our Principles and Purposes speak of "the inherent worth and dignity of every person" and "justice, equity and compassion in human relations" and of the "the goal of world community with peace, liberty and justice for all." Our language as a religious people must constantly reaffirm the equal worth and beauty of all people. As the Hymnbook Resources Commission looks at our current hymnbooks, we see that UUs have a problem here.

Our theological language in general and especially our hymns use light and dark as metaphors for good and bad. The preference for white/light is obvious. The opposition to black/dark is equally obvious. We present only the positive images of light and white . . . in our religious language. Likewise only the negative images of black/dark are used.

Some examples from *Hymns for the Celebration of Life* make this abundantly clear:

- In the darkness drear
- Too long the darkened way we've trod
- Turn our darkness into day
- I saw the powers of darkness put to flight
- On shadowed thresholds dark with fear
- And dawn becomes the morning, the darkness put to flight
- Praise ye, daughters and sons of light
- Ring out the darkness of the land, ring in the light that is to be
- O'er white expanses, sparkling pure the radiant morns unfold

Is there no beauty in darkness? Our hymnbooks contain no negative images of light/white. Our hymnody reflects a bias toward light/white and a bias against black/dark. We've become stuck in a single interpretation of the rich symbolism of dark and light. "We have been trained in our Western culture to see only the light, the masculine 'Yang' of our existence. Yet all creation and wisdom teaches us to seek out and await in the dark, the feminine 'Yin' aspects of our soul," writes John Giannini. As long as we continue to legitimate our hatred of the dark with theological language, we can continue to justify our prejudice, and maintain the racist climate of our culture. . . .

It is vital that we acknowledge that there are negative connotations to *white*. It can be soft, vulnerable, pallid, and ashen. Light can be blinding, bleaching, enervating. We must acknowledge that darkness has a redemptive character, that in darkness there is power and beauty. It is the place that nurtured and protected us before our birth. Welcome darkness, don't be afraid of it or deny it. Darkness brings relief from the blinding sun, from scorching heat, from exhausting labor. Night signals permission to rest, to be with our loved ones, to conceive new life, to search our hearts, to remember our dreams. The dark of winter is a time of hibernation for both plants and animals; seeds in the dark, fertile earth.

The words *black* and *dark* don't need to be destroyed or ignored, only balanced and reclaimed in their wholeness. The words *white* and *light* don't need to be destroyed or ignored, only balanced and reclaimed in their wholeness. Imagine a world that had only light—or a world which had only dark. We could not exist in either. Imagine, if you can, a world where everyone looked and acted just the same. We need to revalue both light and dark, they are both necessary to our continued survival.

—Jacqui James, "Affirming Beauty in Darkness," Mar. 8, 1988, Unitarian Universalist Association Chapel, Boston, Hymnbook Resources Commission (1986) file, Morrison-Reed Collection, Sankofa Archive, Meadville Lombard Theological School Library, Chicago.

AFRICAN-AMERICAN UNITARIAN UNIVERSALIST MINISTRIES 1988

In December 1987, during the administration of William F. Schulz, the UUA Department of Ministry under Rev. Judith Meyer created the Task Force on Affirmative Action for African-American Ministers. The task force included Rev. Rob Eller-Isaacs, Rev. Mel Hoover (hired as the UUA's director for racial and cultural diversity that year), Jacqui James, Rev. Mark D. Morrison-Reed (chair), and Rev. Lindi Ramsden. As they surveyed the situation regarding the settlement of African-American ministers within the UUA, two needs stood out. First was the creation of a process to help congregations searching for a new minister to become open to the possibility of calling an African American. This led to the development of a program called Beyond Categorical Thinking that addressed race and many other ways individuals are marginalized. It included and went beyond the issues of gender and sexual orientation upon which similar programs had focused. Interweave (Unitarian Universalists for Lesbian, Gay, Bi-sexual and Transgender Concerns) and the UUA Black Concerns Working Group initially rejected the proposal. Both feared that if all oppressions were lumped together, their issue would lose out. Over the ensuing years, however, the effectiveness of this approach was proven.

The second need was for the creation of an ongoing support group for African-American ministers. Such a group had never existed before, not even during the late 1960s when the Black Unitarian Universalist Caucus was organized. Clarence Thompson, Ethelred Brown,

W.H.G. Carter, Jeffrey Campbell, Lewis McGee, Eugene Sparrow, and others had labored in isolation from one another. This insight led to a gathering of African-American UU religious professionals.

Like the training of the facilitators for the Beyond Categorical Thinking workshops, the African-American Ministers' Conference was funded by the UU Funding Panel, which derived its funds from the Veatch Program of the UU Congregation at Shelter Rock. The following statement of goals and purposes was written in preparation for that gathering, held in Washington DC, on November 13–16, 1988, at the Howard Inn.

GOALS AND PURPOSES

Goal:

To form an organization to carry out our purposes, among which are the provision of an ongoing structure for communication with and support for one another and the monitoring of the UUA in regard to its response to and involvement of African Americans.

Purposes:

To provide an opportunity for the sharing of information and resources with one another, and to give one another emotional support and nurture.

To reflect together on the current situation of our personal ministries and of the UUA's impact on our work.

To better understand the involvement of African Americans in the UUA by historical, theological and sociological analysis.

To meet with other African-American UUA staff members to understand how we can best use their skills and services and to discover what they need.

To agree on how our congregations and the denomination can and will be a positive force in the lives of African Americans and other marginalized people.

To develop a strategic plan that will be a blueprint for creating a more inclusive, proactive denomination in which African Americans can thrive and be full participants.

In attendance at the conference were Dan Aldridge, Michelle Briggs-Bentley, Yvonne Chappelle-Seon, David H. Eaton, Linda Harris May, Melvin A. Hoover, T. Ewell Hopkins, Jacqui James, Charles Johnson, William R. Jones, Mark D. Morrison-Reed, Thomas E. Payne, Adele Smith-Penniman, Donald Robinson, Thandeka, Toni Vincent, Marjorie Bowens-Wheatley, Ronald White, and Loretta Williams. The meeting led to the formation of African-American Unitarian Universalist Ministries (AAUUM). On June 22, 1989, AAUUM issued a press release announcing its formation, which follows.

AAUUM met twice a year—once for its annual meeting and again at the UUA General Assembly. After nearly a decade during which a group identity formed, an agenda evolved, and its importance proven, AAUUM reached out to other people of color and Latina/o Hispanic peoples in 1997. That conversation had been going for some time, and the emergence of the Latina/o Unitarian Universalist Networking Association in 1995 made it more urgent. From this meeting, a new organization formed, UU Religious Professionals of Color. It in turn evolved into Diverse and Revolutionary Unitarian Universalist Multicultural Ministries.

NEW AFRICAN-AMERICAN UU ORGANIZATION FORMS

A new organization of African and African-American religious professionals affiliated or associated with the Unitarian Universalist Association announced its formation today. The group, African-American Unitarian Universalist Ministries (AAUUM), was formed last fall to "organize, institutionalize and mobilize" African-American UUs working within UUA-affiliated structures.

AAUUM stressed spirituality, power and justice as centerpieces of "a prophetic witness" and distinguished itself from mainstream UUs, saying that they view the African-American experience and heritage, as well as action for justice as part of the "essential feelings and values" which shape their spirituality.

A statement from the new organization outlined the group's understanding of power as "the ability to create and control our social, political and economic realities," and justice as "an equitable distribution of resources and opportunities which work to assist and facilitate individual development and talent in all areas for the ultimate enhancement of the entire community."

The membership organization of UUA-affiliated religious professionals includes, but is not limited to fellowshipped ministers; ministers serving or working for the UU movement; staff of the UUA or affiliated congregations, fellowships or societies; religious educators; and theological students.

Three conveners and several task force chairs, elected annually by the membership, will coordinate the work of the organization. Conveners for 1988–89 are Dr. William Jones, Rev. Mark Morrison-Reed, and Rev. Adele Smith-Penniman. The task forces include Support and Growth (Rev. Yvonne Seon, chair); Social Justice (Rev. Thomas Payne, chair); Education and Communications (Marjorie Bowens-Wheatley, chair); and African-American Theology and Worship (Dr. Thandeka, chair).

—The goals and purposes document and the announcement can be found in the AAUUM file, Morrison-Reed Collection, Sankofa Archive, Meadville Lombard Theological School Library, Chicago.

"PIONEERING MINISTER IS HELPING TROUBLED AREA"
2000

Following Rev. Adele Smith-Penniman (1982), Rev. Dr. Michelle Bentley was the third African-American woman to be ordained (1986) into the Unitarian Universalist ministry. After organizing and serving as minister to two new starts in Chicago, she worked as chaplain to chronically and terminally ill children and with a major substance abuse center before becoming the senior interim minister of the First Unitarian Society of Chicago. From 1993 to 1998, she was a faculty member and the dean of students at Meadville Lombard Theological School, after which she was called to be the senior minister of the Third Unitarian Church of Chicago. Then, from 2002 to 2007, Bentley served as the UUA director of professional development in ministry.

Rev. Michelle Bentley stood outside the Third Unitarian Church of Chicago near the Oak Park border in Austin on a springlike day, admiring a dirt lot.

"We'd like to landscape it. Something for the youth," said the 50-year-old minister, who was called by the congregation in August 1998, the first African-American woman to come to the pulpit that way in a Unitarian Universalist church.

Finding hope, even salvation, in the earth is familiar to her. The church has been working on the one-time eyesore since last

July, and though the church doesn't own the land, the congregation has hopes.

The city landmark church at 300 N. Mayfield, built in 1936 and enlarged in 1956, has for years operated the former Harriet Tubman Center, a two-story structure that has served as everything from a homeless drop-in shelter to an HIV/AIDS counseling center. It's now closed down, but the congregation wants to create a jobs facility, possibly a skills center, to help lift this economically depressed neighborhood.

The lot, if acquired, could bear Tubman's name. Choosing to honor the former slave who became a leading American abolitionist (and whose portrait hangs in Bentley's church office and is also one of 19 ceramic portrait tiles in the sanctuary), reflects Bentley's vision of what the 132-year-old liberal institution can become.

"The pulpit here is the power to transform, the power to teach and to be in the community," she said. "The community sees this church as an anchor. Our vision is to be together. Investing our resources, working with the leaders and residents in the community to make this a model community."

She and her 170 or so members, many of whom are from the suburbs, want to walk the walk by not running away from the problem.

The Austin neighborhood has seen plenty of upheaval. A white exodus in the mid-1960s left this formerly middle-class and largely Catholic area black and impoverished by the mid-1970s.

Members of Third Unitarian were torn. Break-in and vandalism caused many to consider their site several blocks south of the Green Line a dicey haven. The congregation split when a narrow majority voted to move west to Oak Park. About 50 members left to begin a church in Oak Park, which merged in 1994 with the Unitarian Universalist Church in that suburb.

"It hurt a lot," said Betty Harris, chairwoman of the board of trustee and a church member for 33 years. "But we persevered."

The continuing presence of the church there has made a difference, residents said. And under Bentley, that momentum has increased.

"They really have had an impact on the unlicensed salesmen, the drug dealers," said the Rev. Elizabeth Bynum, a board member of the South Austin Coalition. Bynum, a Baptist minister who lives in the neighborhood, credits Bentley with mobilizing the 3M Club, a residents' group from the surrounding blocks. . . .

Ald. Isaac "Ike" Crothers (29th) agreed that things are improving. Beyond crime, he said, Bentley's presence "was symbolic that people can work together and live together. I've been there several times and am impressed that people come from all over, the Far South Side and the suburbs, to join in."

This month, the church hosted a CAPS [Chicago Alternative Policing Strategy] meeting for the first time, and it will become a regular venue for this, Bentley said. . . .

At a recent 11 a.m. celebration of life, as the hour-long services are called, Bentley—dressed simply in a gray outfit—talked about creativity and its powers. Surrounding her were quilts brought by members, some 100-year-old family heirlooms. Pitchfork, hoe and gardening implements nearby.

"I've been saved more than once by plants and dirt," she said.

Her talk was a celebration of those women who used their creativity to quilt, talk, guide escaped slaves by encoding directions, and find the sacred in the everyday. "Creativity," she noted, is leaving "a place better than you found it.". . .

Bentley followed an unusual path to her ministry. Growing up in upper-middle class Lake Forest, she credits her late father, Mitchell Whittingham, and her mother, Edwina, with giving her a strong foundation in agape. "That's unconditional love," she said.

She and her younger sister "learned about racism at an early age. And we learned to go around it, sometimes through it," Bentley said. "Still, there were more drugs in Lake Forest than I saw on the South and West Side."

After graduating from Lake Forest High School in 1967, she became "kind of radical" at Spelman College in Atlanta and embraced the "Black and Proud" ethic. Her search took her through Marx, Islam, Buddhism and other explorations. While working as a principal in an alternative Chicago school, she finally gave up on education when a 16-year-old student, a man/child who still sucked his thumb, was arrested for shooting a Chicago policeman during a scuffle.

"I wanted the credibility of the pulpit," she said.

The Unitarian Universalist tradition was the fit. Not only did she embrace it, she spent time as a dean of students at the Meadville/Lombard Seminary, seeking to broaden the ethnic reach. Yet the call to community reached her.

"I'm glad she left the ivory tower," said her husband, Ray Bentley, an executive with the nonprofit Bethel New Life community development organization in the nearby West Garfield neighborhood.

Bentley said she's coming out of the "transition" period and looking forward. She wants to help the community come along. "It's a constant struggle," she said, mentioning a 20-year-old "nice guy" who was unable to get a job because of his addiction. "When you scratch anything, you start to see the systemic stuff."

She and others want to not only be witnesses, but gardeners, in the struggle to uncover new life. Salvation in the dirt.

—Ernest Tucker, "Pioneering Minister Is Helping Troubled Area," Chicago Sun-Times *Metro Section, March 26, 2000.*

THOMAS ELIRON PAYNE
1942–2001

For me, there is no "one true path" but many paths, perhaps one each, as we struggle for significance and purpose.

—Thomas E. Payne

When, in 1978, Thomas Payne began serving the First Unitarian Church of Roxbury, Massachusetts, the building which seated fifteen hundred was home to a congregation of thirteen, and he was doing what he had always done—ministry. He had been doing that since age five, when he first heard the call.

Born in Washington DC and raised in a liberal National Baptist Convention church, he was a "church brat." Achieving the God and Country Award in Scouting and serving as the president of the Potomac River Baptist Youth Association, he expected to become a Baptist minister. But when the new minister of his congregation began preaching fundamentalist Christianity, and young Payne, who believed "a loving God would not condemn people to everlasting hell," disagreed, he "was backed into a corner of either recanting or being excommunicated."[1] He was excommunicated.

At the age of fifteen, he began attending Universalist National Memorial Church. With the Universalist Church of America's endorsement, he entered college, where he helped start and was first president of the Howard University chapter of Student Religious Liberals. He also came to know James Reeb, who as the assistant minister at All Souls Church, Unitarian, worked with local campus groups. Later still, while attending the Howard Divinity School, Payne taught Sunday school at All Souls.

Payne was in his last year of seminary when he went to the Emergency Conference at the Biltmore Hotel in New York and ended up participating in the initial black caucus meeting. After graduating, he enrolled at Harvard Divinity School, earned a master's degree in urban affairs, and worked as special assistant to Robert West, the new president of the UUA. "Then unable," as he recounted, "to get called to a church, being an African American on one hand, but not a part of the UU Black Empowerment camp on the other, I finally took a job at [a] United Church of Christ College in Ohio."[2] Ordained in 1970 by the First Unitarian Church in Toledo, he served as assistant dean of students for student services at Heidelberg College in Tiffin, Ohio. In this position, he advised minority students, managed a men's dorm, coordinated services for low-achieving students, and taught. He also served as the supply minister for the Lyons Universalist Church, but only after a nearby Universalist church had rejected him as part-time minister. Instead, they hired a white "first-year, foot-washing Baptist seminarian." Payne called it "racism" and remembered, "it was a bad three months between rejection and call. At the end of my three-year non-renewable [contract] at the college, [the Lyons'] church arranged a teaching position at the local high school to keep me."[3]

Payne worked as a prison chaplain for seven years. As a Unitarian Universalist, his "emphasis was on pastoral care (human rights concerns) rather than worship-liturgy; this moved into an ombudsman role and then into administration of an inmate service."[4] Taking a year's educational leave, he completed a doctorate in ministry. His thesis, which addressed the challenges of delivering prison chaplain service in a multifaith context, led him to community and youth work as a way of keeping people from landing in prison in the first place. Returning to Boston, he joined the Benevolent Fraternity of Unitarian Universalist Churches (now called the UU Urban Ministry) as the associate minister-at-large and co-minister of the Roxbury congregation. There, between 1977 and 1987, he served as pastor to the poor and oppressed and especially urban youth. He was active in the school busing crisis, arson prevention, community development, and organizing the Southern Black College Campus Tour, which still exists.

In late 1986, complications from diabetes led to the amputation of his left leg below the knee. He faced his ongoing health problems with a certain aplomb. At the founding meeting of African-American Unitarian Universalist Ministries (AAUUM) in 1988, he detached his prosthesis, placed it in a conspicuous place, and then slyly smiled as those entering the room did a double take. On another occasion after an AAUUM meeting, he gave a driving tour of significant, off-the-beaten-path parts of Washington DC.

In 1987, he turned to interim ministry and said his goal was to work his way around the country. On the way he served the Norwich Unitarian Universalist Church; the Unitarian Universalist Society of Lexington, Kentucky; the Beverly Unitarian Church in Chicago; the Unitarian Universalist Fellowship of Columbia, South Carolina; and the Catawba Valley Unitarian Universalist Church in Hickory, North Carolina, but in 1994, his diabetes and chronic depression forced him to take a medical leave. Chosen by his colleagues in 1995 to deliver the Berry Street Essay, he spoke on suffering in a talk titled "Koheleth Headache." Given his health and his race, it was a subject he knew something about. Ministering all the while as a self-appointed chaplain, Thom Payne lived his final years at Unitarian Universalist House in Philadelphia, Pennsylvania. He died on November 17, 2001, at age fifty-nine, from complications of diabetes.

Payne wrote that "by age ten I experienced doubts about the nature of God and the purpose of humankind. I was active . . . and always asking questions."[5] Ever a questioner, at different times he identified himself as "a discontented theist with growing deistic leanings," "a post-Christian Humanist," and "an agnostic hedonist." "This is where I stand—today!"[6] he said, which meant that tomorrow, he might well be standing elsewhere. Ever a maverick, he quietly and resolutely followed his own path. Ever a minister, which is what he set out to be when he was five years old, he is remembered by his colleagues and friends as a true pastor to seniors, urban youth, the poor, the oppressed, the imprisoned, indeed, whomever was in need.

—Mark D. Morrison-Reed

Sources

The primary sources for this essay include a personal relationship between the author and Payne, beginning in 1978; several autobiographical essays in Payne's UUA Department of Ministry file; the DMin thesis he wrote for the Howard University Divinity School, "Problems in Ministry to Black Prisoners" (1975); Payne's essay for the UUA pamphlet "Soulful Journeys: The Faith of African-American Unitarian Universalists" (2002); a theological reflection he shared at the 1990 AAUUM meeting in Tulsa; and Payne's obituary (http://archive.uua.org/programs/ministry/news/obituaries2002.html).

"WHY CHANGE? WHY NOW?"
2004

The book The Arc of the Universe Is Long: Unitarian Universalists, Anti-Racism and the Journey from Calgary *documents the efforts and initiatives to address the issues of prejudice and power, diversity and inclusiveness within the Unitarian Universalist Association since a resolution passed at the 1992 General Assembly led to the formation of the Task Force on Racial and Cultural Diversity. How to become and remain meaningfully engaged and incorporate these issues into the life of local UU congregations remains an ongoing challenge. For some, it has meant training, for others, community partnerships. The Bowie Unitarian Universalist Fellowship (BUUF) responded in a way that, to date, no other congregation has. In 2004, the eighty-member congregation in Bowie, Maryland, voted to change its name to Goodloe Memorial Unitarian Universalist Congregation. After changing its name, the congregation built a bridge to Bowie State University, where Don Speed Smith Goodloe was first principal, by initiating annual Goodloe celebrations at the church and at the Goodloes' house on the university campus, a structure designed and built by African Americans that is on the National Register of Historic Places. The congregation also established a Bowie State scholarship in Goodloe's name, wrote a pamphlet about him that has been distributed by the Alumni Association, donated a framed portrait of him to the association for display at the Goodloe House, and wrote the Wikipedia entry about him.*

The BUUF newsletter leading up to that vote contained a detailed discussion of the issues involved in and reason behind the proposed name change. An excerpt from that newsletter follows.

Members of the fellowship will vote on whether or not to change the fellowship's name on Sunday, October 24, at a congregational meeting immediately following the service. The Board has asked the Outreach Committee to answer two questions: Why we should change our name to Goodloe Memorial Unitarian Universalist Congregation of Bowie, and why now? . . .

The Committee next considered naming the congregation after a famous Unitarian Universalist, thinking this would have a broader appeal. Davies Memorial Unitarian Universalist Church in Camp Springs was mentioned as a model. This church is named after A. Powell Davies, minister of All Souls Church, Unitarian, in the District from 1944 to 1957. Davies was also an author and a political activist who spurred growth in the denomination in the 1950s. He previously had been a Methodist minister, beginning his career as a Unitarian minister in 1933 in Summit, New Jersey.

In considering a prominent person for our new name, several members suggested Don Speed Smith Goodloe, an African American and the first principal of the school that became Bowie State University.

Early in the 20th century, the state of Maryland hired Goodloe to start a school on a farm in Bowie for training African-American teachers. This he did from 1911 to 1921, obtaining funds from the legislature, erecting buildings, developing curricula, hiring teachers, advertising for students, and supervising the student operation of the farm and staffing a model elementary school on Normal School Road. He put the school on a sound financial footing and made it a reality. He was a dynamic speaker, outstanding leader, and true pioneer. Highly regarded in his time, Goodloe was included in the 1916–1917 *Who's Who in America*.

Goodloe was also, in the words of the noted black Unitarian Universalist author Rev. Mark Morrison-Reed, a "Black Pioneer in a White Denomination." He was Rev. Goodloe, a graduate of Allegheny College and our Unitarian seminary—Meadville Theological School. Although he was reared in the Methodist-Episcopal tradition, Goodloe selected our seminary over all others to receive his religious training.

Why Goodloe? Don Goodloe was a prominent Unitarian, but like other African-Americans of the time, leaders of the denomination discouraged him from following his dream of becoming a Unitarian minister. The Outreach Committee believes that naming ourselves after Goodloe would visibly demonstrate our commitment to diversity, especially in the changing demographic settings of Prince George's and Anne Arundel counties. The Outreach Committee believes that is the perfect opportunity for our denomination not only to honor Reverend Goodloe by bringing to the forefront his proper place in UU history but also to make amends for the past actions that deprived him of his dream.

Why now? Now is a good time to change our name because we have moved to a new location and will be ordering signs and stationery with our new address. Now is especially the time to reach out both to people outside of Bowie and to newcomers to the area.

—George Schulman and Dick Morris, "Why Change? Why Now?" Bowie Unitarian Universalist Fellowship newsletter, October 2004, pp. 2–3.

RECONCILIATION WITH THE CARTER FAMILY

Serving in my first ministry as interim at the Northern Hills Fellowship in Cincinnati, from 1997 to 1998, I preached a sermon on Unitarian Universalism's mixed legacy regarding race. Since I was in Cincinnati, I mentioned Rev. William H. G. Carter, a black Unitarian minister shunned by First Unitarian Church of Cincinnati and St. John's Unitarian Church during the 1930s. At the end of my sermon, a member of the congregation, Leslie Edwards, stood and said, "W.H.G. Carter was my grandfather, and I never thought I would hear his name mentioned in a Unitarian congregation." Everyone was silent, stunned, awed. It was a moment of utter grace.

The next year (by coincidence), I became the settled minister at First Unitarian Church of Cincinnati. Again I preached the sermon, this time titled "Get Back on the Bus," but added the story about Leslie Edwards. After the service, members swarmed me, all saying the same thing: "We have to do something."

Two years later, with much planning and trepidation, we did. It took that long to plan a reconciliation service between First Unitarian Church, Northern Hills, the UUA, and the descendants of W.H.G. Carter. Carter died in 1962. He and his wife, Beulah, had fifteen children. By 2000, only two sons were living, but hundreds of other Carters were spread across the United States.

The logistics, however, were not as complicated as the relationship building. First, we had to earn the trust of the Carter descendants. Leslie Edwards led us in this venture, and two of our lay members, Walter Herz and Dick Bozian, were unflagging in their interest and openness to meeting the Carters and learning more. And learn we did. We learned that the Carters themselves were divided on the legacy of W.H.G. Carter. We had to move slowly.

At some point, I came to an understanding that we needed to formally apologize on behalf of First Unitarian, St. Johns, and the American Unitarian Association (AUA) (the Unitarian Universalist Association did not exist in the 1930s). This came from reading the work of Elazar Barkan, who maintains that apology opens the doorway for reconciliation. But apology comes hard.

During the next two years, concerned members questioned why we should apologize. None of us had been alive then. What our congregation had done was what any white congregation would have done. To prepare us and address these questions, I preached sermons about grace, atonement, collective responsibility, reconciliation, and sin, which I identified as wrong relationship. I preached that this was an opportunity to redeem our ancestors now that we knew better.

As the event drew closer, the anxiety grew. I was regularly asked what would happen. I said, "I do not know." I taught that we embraced reconciliation because it was right, not because we knew what would happen; that this was an important lesson to teach our children, for they are always watching.

Members volunteered to send invitations, make food, and host weekend events. We invited the Carters, having no idea how many would attend. Maybe fifteen? How would they feel? What would they think? We did not know. I said that we did not need to know, we needed only to be sincere. Members were not comforted. People come to services for stability, not alarm. I tried to create a framework that would safely hold the growing anxiety.

The content of the service, beyond the apology, also plagued me. We knew we wanted Rev. Dr. Mark D. Morrison-Reed to preach. He agreed. Beyond that, what? We asked Rev. Dr. Morris Hudgins, minister at Northern Hills Fellowship, to participate since he had been so helpful in both historical research and support. The Unitarian Universalist Association sent a formal letter of apology, which I planned to read during the service. But I could not figure out how widely to advertise this event. I wanted people to know, but I also wanted it to be sincere; not a show, but a living worship experience that would be real and, if we were lucky, a reconciliation.

I have a particularly painful memory of a conversation with a black Unitarian Universalist colleague. I called to ask his advice on the service, and by the end of our conversation, I was sweating. I was trying so hard to say the right thing and not the wrong thing, but the story of race and its complexity in America and how to name and respect it is so tortured that our conversation exhausted me. We both exhaled a sigh of relief when the conversation was finished, and he reflected, "In America, race is the wound that will not heal." Race is the wound that will not heal because we have so few opportunities to sit with our knees touching and safely discuss our thoughts and feelings—all we know and live and can never possibly understand.

In the midst of anxiety and doubt (whoever said reconciliation is easy?), I kept reminding myself, and telling others, that an active faith life should challenge and leave us unsettled so that change is possible. Now was that time. We could do this and would emerge transformed. And yes, I silently said, "Lord, I hope this turns out okay."

On the day of the reconciliation service, over one hundred Carter descendants arrived from all over the country. We were stunned. For the first time in my experience, our sanctuary was filled to capacity. Later, several of the Carters told me that our work had enabled the extended family to come to terms with the full legacy of W.H.G. Carter, a gift of healing. Unexpectedly, one reconciliation led to another.

Music healed us all. Our music director at the time, Dr. David Jackson, invited a former student of his, now Rev. Todd O'Neal, and his exceptional black church choir to sing with our choir. No one who was there that day will ever forget the soloist who sang "The Battle Hymn of the Republic." She blew the rafters down.

There was another moment that no one there will ever forget. Unbeknownst to us, Leslie Edwards had commissioned another Carter descendant, Starita Smith, to deliver a response to my formal apology. After my apology, Starita came forward and delivered words of truth ending with "We accept your apology." There was a moment of silence and then noise and cheering, crying and shouting. I had never let myself believe that the Carters would accept our apology. I hadn't considered it. Reflecting later, I learned that we need to be forgiven as much as we need to make amends, without ever expecting forgiveness.

I could not have predicted the events that followed. Three months later, Cincinnati was shocked by race riots that placed our city on national television. The riots began after an unarmed black man, Timothy Thomas, was shot dead by a white police officer. Citizens rioted for days. A curfew was declared. Stories of years of racial profiling and abuse poured out.

In my study at church, near those riot-torn neighborhoods, I looked at the photo of Carter and his wife and children given to me by his descendants and wondered what to do. I looked at the face of William H. G. Carter and figured that he had been through worse and I needed to do something, so I did. I joined a group of local clergy who began to talk about racial profiling. First Unitarian Church was deeply mixed about my public response to the riots, some supporting my conversations about injustice, others concerned I was spreading controversy. It was not easy.

This was also my first foray into urban clergy relationships. I regularly found myself as the only female, white, non-Christian at the table. It was an enormously stressful opportunity, but if I learned anything from our Carter reconciliation, it was to stick with the relationships; and as awkward and slow as they were to develop, I stuck with them. It took a decade, but I "earned" my place in our neighborhood.

There have been other amazing connections along the way. We discovered that W.H.G. and Beulah were buried in unmarked graves behind the Northern Hills Fellowship. Money was raised to place markers. In the last few years, the Carter family learned that W.H.G. Carter was the grandson of a man who was most likely the biracial son of a female slave and an antebellum governor of Virginia. The two branches of the family made contact, and recently, black Carter descendants attended the family reunion of the wealthy white descendants of a former governor of Virginia. They are one large family with a very American story.

Since the first reconciliation service in 2001, we have given away over $30,000 through the Carter Fund, established in 2001, which helps families in need. Our congregation also created a mission statement firmly stating our existence as an urban church and the commitment this entails. As a congregation, we have supported city public school levies, hosted homeless families, funded peace education camps, and marched in support of antigun violence initiatives. And Andrew Carter, one of W.H.G. Carter's two living sons, joined the congregation. These, too, are the benefits of reconciliation.

There has been much healing, more positive relationship, and forgiveness than I had ever hoped. Indeed, during the 2009 Carter service, Leslie Edwards told us we could stop apologizing. Nonetheless, the wound that will not heal is still there and accompanies us to every social justice venture in our city. We take one step at a time and live one day at a time in an unknown land of hope and pain, where transformation is possible.

—Sharon Dittmar

THE FIRST

I found Unitarian Universalism at age fourteen, when my mother dragged me, almost kicking and screaming, into First Unitarian Church in Cincinnati, Ohio. I found there a community that welcomed all of me, where I did not have to check any part of myself at the door. The welcome I experienced, the sense of finding "home" was real, and I've heard so many other Unitarian Universalists say the same thing about finding our faith.

But what Unitarian Universalism did I find, and find so welcoming? It is my observation that each Unitarian Universalist congregation believes it is unique, one of a kind. That, in the view of every student of religion who has studied our faith, is simply not accurate. Unitarian Universalist congregations share more similarities than most of us acknowledge. We prefer to dwell on the differences. Many Unitarian Universalists from small fellowships find worship at one of our largest churches somewhat foreign. A visit to King's Chapel, with its Episcopalian liturgy, leaves many Unitarian Universalists scratching their heads. Is that Unitarian Universalism? For them, the answer is no, at least it's not the Unitarian Universalism that feeds their spirit, nor the Unitarian Universalism they know in their home church.

What Unitarian Universalism did I find at age fourteen? My sample of experience was modest, to say the least. I'd been unable to wrap my head around the liturgical mysteries of transubstantiation and the triune God taught in Episcopal church school, nor could I believe in the hellfire preached from the Southern Baptist pulpit. Based on those experiences, I had decided that Christianity was not for me. I proclaimed a "stand up" atheism. I had no need of God and thought that people who did were either weak or unenlightened, unlike myself.

I was accustomed to proclaiming those beliefs and, frankly, enjoying the reaction of adults as they squirmed between discomfort and outrage. At fourteen, I had far more answers than questions.

But when I made my proclamations with adults in the coffee hour after the service and in the youth group meeting that first night, the reaction was one of interest rather than shock. This was a Unitarian congregation in 1960, one year before merger with the Universalists. The long and strong history of reason in religion tempered the response I got. Humanism was without a doubt the dominant theological stance of the adults. My point of view seemed well within the bounds of acceptability. And the adults and my high school peers in the youth group wanted to discuss my views—and their own.

So far so good. I felt at home theologically, but Rev. Bill Jones cautions that we should do our sociology before we do too much theology.

When I entered the doors of that church, I found an integrated congregation. Primarily as a result of prominent witness for desegregation and racial justice in Cincinnati, blacks had joined the church. I don't know whether the congregation was 10 percent, 15 percent, or 20 percent black, but dark faces were clearly present.

It seemed that as soon as Mother and I crossed the threshold, we were introduced to the director of religious education, Pauline Warfield Lewis, an African-American woman of about my mother's age. When I read the history of the Liberal Religious Educators Association (LREDA) recently, I was surprised and pleased to see a picture of Mrs. Lewis at one of the first LREDA conferences. Hers was the only dark face in the crowd.

I went to the youth group that first Sunday evening and found that of the ten or so young people in the group, four were African American. This church was clearly a place where it was acceptable to be black in the company of whites. When I say I found my religious home that day, the presence of that easy, unforced, natural-seeming diversity was a huge element. For persons of color who check out a Unitarian Universalist church where there are no dark faces or very few, the decision to come again, let alone to stay, must be far more difficult. How can you be at home when everyone else in the room is white? Are you willing to sign up to be a token? That one of the religious professionals at the church was a person of color said volumes.

My experience in Liberal Religious Youth (LRY), the name for the UU youth ministry at the time, was similar. There were always other dark faces, especially in leadership. When I was elected continental LRY president (my first Unitarian Universalist Association presidency), the executive committee of seven also included two other African Americans (Toni Reed of St. Paul, Minnesota, who was treasurer, and Cappy Pinderhughes of Boston, who was social action chair). The previous executive committee had included a Native American woman as vice president.

I, and we, assumed that Unitarian Universalism was naturally diverse, normatively diverse racially. The way First Church Cincinnati looked, the way my executive committee looked, was what our faith was supposed to look like. The Unitarian Universalism that I embraced was theologically open and racially inclusive. That is the Unitarian Universalism where I found home.

The desire for greater racial and cultural diversity in Unitarian Universalism always bumps up against a Catch-22. The lack of diversity is the greatest obstacle to creating more diversity.

The racial diversity that I found in Cincinnati and my experience in LRY paved the way for me to consider the ministry as a young man. But it was a shock to discover that most UU congregations did not look like my home church. There were few people of color in the pews. I advised two youth groups in the Boston area after college in which every young person was white. More stressing and distressing still was learning that there were virtually no UU ministers of color. I experienced what I can only describe as a crisis of faith. Could this very white faith really be my spiritual home?

What is called the black empowerment controversy of the late 1960s and early 1970s and its aftermath sent me over the edge. The divisiveness of the controversy, the ultimate withdrawal of support for black Unitarian Universalists and black economic development and the general retreat from engagement with racial justice all led to a sense of betrayal that I could not bear.

I left the faith where I had found a religious home and did not enter one of our churches for more than a dozen years. I didn't join another church or even attend one. I still identified myself as a Unitarian Universalist theologically, but the sociology of this faith and its actions forced me away. I left Unitarian Universalism to wander in the spiritual wilderness.

After working in the corporate world, I started my own housing development and rehabilitation business in 1979, and now with a young family, moved that business back to Cincinnati when my mother became ill. It was her death in 1984 that helped me return to Unitarian Universalism. A few days after her death, an old friend from my home church showed up on my doorstep with a truly bad casserole and stories of my mother that allowed me to begin grieving.

I didn't know, when I opened the door, that her caring and perfectly ordinary action would transform my life. First Church Cincinnati, where I had found Unitarian Universalism as an adolescent, wanted me to come back. "We want to be your church," the woman said. It was enough to allow me to begin reclaiming my faith.

Within a year, I became one of those lay leaders who serves on every committee, volunteers for every work project, and never misses worship. I yearned so much for what I had known, for the home I had found and then lost. The church became the center of my life and that of my family.

Six years later, trying to figure out what was next for me after my business failed, the interim minister at the church asked me a simple question: "Have you ever considered the ministry?" I knew immediately that I had just heard my call to ministry.

Not every call to ministry is answered, of course. I had not forgotten my previous experiences with Unitarian Universalism outside of my home church. Thankfully, by then there were a small number of ministers of color and an organization called the African-American Unitarian Universalist Ministry (AAUUM). I attended my first meeting in 1991, before I applied to seminary. I recall little of the content now, but I remember vividly being in the presence of other persons of color who were UU ministers and seminarians. All ten of them told the stories of their struggles with Unitarian Universalism honestly, just as I did. But they had found the strength to stay. If they could, I could. AAUUM became a critical part of my support system as I moved toward and into ministry.

Studying at Starr King School for the Ministry followed, then serving on the Unitarian Universalist Association (UUA) staff. In 1998, lay and ordained leaders began asking me if I had ever considered running for the UUA presidency. I brushed their questions off. I'd come late in life to the ministry. I'd never served a church. And I was African American. But they were persistent, and I eventually heard a calling to the ministry as president.

When I was elected UUA president in 2001, there was considerable national attention. Within hours, I was on the phone with Gus Neibuhr, the religion reporter for the *New York Times*, and a host of other interviews followed. My picture was at the top of the front page of the *Boston Globe* the next day, on the second page of the *New York Times*, and dozens of other papers picked up the story. "First African American to lead a traditionally white denomination," read the headline; "black pastor, white flock," declared the sound bite.

Such attention can be heady, and I must confess that I enjoyed the attention and the opportunity it provided. It was a chance to begin raising the profile of Unitarian Universalism in the public square, the central promise I had made in my campaign for the presidency. For the press, my election offered a ray of hope that our nation might finally be making some progress in overcoming the legacy of slavery and racism so deeply embedded in our national character, a sign that progress on racism could be and was being made.

Among Unitarian Universalists, there was a palpable feeling that our faith had accomplished something. I believe that we longed for a sense of hope about "putting racism behind us," just as the national culture did and still does. There was and continues to be a genuine sense of unfinished business about race that most progressive communities share.

Unitarian Universalists like to see ourselves as working on the cutting edge of justice making. We point to our early commitment to civil rights, to women's rights, the reality that more than half of our ministers are now women, and our advocacy for the BGLT community with pride. We forget that coming to consensus about each of those issues was a long, difficult struggle. Perhaps it is most accurate to say that Unitarian Universalism has been precocious, an "early adopter" of progressive positions. As one reporter commented, we have a history of being proven right on issue after issue. My being "the first" appealed to our faith's collective vanity.

In those early days, as press attention continued, and indeed throughout my eight-year service, I knew that I was walking through a minefield. Unitarian Universalists, and many others, expected me to offer answers to racism, to point a confident way forward toward the Beloved Community. "How can we attract more people of color to our congregation?" was the most frequent question I received as I traveled for the association.

I knew how complicated and difficult race and my racial identity had been for me to deal with. I'm light skinned with what, when I was growing up, was called "good hair" (wavy, not kinky). There is no doubt that as much or more "white" blood flows in my veins than "black." Without a suntan, I could pass as white in many places.

I lived all of my young life and have lived most of my adult life in African-American communities, but although I lived in the 'hood, I was never of the 'hood. Since high school most, but not all, of my friends have been white, and I've worked in white environments. Although I certainly have scars from the effects of racism, as does every person of color in this country, I have probably benefited more than been penalized for being an African American, thanks to affirmative action.

The idea that I could speak for all people of color is laughable, and I knew it. The request, by whites, for me to tell them how to end racism falls in that same category. If racism could be ended based on advice from people of color, we would have been living in the Beloved Community for generations.

I managed the minefield of expectations by turning the questions back on the questioners. I reminded them that the goal of acquiring a few more dark faces so that white Unitarian Universalists would feel better about themselves is not a spiritually grounded approach. I suggested that they reflect on where they have chosen to live, where their churches are located, who their friends are, and who is invited to their dining room table before lamenting the absence of people of color in their congregations. I called my white co-religionists to engage once again with race as one of the most important pieces of unfinished business in our faith and in our nation.

I did, and do, have things to say about race to the white community. But long before I was elected president, I realized that I could not make race the focal point of my campaign. The danger was that I would be considered a one-issue candidate without the breadth of concern for our faith that Unitarian Universalists want and deserve in a president. I didn't avoid talking about race, people wouldn't allow that, but I talked first about increasing our public visibility and voice, about growing our faith, about youth and young-adult ministry. Addressing race and racism took a back seat to these other issues on the campaign stump.

Politically, I didn't think I could win with race as the first plank of my platform. Did this mean that I campaigned with tongue in cheek, editing my self-presentation in the quest for victory? I hope not. I was and remain passionate about public witness, growth, and youth ministry, as well as race. I have broad and deep concern for Unitarian Universalism and strongly held opinions about what we need to pay attention to.

To put it another way, I think my identity as a Unitarian Universalist is as important to me as my identity as a black man. The two are not equivalent, of course. I don't have a choice about my race. To try to deny who I am racially would be to cut myself off from my roots, to live in a fantasy of self-creation and disconnection. That was never an option for me, whatever convenience and ease it might have brought.

Unitarian Universalism is, for me, a chosen faith. But my choosing happened early, and somehow our open and welcoming theology took hold of my heart. That identity stayed with me even when I had to leave, and it made my return so much sweeter.

The most accurate statement is that I am both a black man and a Unitarian Universalist. Often those two identities coexist comfortably, but not always.

The UUA president's office on Beacon Hill is lovely, spacious, and has a gorgeous view of Boston Common. The building sits right next to the Massachusetts State House, a location we used to good advantage in our advocacy for marriage equality. The Beacon Hill location fit Unitarian Universalism when its presidents and its members were Boston Brahmins, members of the elite. It is still one of the whitest and most privileged neighborhoods in America. I always felt just a bit like I was entering foreign territory when I walked up to Beacon Hill.

I was able to do a few things to ease the fit. I removed most of the pictures of "dead white guys" from the entryway and grand staircase, replacing them with photographs of living Unitarian Universalists that reflect the reality of our present diversity. The pictures changed in my office as well. I hung a Haitian oil painting behind my desk and an American primitive painting of a church with black, red, and white worshipers (given to me by the Mid-South District) over the mantel.

Print and web images of Unitarian Universalism always tried to present racial diversity while I served as president. All of these efforts were aspirational. I thought it was important to present the Unitarian Universalism we wanted to see both to ourselves and to the outside world. It was certainly preferable to presenting our faith as it had been a century ago.

I had assumed, when I was elected, that racial justice would be the central public witness issue during my tenure. How wrong I was. Three months in, the 9/11 attacks took place and crowded all else to the background. Our churches, which like all places of worship were filled with people looking for solace and support, needed pastoral care. I did manage to highlight how race and culture played into our collective reaction as Arab-looking people eclipsed even African Americans as people to be feared. I'm proud of our support for the Muslim and Sikh communities during that period. The war in Afghanistan and the run-up to the Iraq occupation that followed demanded attention next.

But it was the decision by the Supreme Judicial Court of Massachusetts to mandate legal civil marriage for gay and lesbian couples in 2003 that dictated the shape and focus of Unitarian Universalist public witness during my presidency. Marriage equality became the issue with which I was most closely associated.

I want to be clear that my support for marriage equality has always been heartfelt. Support for BGLT rights runs deep in our faith, no less for me than for others. But it is ironic that it was marriage equality, not racial justice, that got my picture in *People* magazine (officiating at one of the first legal same-sex marriages in the United States) and got me named one of the ten most influential African-American religious leaders in the United States three years running.

Serving as UUA president had personal costs for me, among them a change in my relationship to most of my colleagues of color. When I showed up for gatherings of Unitarian Universalists of color, I had to show up as the UUA president, not just as another person of color. The community of color in our faith deserved to have a president, not just a friend. Even with good friends there was a change.

Some of the most difficult work I did as president involved reframing and reshaping the association's work on race. After commitments by the General Assembly, in 1992 and 1997, to the creation of an antiracist, multicultural Unitarian Universalism, we had become stuck. The training and educational resources offered were controversial, the analysis seen as fundamentalist and theologically inappropriate for our liberal religious faith. Something had to change to open the hearts and minds of our people. Too many had shut down around issues of race.

I made difficult personnel decisions, helped imagine a new and more flexible consultancy approach, and reorganized the staff to spread responsibility for this work more broadly. I paid a price for those changes. The UU leaders most committed to the initial approaches, almost all of them good friends, felt that I was retreating from our commitments. They felt that I was betraying a trust. I was called names that still cause me pain. Interestingly, it was the group of white allies who were most disappointed, most angry, and most vocal. The community of color was either willing to try a new way or at least give me the benefit of the doubt.

Looking back, I understand that the anger was in direct proportion to the hope that my election had created. The voices of disappointment and anger had expected me to use the bully pulpit of the presidency to demand that our faith fall in line with the initial program. They acknowledged the resistance but expected me to push through it to a brighter day.

The changes worked, however. More congregations were willing to engage, and the new approaches proved their value over time. It is far too soon to assess the long-term impact, but at least I helped create an opening through which the discernment could begin again. With conversations about race still rife with political correctness and the white community fearful of challenging the leadership of persons of color, perhaps only an African-American UUA president could have made such changes and survived to tell the tale.

What was accomplished by my election and service as president? Did my time prove, once and for all, that Unitarian Universalism can be a welcoming home to African Americans and other persons of color? The stories in this book prove that African Americans have always been drawn to this faith, but also what a struggle it has been for them to find acceptance. Was my election the fulfillment of our promise? Was it a productive step on a long and complicated journey? Time will tell.

I remember interviewing for my job on the UUA staff in 1994, when considering a position as director of district services, a position that would make me the first African American on the association's executive staff. I was greeted at 25 Beacon Street by candy and flowers in a beautiful basket from the African-American staff. It was an expression of their joy that a person of color might be in senior leadership and hope for what I might be able to do.

At one point during my interview, Kay Montgomery, the executive vice president, commented that my service would change things at the association. "What things do you expect will change?" I asked. "I don't know. I just know that things will change somehow."

My service was certainly not the fulfillment of a promise. Unitarian Universalism did not magically change as the result of having a black man in the president's office. The acceptance of me as president has not made it simple for people of color in our faith. The reality is that "the first" only has meaning if it is followed by a second and a third and . . .

Unitarian Universalism has chosen the first Hispanic president to follow me. I hope that my service will be a foundation on which he can build.

Perhaps the helpful question is whether I think it's easier, more comfortable, more welcoming for African Americans and people of color generally in our congregations now than it was, say, when I entered the ministry in the early 1990s. That is a span of twenty years, enough time for cultural shifts to be visible. Is change taking place or are we stuck?

Some things are clear. Unitarian Universalist church schools, thanks to transracial adoptions and blended families, have come to look a great deal more like our multicultural world than do our pews.

There is a discernible, though not dramatic, increase in the number of dark faces in our pews in many of our congregations. All Souls Unitarian Church in Tulsa, Oklahoma, has welcomed members of the mostly black New Dimensions evangelical church into its membership, creating in a year what is one of the most thoroughly integrated UU congregation in the United States. Other congregations, like First Parish in Concord, Massachusetts, have found ways to be in relationship and helpful to poor and person-of-color communities near them. More congregations are taking advantage of educational and training opportunities around race, culture, and class.

The measure of progress that is closest to my heart is the growing number of UU religious professionals of color. In 1993, there were seven ministers of color, Latina/o, Hispanic, or Asian-American, serving our congregations. By 2001, when I was elected, there were seventeen. Today, there are forty ministers of color serving our congregations and another fifteen serving in community ministries and on the UUA staff. There are more than forty seminarians of color currently preparing for our ministry. We should be pleased with this trajectory. At least the numbers are going in the right direction.

People of color continue to be called to our ministry. Our theology draws them in, as it did me. I had what often seemed a full-time job of speaking at the ordinations and installations of ministers of color during my last years as UUA president. The presence of these persons in our faith is perhaps the most hopeful sign on our collective horizon.

The good news is that these ministers are finding settlements. The bad news is that those settlements tend to be dramatically shorter than those of white ministers and more often end in negotiated resignations. Cultural differences and differing expectations too often overwhelm the goodwill of our congregations and their leaders.

One of the most important initiatives of my second term was the creation of the Diversity of Ministry Initiative, which is designed to work with congregations expressing an interest in settling a minister of color. The task is to prepare them to deal in a direct way with race and culture so that the conversations don't go underground and undermine the ministry.

In my last General Assembly, which was filled with thanks and honors for my service as president, I was joined on the stage by some fifty ministers, seminarians, and other religious professionals of color. I could not, and I doubt that anyone else could have imagined such a hopeful reality twenty years ago.

There are, indeed, signs of progress, or at least signs of change. But we are still far from a tipping point in terms of the racial and cultural profile of our faith. Though it may not be helpful, it is still accurate to describe Unitarian Universalism as a predominantly white faith. We can predict that, when and if we reach that tipping point, resistance to the changes will be strong. Don't forget the fear of "feminization" of our ministry as women ministers became more common.

The capstone of my service as UUA president was a three-week trip to Africa in November 2008. There were many high points but right at the top was meeting African Unitarian Universalists in Uganda, Kenya, and Nigeria. I saw our faith practiced by congregations made up of Africans, worshiping in African languages, with music in their rhythms from their own instruments. I saw the same thing in the Khasi Hills of India. I know, because I've experienced it, that the Unitarian Universalist message can minister to a diversity of experience we can only imagine here in the United States.

I hope and pray that our faith can someday fulfill the promise of its theology. That possibility is an article of faith for me. Our theology is open-hearted enough to embrace a future in which our congregations look more like our multicultural world. The open question is whether, as a broad faith community, we will recognize the challenge and the opportunity, whether we will work to make it happen. Hope alone will fail.

—William Sinkford

AFTERWORD

February 2008. I am on the Unitarian Universalist Living Legacy Civil Rights Pilgrimage bus tour. We are a diverse group in an early twenty-first-century Unitarian Universalist way: more seniors than young adults, female and male ministers split about evenly, four families, about a quarter of us identified as lesbian, gay, bisexual, or transgender, another quarter as people of color, one Latina, and one Canadian. The tour also includes Rev. Bill Sinkford, the first African-American president of the Unitarian Universalist Association (UUA).

On day five, we reach Selma, Alabama, the epicenter of events that reshaped American history. I have never been to Selma before; indeed, I have never been in the Deep South. Standing on the curb in front of Brown Chapel, ready to tour the simple red brick row houses that surround it, I imagine what it was like back then. Clusters of people. Black folks taking in their comrades in arms, providing places to sleep, food to eat, and thanks. I imagine how out of the ordinary it was for all of them, black and white, to live and link arms together, to form lines and find in one another the courage to meet phalanxes of police with prayer and song.

I am waiting and musing when a distant low rumble wafts toward me. I turn. Looking down Martin Luther King Jr. Street, I see a few motorcycles. But the rumble grows as more motorcycles come into view. And more. And more. The rumble becomes a roar. Now I can distinguish the three leaders. They are police officers—two white and one black. For an entire block, the street is filled with motorcycles. The roar is deafening. They cruise up to the chapel, cut their engines, and dismount. What bikes! BMW Roadmasters. Honda Gold Wings. Harley-Davidsons. The black-leather-clad riders head into Brown Chapel, and as they walk past, I see the insignia on the back of their leather jackets: "Buffalo Soldiers." Over two hundred of them from across America, all of them black and, like us, come to pay homage.

In March 1965, no one who lived in Selma and no one who went to Selma could have envisioned this. Those protesters thought it was about gaining the right to vote. It was that, and much more. March 1965 was a continuation of the American Revolution and the precursor to an economic and a political revolution that led to an African American becoming president of the United States of America. King delivered many a biblical turn of phrase that held up a vision of freedom and justice. But it was impossible to imagine that would look like this.

Nor could Unitarian Universalists have known that Selma would become a pivotal moment in their history. Many times, they had stood at a moment that could have made a difference and shunned the opportunity. But not this time. Called, sent, drawn, compelled, hundreds came. They left with two UU martyrs in their hearts and conviction in their stride.

It is neither possible nor necessary to know the outcome of our actions. We are not called to succeed; we are called to try. Called because it is right. Conscience urging us on because we yearn to live out our values. Responding because we have dreamed of a better, more just tomorrow; we are sustained by love and by hope. We care; therefore, we act. In acting, we risk having our hearts broken a thousand times. That is the price our African-American religious forebears accepted; it is what living fully, deeply, and with integrity requires.

The second half of the second verse of "Lift Every Voice and Sing," the African-American national anthem, begins, "We have come over a way that with tears has been watered." That is what Unitarian Universalists are about today—following the way marked out by the black trailblazers who brought us thus far on our way. From the beginning it was a long, slow and treacherous way. The Unitarians who heard William Jackson testify to his conversion to Unitarianism at the 1860 AUA meeting in New Bedford would have all been familiar with William Ellery Channing's essay "Emancipation." In 1840 the progenitor of American Unitarianism wrote, "I should expect from the African race, if civilized, less energy, less courage, less intellectual originality than in our race. . . . There is no reason for holding such a race in chains: they need no chains to make them harmless."[1] Despite his depth of thought and moral integrity, in regard to race, it seems the best Channing could do was mimic the sentiment of his age. It is no wonder that Jackson was spurned. Racism is, indeed, inveterate. Similarly in 1939, one hundred years later, when Universalist John van Schaick wrote, "marriages of white and colored people are unwise, and that it is no lowering of Christian ideals to say so," he too was echoing the prejudice of his era.[2] Our faith, which has been denouncing racism since the 1940s, is now seeking a way to become as diverse as we, at long last, aspire to be. It is a yearning we feel but do not understand much less know how to attain. Given such a history, how could we?

After eight days in the South, I return home to one of the most diverse cities in the world. My little pocket of Toronto is called Korea Town. Nonetheless, I step out the front door of our condo, look west across Christie Pits Park, and above the tree line, spy the domed spires of the Holy Protection Mother of God Ukrainian Catholic Church. Walk north, and the first church I pass is the Korean Beacon Church. Keep going and there is a Jehovah's Witness Kingdom Hall with Portuguese language services. A little further north and west, I pass the Metropolitan Korean Church and then St. Paul's Slovak Evangelical Lutheran.

For many living in an urban environment, this pattern is familiar. You may come across a Filipino Baptist or African Methodist Episcopal church, a Catholic church with services in Spanish, or a Buddhist temple, a mosque, or a synagogue. In the North, as in the South, we still manage to segregate ourselves when it comes to religion.

Where do Unitarian Universalist congregations fit in this ethnic mix? The question leaves UUs flummoxed. We do not think of ourselves as an ethnic religion. The numbers, however, say that we are: our race (91.5 percent Euro-American),[3] our education (17.2 years on average), our language (Inglés por favor), our style of worship (no amen corner here), our Principles (seven of them, and not a word about Jesus), and our social norms (many of ours are Welcoming Congregations). Who we are reflects our Yankee heritage and upper-middle class, progressive, NPR, North American values.

Our brother and sister Unitarians in Transylvania find queries about their ethnic identity perplexing. An ethnic church? Of course, they are ethnic—Hungarian Unitarians. Preserving their language, culture, and faith is their *raison d'être*. There is a tribal element even in the most universal of faiths, and institutional religion is always a marriage of religion with culture. The Transylvanian Unitarians know this. American Unitarian Universalists choose denial.

In 1967, the UUA "Report of the Committee on Goals" found that in regard to "Negro" ministers, 27 percent of Unitarian Universalists agreed that such a person's "race might hamper his effectiveness."[4] The percentage that said the same about women was 47. What happened in the ensuing years? The number of women grew from about 21 in 1968 to 199 in 1987, and in 2010, women make up over half of our active ministry. "Might hamper her effectiveness"? Apparently not. Meanwhile, how many African Americans were there? Five in 1948, around eight in 1967, an increase to seventeen by 1987, and currently around thirty.

In a 1989 UUA Commission on Appraisal (COA) survey, Unitarian Universalists made a similarly lopsided prediction about whether being openly lesbian, gay, or bisexual would hamper one's ministry. Twenty-six percent still said being an African American would hinder one's ministry, but a whopping 66 percent said so about LGB ministers. What happened? Today, there are over seventy LGBTQ ministers. Take note: It was thirty years ago, during the late 1970s, that the first openly gay and lesbian ministers were fellowshipped and, not without difficulty, settled. The first African American, Rev. Joseph Jordan, was ordained by the Universalists in 1889, 121 years ago. We guessed wrong again, and so profound is UU cultural chauvinism that in neither 1967 nor 1989 did surveyors think to ask about Hispanic ministers.[5]

Culture prevails. The UUA would be different today had the AUA welcomed Rev. William Jackson into the Unitarian fold in 1860, or William H. G. Carter in 1938, or if the Universalist mission church in Suffolk, Virginia, had survived Joseph F. Jordan's death in 1929. As Bill Sinkford observes, "lack of diversity is the greatest obstacle to creating more diversity." Diversity in the Unitarian Universalist context progresses more quickly when the primary barrier to inclusivity is not culture but gender or sexual orientation. And history, from Frances Ellen Watkins Harper to Sinkford, shows that the people of color who became Universalist or Unitarian, and more recently, Unitarian Universalist, have always been those who operated within our white liberal cultural norms. It bears repeating: Although we are no longer upper- and middle-class Anglo-Saxons from New England, we are still an ethnic-like faith.

The difficulty, and why Unitarian Universalists keep guessing wrong, is that who we are conflicts with who we aspire to be. In the same 1989 COA survey, "embracing diversity" ranked very high as a necessary characteristic of a "vital congregation." Indeed, whenever diversity is advanced we salute; it is apostasy to do otherwise. In 2007, Sinkford wrote in the *UU World* that he hears among Unitarian Universalists "a deep sense of failure" and that "to sing 'We Shall Overcome' felt like a lie" to him. Why? Because we aren't as diverse as many wish. Therefore, he went on to announce, "the UUA Diversity of Ministry team . . . has outlined a plan for welcoming the forty-two seminarians preparing for our ministry who are persons of color and Latino/Latina/Hispanic people."[6]

What is it we aspire to be? Wouldn't it be great if, in our congregations, a large population of people used American Sign Language? Of course, but that is not what we mean when we say diverse. Wouldn't it be great if we attracted even a handful of individuals who are developmentally challenged? Of course, but that is not what we mean when we say *diverse*. Suppose ours were a faith to which working-class people came in droves. That would be something to celebrate, but it is not what we mean either. And we all know it doesn't mean religious diversity; the goddess knows we have enough of that. The word *diversity* is UU code for "persons of color and Latino/Latina/Hispanic people," which seems to be the current politically correct mouthful. Why do we say *diversity*? It saves time. If we had to list everyone—Asians and South Asians, Native Americans and Inuits, Filipinos and Pacific Islanders, Latino/Latina/Hispanic peoples and, of course, members of the African diaspora, and whomever else I have missed—we would not finish the sentence until tomorrow.

This attention to naming looms large, and the awkwardness of the nomenclature reflects an awkward relationship. People want to have their cultural identities recognized and respected in a way they have not been. So in a denomination that, first and foremost, "respects the inherent worth and dignity of every person," we try. We are awkward, in part, because we are afraid of offending. That fear makes us cautious, and being cautious, whether looking for offense or fearful of offending, makes for stilted conversations and hesitant relationships. The voice in the back of one's mind whispers, "It'll be over soon," while we scan ahead for cultural land mines.

We alternate between tiptoeing and stumbling along. Who we are isn't who we want to be, and the way we are going about addressing this challenge isn't working as fast as we wish. We know it when we look around the room at UU gatherings and notice the lack of racial and cultural diversity. The reality that we do not reflect the world in which we live calls our liberality into question. Many, feeling a vague sense of discomfort, worry and ask, "Why, when we have such good intentions, can't we change?" A growing number, not seeing their multicultural families reflected, are frustrated. Others, not seeing people like themselves, ache.

The numbers, not our hopes, wishes, or impatience, indicate change. The number of female and LGBTQ ministers has moved toward reflecting their percentage in our UU population. The same is true of ministers of color. Adding the handful of other ministers of color to the African-American ministers, it looks like this: Over the past seventy years, the number of ministers of color serving congregations grew from five to eight to twenty-one to sixty; in other words, it about doubled every fifteen years. This increase happened throughout the 1940s and 1950s, when it was nearly impossible to settle an African American; in the 1960s when we marched in Selma and then scrambled to respond to black power; during the retrenchment of the 1970s; finding our feet again in the 1980s; or in the middle of the current antiracism, anti-oppression, multicultural effort. This suggests that the determining factor is not our indifference, our efforts, or our fretting. In fact, it may have little to do with the UUA.

The characteristics of African Americans who have been drawn to liberal religion become obvious after reading the essays in this collection. From Joseph F. Jordan to Yvonne Seon, they were and are independent-minded religious seekers, or they would not have chosen to be Unitarian Universalists. From Fannie Barrier Williams to Lewis A. McGee, they are refugees from other faith traditions and practiced at living in both white and black worlds. From William H. G. Carter to David Eaton, they are progressive, socially concerned, and engaged individuals who differ from other Unitarian Universalists in having inherited, via black suffering, a deeply ingrained understanding that salvation is a collective reality in which we leave no one behind. All of them dedicated themselves to the good of the black community but not always to its social and theological dictates. And from Don Speed Smith Goodloe to Annie B. Willis, they have been individuals who placed education, their own and others, before all else. Religious liberals they were, but earlier generations of Euro-American Unitarians and Universalists were blind to this for one reason—their color.

These black trailblazers were all educated, and that is the quality one can most easily track. Repeatedly, surveys tell us that education is an indicator that correlates strongly with being Unitarian Universalist. This is not to conflate an inquiring approach to life with education, but the one can be measured, the other not. The average academic level attained among UUs is 17.2 years, close to what it takes to earn a master's degree. In 1940, 1 percent of the African-American population over twenty-five held a BA degree; by 2000, that had increased to 16.6 percent. In 1940, there were two Unitarian African-American ministers, Jeffrey Campbell and Ethelred Brown; by 2000, that two had increased to twenty-six.

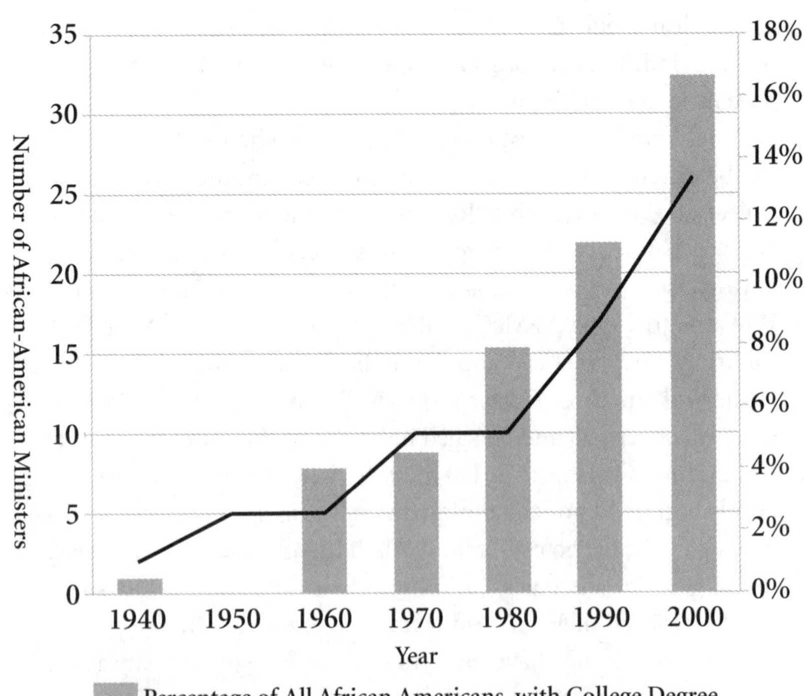

If we plot the increase in African Americans with BA degrees alongside the increase in the number of African-American UU ministers, the percentage increase in the number of ministers lags slightly behind the percentage of African Americans holding a BA. Not surprisingly, after the UUA's engagement with civil rights and Black Power there was a jump in 1970 that flattened out afterward (see graph).

The overall trend seems to apply to other people of color and Latino/Latina and Hispanic UUs. The first Latino minister, John Burciaga, was fellowshipped in 1965; the first Latina, Patricia Jimenez, in 1994. There are now about fifteen Hispanic ministers, including the current president of the UUA, Peter Morales. This represents a doubling every 11.5 years. Speaking on a panel in 1998, Jimenez said, "Take for example the three of us [Latinas/os on the panel]. All three of us come from other faith traditions; we all three have graduate degrees; and we are all professionals. We fit the profile of a lot of UUs. In addition, we all speak English. What I do suggest is that here among the educated, professional, and bilingual Latinas and Latinos is a good place to start."[8]

Anecdotally, quantitatively, historically, and demographically, the story is the same. What happened? Over the past seventy years, the make-up of the group our congregations draw from has changed. With the growth of the African-American and Hispanic middle classes; the substantial increase in the number of people of color graduating from college; the growth in the number of mixed marriages, and the children of those marriages—a group that is overwhelmingly middle class—we changed. Why? Because we are an ethnic-like faith community, and these individuals fit into a Unitarian Universalist culture whose values, regarding race and ethnicity, have changed. The growth has been incremental, but the numbers indicate it will continue regardless of what we Unitarian Universalists do or don't do. Rather than leading, we are mirroring a changing, evolving society.

In the 1989 COA survey, not only did embracing diversity rank as the third highest factor in being a vital congregation, but it also ranked second lowest in being met. Twenty years later, Bill Sinkford was still hearing that we feel "a deep sense of failure" in this regard.

Why the fretting? Unitarian Universalists have a self-image problem. In 1967, our self-image was that of civil rights activists, which led us to say that it would be more difficult to be a female minister than an African-American one. In 2010, we think of ourselves as open, tolerant, justice-seeking, feminist, gay-affirming, eco-sensitive liberals attuned to a multicultural world; seduced by our "precocious" self-image, we make far-fetched predictions and set unattainable goals. Then, of course, we don't live up to one particular racially focused set of expectations, which were unrealistic from the beginning. This failure leaves us feeling deficient, so we flagellate ourselves because our efforts at racial diversity have not kept pace with our achievements vis-à-vis women and LGBTQ people.

This reaction is not really about social change or spiritual transformation or even diversity in its broadest sense; it is about self-esteem. We want to be different than we are because we want to feel better. We want to look around and be able to say, "Yes, this reflects the world I see around me," rather than feel ashamed that it does not. We want UU congregations to reflect the emerging multicultural, pluralistic society, and we want to think of ourselves as on the forefront of that transformation. But we cannot.

What are Unitarian Universalists to do about the situation in which we find ourselves vis-à-vis our lack of racial and cultural diversity?

First, lecturing, cajoling, and saying "shame on you" will not work. Pulling the race-card and kicking white Unitarian Universalists in the teeth by telling them what low-down racist honkies they are is not the answer. Neo-sinners? We have jettisoned the orthodox language but held on to the attitude, and that is not the way. Earnestness is sure to sabotage this endeavor, for as William Schulz warns, guilt always deals "cruelly with vision."[9] What kind of enthusiasm and commitment does one bring to the task one ought to do? A person cannot try something different and, at the same time, be too careful, because taking risk is how we learn. Trepidation only encourages timidity—lighten up and laugh at the mistakes. Afterward we can apologize for the gaffes and forgive the inevitable blunders. The sort of transformation we are seeking cannot be rooted in "I should" but will only grow out of what we want and yearn for.

Second, as we move on, we need to be honest with ourselves about who we are, why we want to be different than that, and what is possible. Who are we? Bound by class and culture, Unitarian Universalism is an ethnic-like faith, and that defines who we can, at this moment, successfully attract. Why do we want to be different? Frankly, so we can feel better about ourselves, and the people of color and Latinas/os among us can feel more at home. What is possible? Let us be realistic and stop setting ourselves up for frustration and failure by creating expectations we cannot meet. What do we need to remember? To apply Unitarian Universalism's first Principle, "the inherent worth and dignity of every person," to ourselves as well as others. We are lovable even when we fail. We need to forgive ourselves, over and over again.

Third, if we want to be diverse, we must appreciate the diversity we have achieved. Find that diversity; it is there. Then treasure the complex and unique identities that are already represented among us. Who we are is worth celebrating, and the more we celebrate, the more inviting a place we will become, because praise, joy, and affirmation will serve us better than blame, guilt, and earnestness.

Finally, accept that we are caught in a paradox and that there is a perversity to our call for more diversity. We do not want change. Having found a comfortable religious home—no small challenge—we fear it might slip from our grasp. While it is important to be a justice-seeking and openly tolerant community, we also yearn for stability, familiarity, and people like "us," companions we can trust. We want a religious home where we can come when facing life transitions and personal challenges, seeking solace from the emotional wounds an unpredictable world lays upon us. If who we are now—the community that has nurtured us—were going to appeal to more people of color and Latina/Latino and Hispanic people, it would have happened. Indeed, we find it a challenge to attract people regardless of color or culture. Intellectually, we understand the need for change. Emotionally, however, we don't want change, at least not too much. Reluctant to voice this heresy, we say we want diversity. What we would actually prefer is a change of appearance rather than substance. We would settle for looking different rather than being different. But when you pursue diversity, you invite change, and you become something different than you were drawn to in the beginning. A paradox? Yes. A choice? No. There are only two options: change or die.

Now and then, someone dares to ask, "Why go through all this trouble to attract a few people of color?" Because it is not about bringing in people of different hues and cultures or about doing what seems morally correct. It is not about them. It is about healing ourselves and transforming Unitarian Universalism. This yearning is spiritually rooted in an intuition. It is a reality that Unitarian Universalism's seventh Principle points toward: "the interdependent web of all existence of which we are a part." We are deeply and inextricably connected to one another and all that ever was or shall be. We want one another. We yearn to feel connected—and whole. Each of us is a unique manifestation of the eternally unfolding creation, each a member of one human family, each entwined in the arms of the Divine Mystery that is both parent and partner, all of us sharing a common destiny. As we love, are loved, and act out of that love, we are proclaiming twenty-first-century Universalism with our lives.

If Unitarian Universalism stands for love, it is wed to freedom. Freedom invites vision. Vision leads to change. Change causes anxiety. Anxiety awakens resistance. Abolitionist Frances Ellen Watkins Harper sought freedom from bondage for blacks and suffrage for women. Mary and Joseph F. Jordan sought to free blacks from poverty through education. So too, Brown's black radicalism, Jones's black humanism, Eaton's activism, and Seon's spirituality are all about freedom—freedom for all and freedom for each, freedom to be and believe as one will.

Freedom begets vision. Vision leads to change. To embrace change means welcoming someone with an open mind and responding with interest to different behavior or beliefs rather than with a raised eyebrow, frozen smile, and silence. See that reaction for what it is—a sophisticated way of masking fear. Hold that fear at bay and let your heart lead the way. Change means discomfort, and because of that discomfort, some people will leave. They have in the past and will again. Let them go. For those who remain and commit, the discomfort becomes bearable when we recognize that it is for our benefit, that transformation is its result. Healing the systemically transmitted virus that is racism is nothing less than grace. Grace—the moment when we sense within ourselves that something broken has become whole—cannot emerge without freedom. Stasis and control are fear's bastion. Welcoming change means being open and adventuresome. It asks us to celebrate the breadth of theological and social diversity Unitarian Universalism already encompasses, and then to reach beyond it. It means recapturing the excitement we once felt about the new: the wonderment, the curiosity, the openness we knew as children before fear shut it down. It means seeing diversity as a gift we cannot wait to get our hands on. Change will come whether we work for and celebrate it, or distrust and resist it, or simply wait. Our history says it will come whether we want it or not. For that we can be thankful.

—Mark D. Morrison-Reed

CHRONOLOGY
1785–2001

1785 Gloster Dalton is one of eighty-five signatories of the Charter of Compact of the Gloucester Universalist Society.

1801 Amy Scott is one of the incorporators of the First Universalist Society organized in Philadelphia.

1830s Nathan Johnson, a prominent citizen of New Bedford, Massachusetts, and conductor on the Underground Railroad, becomes a member of New Bedford's Universalist church.

1845 Itinerant George Rogers reports meeting "a free colored man, who with his family are members of the Mt. Olympus" Alabama Universalist Society.

1860 Rev. William Jackson of New Bedford—who would later serve as chaplain of the Fifty-fourth Massachusetts Volunteer Infantry Regiment under Unitarian colonel Robert Gould Shaw and then the Fifty-fifth Regiment—announces his conversion to Unitarianism at the American Unitarian Association (AUA) autumnal convention. They "took up a collection and sent him on his way."

1868 Peter H. Clark—abolitionist, educator and politician—joins the First Unitarian Church of Cincinnati.

1868 William White, a white Unitarian, proposes to the AUA that it organize a "Unitarian Colored Church" in Washington DC. This is endorsed at a regional AUA meeting, but nothing materializes.

1869 William Henry Brown becomes the first of five African Methodist Episcopal and one African Methodist Episcopal Zion students to attend Meadville Theological School between 1869 and 1910.

1870 Frances Ellen Watkins Harper—abolitionist, writer, lecturer, and friend of Peter H. Clark—becomes a member of the First Unitarian Church of Philadelphia.

1887 Rev. Joseph Jordan starts a Universalist mission in Norfolk, Virginia.

1889 Joseph Jordan becomes the first African American to be ordained as a Universalist minister.

1893 Fannie Barrier Williams, a member of All Souls Church in Chicago, delivers "The Religious Mission of the Colored Race" at the World's Parliament of Religions.

1894 Rev. Henry Holmes of Henderson, Tennessee, is ordained as a Universalist minister.

1895 Hester C. Whitehurst Jeffrey—national organizer for the National Association of Colored Women's Clubs, suffragette, and friend of Susan B. Anthony—joins the First Unitarian Church of Rochester, New York.

1895 Rev. Thomas E. Wise is fellowshipped as a Universalist and assists Joseph Jordan in beginning a mission in Suffolk, Virginia.

1899 J. A. Murphy converts to Universalism and, with the help of Quillen Shinn, attempts and fails to establish a mission in Barstow, Georgia.

1904 Wise leaves the mission in Virginia and returns to the African Methodist Episcopal church.

1904 Rev. Joseph Fletcher Jordan and his wife, Mary J. Jordan, herself a graduate of Shaw University, take over the Suffolk mission after Joseph spent a year training at Canton Theological School.

1906 Don Speed Smith Goodloe enters Meadville Theological School in 1904 and graduates in 1906. Rather than pursue ministry, he returns to teaching and, in 1910, becomes the first principal of the Maryland Normal School No. 3, which would become Bowie State University. Goodloe's son Donald Goodloe later became a member of All Souls Church, Unitarian, in Washington DC.

1906 Clarence Bertrand Thompson receives fellowship with the American Unitarian Association (apparently without mentioning his race) and then goes on to serve for three years as minister of the Unitarian Church of Peabody, Massachusetts.

1907 Maria Louise Baldwin—educator, administrator, and lecturer—joins the Unitarian Church of the Disciples in Boston. In 1895, she helped organize a conference of representatives from African-American women's clubs that will lead to the founding of the National Association of Colored Women's Clubs (NACW) in 1896. Her partners in that effort were Florida Ruffin Ridley, an educator, journalist, and member of Second Unitarian Church in Brookline, Massachusetts, and Josephine St. Pierre Ruffin, Florida's mother, a charter member of the National Association for the Advancement of Colored People (NAACP).

1908 Lewis Latimer, a draftsman and inventor, is a founding member of the Flushing Unitarian Church in New York.

1909 John Haynes Holmes, minister of the Community Church of New York, participates in the Niagara Movement and, along with Unitarian Mary White Ovington, is one of the five founders of the NAACP. Holmes asked his African-American associates to integrate the church. Among these was Augustus Granville Dill, the business manager of the NAACP magazine *Crisis*.

1911 African Americans with Universalist sympathies in Rusk, Oklahoma, ask the state superintendent, C. H. Rogers, to help organize a church; acquiescing to white resistance, Rogers declines.

1912 Rev. Egbert Ethelred Brown, after two years at Meadville Theological School, returns to Jamaica and founds a church.

1913 Rev. C. W. Jones, licensed by the Universalist Convention, joins an effort in Norfolk, Virginia, to merge old congregations together. The effort failed.

1920 E. E. Brown moves from Kingston, Jamaica, to Harlem and founds the Harlem Community Church. Among its founding members were some of the most prominent socialists in Harlem: W. A. Domingo, Thomas B. Moore, Grace P. Campbell, Frank A. Crosswaith, and Thomas A. Potter.

1927 Errold D. Collymore integrates the White Plains Unitarian Church, New York, and later becomes chair of its board.

1927 Rev. Lewis Allen McGee, an African Methodist Episcopal minister, approaches Curtis Reese and is told, "If you want to be a Unitarian you'd better bring your own church."

1929 Joseph F. Jordan dies, and his daughter, Annie B. Willis, takes over the school.

1929 E. E. Brown is removed from fellowship by the American Unitarian Association (AUA).

1930 Rev. Harry V. Richardson is refused admission by the AUA. He will graduate from Harvard Divinity School in 1932, earn a doctorate from Drew University, and become cofounder and first president of the Interdenominational Theological Center in Atlanta.

1932 William H. G. Carter founds the Church of the Unitarian Brotherhood in Cincinnati. Local Unitarian ministers know of him but do not inform the AUA. Carter's sons Daniel and Andrew later become Unitarians, and a grandson, Leslie Edwards, will join Northern Hills Fellowship in 1993.

1935 Rev. Jeffery Worthington Campbell graduates from Canton Theological School, and the Universalists grant him fellowship.

1935 E. E. Brown is reinstated when the American Civil Liberties Union threatens to sue the AUA.

1938 Rev. Felix D. Lion comes across Brotherhood Church in Cincinnati and tells the AUA. AUA official Lon Ray Call visits, but neither Carter nor the congregation is welcomed.

1938 Jeffrey Campbell is fellowshipped as a Unitarian. Later he recalls that AUA president Frederick May Eliot would make excuses for not being able to settle him, every time the two met.

1939 Marguerite Campbell, Jeffrey's sister, marries Francis Davis. Their interracial marriage is attacked in the *Christian Leader*. Davis will never be settled but goes on to work for the Boston Urban League. Marguerite will spend thirty-three years working for the Universalist Church of America and the Unitarian Universalist Association.

1942 Alvin Neeley Cannon, while attending Meadville Lombard Theological School in Chicago, participates in a black and white cooperative in a racially restricted area. Subsequently, he graduates from Starr King School for the Ministry, in 1945.

1946 Cannon is recruited to explore the possibility of founding a "Negro Unitarian Church" in Des Moines, Iowa. The effort fails.

1946 Donna Sparrow, wife of Eugene Sparrow, works at the AUA while he attends Harvard Divinity School preparing for the Unitarian ministry.

1947 Lewis McGee is granted fellowship and with his wife, Marcella Walker McGee, helps found the interracial but predominantly African-American Free Religious Fellowship (FRF) in South Side Chicago.

1948 Rev. Maurice Dawkins is granted affiliated fellowship and becomes minister of education at the Community Church of New York. The AUA has five black ministers: three settled, one in a student pastorate, and one working as a teacher.

1948 Pauline McCoo joins the First Unitarian Society of Chicago, thus beginning its process of integration. The Unitarian Universalist Association (UUA) will later recognize her contribution by awarding her an Unsung Unitarian Universalist Award in 1999.

1949 Rev. Eugene Sparrow graduates from Harvard Divinity

School and receives fellowship, but seeing no job opportunities, takes a position as a college dean.

1950s Margaret Moseley, an activist and organizer, serves as president of the Community Church of Boston; she will later chair the Board of the Unitarian Church of Barnstable, Massachusetts.

1950 Margaret Young, the wife of Whitney Young Jr.—social worker, educator, administrator, and activist—joins the First Unitarian Church of Omaha. Whitney is active in the congregation and he later joins the Unitarian church in Atlanta and the UU church in White Plains, New York.

1950 Rev. Eugene Sparrow is refused the call to be assistant minister in Detroit.

1951 Jeffrey W. Campbell, after eleven years away, returns from England and becomes a teacher at the Putney School in Vermont.

1954 William Y. Bell Jr. is appointed director of adult education and social relations for the Council of Liberal Churches (Universalist-Unitarian).

1954 Maurice Dawkins is recruited for the FRF but goes to People's Independent Church of Los Angeles, one of the oldest and second-largest community churches in the United States.

1954 Rev. Benjamin Richardson is fellowshipped and settled at FRF.

1954 The AUA Commission on Intergroup Relations, which includes Rev. Howard Thurman and Errold Collymore, reports: "One-third of the congregations responded and of these 170 societies 52 had AA [African American] members and 13 had more than 5." The report recommends that the AUA meet at Fisk University following the annual race relations conference. No action is taken.

1954 Collymore becomes the first African-American AUA board member and serves until 1957. He will be followed by Wade McCree, Edna Griffin, Dalmas Taylor, Gwendolyn Thomas,

Loretta Williams, Gustavia Gash, Norm Lockman, Winifred Norman (the granddaughter of Lewis Latimer), Edward Simmons, Leon Spencer, William Jones, Norma Poinsett, Adele Smith-Penniman, William Sinkford, Tamara Payne-Alex, Charles Redd, and Rosemary Bray McNatt.

1955 Beacon Press publishes *Notes of a Native Son* by James Baldwin and *Prejudice and Your Child* by Kenneth B. Clark.

1956 Eighty out of 287 congregations have African-American members, and African Americans are active as officers in 49 congregations, according to a *Christian Register* survey.

1956 Howard Thurman delivers the Ware Lecture.

1956 Pauline Warfield Lewis becomes director of religious education at First Unitarian Church of Cincinnati.

1956 While serving both the American Humanist Association and the Springfield, Ohio, fellowship, McGee is refused a call to Flint, Michigan, a Unitarian and Congregational congregation that has five African-American families.

1957 All Souls Church, Unitarian, in Washington DC hires Bernice Bell Just as director of religious education.

1958 Rev. William R. Jones is fellowshipped and serves as assistant minister in Providence, Rhode Island.

1958 Rev. David H. Eaton approaches AUA president Dana Greeley and is told, "I'd love to have you but we'll have trouble settling you."

1958 McGee is called to be associate minister to the First Unitarian Church of Los Angeles.

1960 Marcella McGee is elected to the UU Women's Federation Board.

1960 Sparrow becomes director of field service for the Western Unitarian Conference. Two years later, he will leave the ministry for good, first working for several human relations commissions before becoming a college professor.

1961 McGee becomes minister of a fellowship in Chico, California, and thus the first African-American senior minister of a white congregation since Clarence B. Thompson.

1962 Richardson leaves FRF to become a professor at DePaul University.

1962 Harold B. Jordan is elected to the Board of All Souls in DC; in 1964, he will become its chairperson.

1963 Henry Hampton is hired as UUA associate director of information and publicity; he remains at the UUA until 1968.

1963 At the UUA General Assembly in Chicago, a resolution requiring congregations to adopt a nondiscrimination clause is defeated, but a subsequent resolution encouraging this clause for existing congregations and requiring it of new ones passes. The GA also establishes the Commission on Race and Religion.

1965 Following the shooting of Jimmy Lee Jackson and the beating of voting rights protesters, UUs respond to Martin Luther King Jr.'s call for people of all faiths to come to Selma, Alabama, and participate in the voting rights demonstration. Rev. James Reeb, part of the first wave, dies after being clubbed. More UUs, including Lewis McGee and the UUA board, then come to Selma. A UU volunteer Viola Liuzzo, is also killed.

1965 Judge Wade McCree is elected vice-moderator of the UUA.

1966 Dr. Martin Luther King Jr. delivers Ware Lecture.

1966 Margaret Williams follows Bernice Just as director of religious education at All Souls, DC.

1967 Black Unitarians for Radical Reform (BURR) is founded in August by black members of First Unitarian Church of Los Angeles and other Los Angeles area UU churches as a means of reforming the Unitarian Universalist faith to be more inclusive of blacks.

1967 The UUA Commission on Race and Religion, chaired by Cornelius McDougald, convenes the Emergency Conference on the Black Rebellion. Approximately 150 people attend. Instigated by BURR, thirty-three of the thirty-seven African Americans withdraw to form a black caucus, later called the Black UU Caucus.

1967 Jeffrey Campbell, while teaching at the Putney School, is settled in a part-time ministry in Amherst, Massachusetts.

1967 The UUA Goals Report finds that 11 percent of UUs say that being black would improve a minister's effectiveness, 63 percent say it would make no difference, and 27 percent say it would hamper a minister's effectiveness. The corresponding percentages for women are 5, 48, and 47.

1968 The National Conference of Black Universalists is held in Chicago with 207 attendees.

1968 Martin Luther King Jr. is assassinated.

1968 The Black Affairs Council (BAC) and Black and White Alternative (BAWA) are formed.

1968 Carl B. Stokes, mayor of Cleveland, delivers the Ware Lecture, and the Cleveland General Assembly commits $1 million dollars to the BAC.

1968 Revs. John Frazier Jr., Thomas Payne, and Mwalimu Imara (nee Renford Gaines) are granted fellowship. There are eight African-American ministers and about 1,500 African-American laity.

1969 BUUC and its supporters walk out of the Boston General Assembly.

1969 Joseph Samples and Harold Wilson are elected to the UUA Commission on Appraisal. They are followed by Norma Poinsett, Dalmas Taylor, Mark D. Morrison-Reed, O'Ferrell Nelson, Marjorie Bowens-Wheatley, Charles Redd, Janice Marie Johnson, Arthur Morrison, and Jacqui C. Williams.

1969 David H. Eaton is called to All Souls Church in DC.

1969 Rev. Harold Wilson is granted fellowship. He serves in Walnut Creek, California, as co-minister from 1968 to 1972.

1969 John Frazier Jr. begins serving the Black Humanist Fellowship of Liberation in Cleveland.

1970 Imara is called to Arlington Street Church in Boston.

1970 Margaret Williams joins UUA staff as an educational consultant in the Dept. of Education and Social Concerns.

1970 The BAC disaffiliates from the UUA.

1973 Henrietta McKee becomes the first African American elected to the UUA Nominating Committee. She will be followed by Cornelius McDougald, Winifred Norman, Gustavia Gash, Etta Green Johnson, David Eaton, Sayre Dixon, Charles Yielbonzie Johnson, Daniel Aldridge, Michelle Bentley, Laura Spencer, Hope Johnson, James Coomes, and Leon Spencer.

1974 Imara leaves Arlington Street Church for the Benevolent Fraternity of UU Congregations (later named UU Urban Ministry).

1977 Thomas E. Payne begins working for the Benevolent Fraternity of UU Congregations.

1979 Rev. Jesse Jackson delivers the Ware Lecture.

1979 UUA President Eugene Pickett convenes a meeting of all African-American ministers.

1980 The UUA undertakes an Institutional Racism Audit.

1980 Skinner House Books publishes *Black Pioneers in a White Denomination* by Mark D. Morrison-Reed.

1981 Vernon Jordan delivers the Ware Lecture.

1981 Rev. Yvonne Chappelle Seon is the first African-American woman granted fellowship.

1982 Rev. Adele Penniman-Smith becomes the second African-American woman granted fellowship.

1982 The Network of Black UUs is formed. It meets primarily at General Assembly.

1983 The UUA Commission on Appraisal publishes *The Empowerment Controversy: One Denomination's Quest for Racial Justice, 1968–1972.*

1984 The Jordan School closes.

1985 The UUA Black Concerns Working Group is established.

1985 Congresswoman Shirley Chisholm delivers Ware Lecture.

1986 Yvonne Seon is the founding minister of Sojourner Truth, a new congregation in southeast Washington DC.

1986 Rev. Michelle Bentley is the third African-American woman granted fellowship.

1987 Rev. Mark D. Morrison-Reed chairs the UUA Department of Ministry's Task Force on Affirmative Action for African-American Ministers, which is staffed by Jacqui James, worship resources coordinator, and Mel Hoover, director for racial and cultural diversity. This task force develops the Beyond Categorical Thinking program and calls the conference of African- American UU religious professionals from which African-American Unitarian Universalist Ministries (AAUUM) will emerge.

1988 AAUUM is founded. There are now seventeen African-American ministers.

1988 Rev. Charles Johnson (later Yielbonze Johnson) founds Church of the Restoration, in Tulsa, Oklahoma.

1989 Rev. Dan Aldridge founds the Thurman Hamer Ellington congregation in Decatur, Georgia.

1989 *How Open the Door? The African-American Experience in Unitarian Universalism*, an adult religious education curriculum, is published. Stories about African-American UUs are included in the other curricula produced by the UU Identity Curriculum Team.

1989 The Commission on Appraisal's study, "Quality of Religious Life in Unitarian Universalist Congregations," finds that, when asked if being black would help, make no difference to, or hinder ministers' effectiveness, UUs responded, 3 percent, 71 percent, and 26 percent, respectively. For women, the corresponding percentages were 9, 78, and 13. For gay, lesbian, and bisexual people, 2, 33, and 66.

1991 *Been in the Storm So Long*, a collection of writings by African-American UUs, edited by Mark D. Morrison-Reed and Jacqui James, is published by Skinner House Books.

1992 The Continental Congress of African American UUs is held in Philadelphia.

1992 Following the passage of the General Assembly "Resolutions on Racial and Cultural Diversity," the UUA Office for Racial and Cultural Diversity is established.

1993 James Brown is hired as the Southwest District executive, the first African American to hold such a position.

1993 *Singing the Living Tradition* is published. The Hymnbook Resource Commission included Fred Wilson (later replaced by T. J. Anderson) and was staffed by Jacqui James, who was also the UUA's affirmative action officer.

1993 Michelle Bentley becomes dean of students at Meadville Lombard Theological School.

1993 Marion Wright Edelman delivers the Ware Lecture.

1994 Rev. William Sinkford becomes the UUA's director of congregational and district services and the first African American on executive staff.

1997 The Journey Toward Wholeness resolution is passed by General Assembly.

1997 Diverse Revolutionary UU Multicultural Ministries is founded.

1999 Rev. Adele Penniman-Smith and Rev. Kristen Harper become the first regularly settled African-American women as senior pastors.

1999 Qiyamah Rahman becomes first female African-American district executive, serving the Thomas Jefferson district.

2000 There are twenty-six African-American ministers.

2001 Mark D. Morrison-Reed is the first Afro-Canadian president of the Canadian Unitarian Council.

2001 Rev. Dr. James Forbes delivers the Ware Lecture.

2001 William R. Jones receives the Award for Distinguished Service to the Cause of Unitarian Universalism.

2001 William Sinkford is elected the first African-American president of the UUA.

FOR FURTHER READING

Marjorie Bowens-Wheatley and Nancy Palmer Jones, eds. *Soul Work: Anti-racist Theologies in Dialogue*. Boston: Skinner House Books, 2002.

Victor H. Carpenter. *The Long Challenge: The Empowerment Controversy (1967–1977)*. Chicago: Meadville Lombard Theological School, 2004.

Dorothy May Emerson, ed. *Standing Before Us: Unitarian Universalist Women and Social Reform, 1776–1936*. Boston: Skinner House Books, 2000.

Juan M. Floyd-Thomas. *The Origins of Black Humanism in America: Reverend Ethelred Brown and the Unitarian Church*. New York: Palgrave Macmillan, 2008.

Paula Cole Jones, ed. *Encounters: Poems About Race, Ethnicity and Identity*. Boston: Skinner House Books, 2010.

Mel Hoover and Jacqui James, eds. *Soulful Journeys: The Faith of African-American Unitarian Universalists* (pamphlet). Boston: Unitarian Universalist Association, 2002.

Richard D. Leonard. *Call to Selma: Eighteen Days of Witness*. Boston: Skinner House Books, 2002.

Russell E. Miller. *The Larger Hope: The Second Century of the Universalist Church in America, 1870–1970*. Boston: Unitarian Universalist Association, 1985.

John Gibb Millspaugh, ed. *A People So Bold: Theology and Ministry for Unitarian Universalists*. Boston: Skinner House Books, 2009.

Mark Morrison-Reed. *Black Pioneers in a White Denomination*. 3rd ed. Boston: Skinner House Books, 1994.

———. *In Between: Memoir of an Integration Baby*. Boston: Skinner House Books, 2009.

———. *The Selma Awakening: How the Civil Rights Movement Tested and Changed Unitarian Universalism.* Boston: Skinner Hosue Books, 2014.

Mark Morrison-Reed and Jacqui James, eds. *Been in the Storm So Long: A Meditation Manual.* Boston: Skinner House Books, 1991.

Leslie Takahashi-Morris, Chip Roush, and Leon Spencer. *The Arc of the Universe Is Long: Unitarian Universalists, Anti-Racism and the Journey from Calgary*. Boston: Skinner House Books, 2009.

Joyce Moore Turner. *Caribbean Crusaders and the Harlem Renaissance*. Chicago: University of Illinois Press, 2005.

Unitarian Universalism and the Quest for Racial Justice. Boston: Unitarian Universalist Association, 1993.

Robert Nelson West. *Crisis and Change: My Years as President of the Unitarian Universalist Association, 1969–1977*. Boston: Skinner House Books, 2007.

Unitarian Universalist Women's Heritage Society. *Unitarian and Universalist Women: Liberating History*. Providence: Blackstone Editions, 2008.

ABOUT THE CONTRIBUTORS

BRUCE BEISNER is a candidate for the Unitarian Universalist ministry and a student at Meadville Lombard Theological School, studying for his master of divinity degree. Bruce has a bachelor's degree in graphic design from the University of Cincinnati. He has served as administrator at the Northern Hills Unitarian Universalist Fellowship in Cincinnati and has been an active lay leader at St. John's UU Church. Bruce was the editor of the *Greater Cincinnati GLBT News* and is a former president of the Gay and Lesbian Community Center of Greater Cincinnati.

COLIN BOSSEN serves as the minister of the Unitarian Universalist Society of Cleveland. He is the cofounder of CASA, an international human rights and solidarity organization based in Mexico, and has helped organize labor unions in Chicago, Los Angeles, and Washington DC. His publications include two religious education curricula—"The Bridging Program" and "Resistance and Transformation"—as well as articles in the *UU World, Long Beach Press Telegram, Industrial Worker*, and the *Journal of Liberal Religion*. A graduate of Meadville Lombard Theological School, he lives in Cleveland Heights, Ohio, with his family.

JOHN BUEHRENS served as president of the Unitarian Universalist Association from 1993 to 2001. He is the author of *Universalists and Unitarians in America: A People's History* and *Understanding the Bible: An Introduction for Skeptics, Seekers, and Religious Liberals*; and co-author (with Forrest Church) of *A Chosen Faith: An*

Introduction to Unitarian Universalism and (with Rebecca Parker) of *A House for Hope: The Promise of Progressive Religion for the Twenty-first Century*. He is minister of First Parish in Needham, Massachusetts, and adjunct faculty at Harvard Divinity School.

PAULA COLE JONES, a management consultant specializing in group facilitation and diversity, is a lifelong member of All Souls Church, Unitarian, in Washington DC. Her experience in this multicultural congregation led to involvement as a leader in antiracism, anti-oppression, and multicultural training and consulting with the Unitarian Universalist Association. She is a past president of Diverse & Revolutionary Unitarian Universalist Multicultural Ministries, and the founder of A Dialogue on Race and Ethnicity. Paula is the author of "Reconciliation as a Spiritual Discipline," which appeared in the March/April 2004 issue of *UU World* magazine; a contributing author to the book, *A People So Bold: Theology and Ministry for Unitarian Universalists*; and editor of *Encounters: Poems about Race, Ethnicity and Identity*.

SHARON DITTMAR, a graduate of Harvard Divinity School, has been the minister of First Unitarian Church in Cincinnati since 1998. She initiated the congregation's reconciliation project with the descendants of Rev. W.H.G. Carter. Within the city of Cincinnati, she is recognized and sought out for her interfaith work on social justice issues, particularly involving race, class, and gun violence reduction. Under Rev. Dittmar's leadership, First Unitarian Church has won numerous local and district awards for its social justice work and commitment to right relationships.

NANCY J. DOUGHTY, a fifth generation Universalist, graduated from Miami University with a BS in Education, and received her MDiv from the Theological School at St. Lawrence University. Ordained in 1962 as minister of education, she served the First Unitarian Universalist Church of Detroit. During her five years of ministry there and thirty-five years living in Detroit, she learned about Eugene Sparrow's failed candidacy. Over the years, Nancy has been a member of the UUA Board, member of the Ministerial Fellowship Committee, and most recently board president of the UU Retired Ministers and Partners Association. She lives in Traverse City, Michigan, with her husband, Bob.

JUNE EDWARDS is professor emeritus at the State University of New York at Oneonta, where she received awards for Academic Excellence and Excellence in Teaching. She is the author of *Women in American Education, 1820–1955: The Female Force and Educational Reform* and *Censorship in the Public Schools: Religion, Morality, and Literature*. She was the section editor on education for *Standing Before Us: Unitarian Universalist Women and Social Reform*, and has contributed three articles for the online "Dictionary of Unitarian Universalist Biography," including one about Fannie Barrier Williams. Her numerous articles in professional journals concern conflicts over religion and civil rights within public schools.

WILLARD C. FRANK JR. holds degrees from Brown University, the College of William and Mary, and the University of Pittsburgh. He is a professor emeritus in history at Old Dominion University, in Norfolk, Virginia, and a former board member of Meadville Lombard Theological School. A member of the Unitarian Church of Norfolk (Unitarian Universalist) since 1958, he discovered its link to the Jordan School in Suffolk and since the late 1970s has been researching, teaching, and writing about the African-American Universalists in the Tidewater Region. This was also the focus of two denomination-wide conferences and several programs he organized. He has published several articles on Unitarian Universalist history and in 1984 published *A Year With Our Liberal Heritage.*

DAN HARPER is the assistant minister of religious education at the Unitarian Universalist Church of Palo Alto, California. He researched Rev. William Jackson while serving as minister at First

Unitarian Church of New Bedford, Massachusetts, two blocks away from the site of Jackson's Salem Baptist Church. Harper, a lifelong Unitarian Universalist, has also worked as interim minister, carpenter's helper, salesman, and retail clerk. He writes daily at the blog, "Yet Another Unitarian Universalist" (www.danielharper.org/blog).

WALTER P. HERZ received his AB from Harvard University after serving in the U.S. Navy in World War II. He devoted his business career to marketing communications for health care companies. Herz and his spouse joined First Unitarian Church of Plainfield, New Jersey, in 1958. Now a member of the First Unitarian Church of Cincinnati, Herz has been active in congregational, district, and denominational affairs. He has published articles on local UU history, contributed seven biographies to the online "Dictionary of Unitarian Universalist Biography," and was editor of *Redeeming Time: Endowing Your Church with the Power of Covenant*, published in 1999.

JOHN HURLEY first learned of the intertwined stories of Jeffrey Campbell, Marguerite Campbell, and Francis Davis while doing research on the black Universalists in Virginia in advance of the Universalist Bicentennial in 1993. A graduate of Fordham College and the University of Wisconsin-Madison, he joined the staff of the Unitarian Universalist Association in 1995 and became director of communications in 2006. He has served on the Board of the Unitarian Universalist Historical Society and as staff liaison to the Emerson Bicentennial Committee and the 50th Anniversary Task Force.

RICHARD (DICK) MORRIS is a graduate of Haverford College (BA) and Harvard University (MBA). A longtime member of what is now the Goodloe Memorial Unitarian Universalist Congregation, he began researching Don Speed Smith Goodloe in 1993 for Mark D. Morrison-Reed's *Black Pioneers in a White Denomination.* Morris spent most of his career in the housing industry, doing research and writing books and articles. He now writes novels, including *Cologne No. 10 for Men* (2007) and *Well Considered* (2010).

MARK D. MORRISON-REED, a lifelong Unitarian Universalist, has written extensively about the African-American experience in Unitarian Universalism. He is author of *Black Pioneers in a White Denomination* (1980), now in its third edition. He also developed the multimedia curriculum *How Open the Door? The African American in Unitarian Universalism* (1989), co-edited *Been in the Storm So Long* (1991), wrote the entry on the Unitarian Universalist Association to *The Encyclopedia of African-American Culture and History* (1996), and wrote *In Between: Memoir of an Integration Baby* (2009). He is an affiliated faculty member at Meadville Lombard Theological School and former president of the Canadian Unitarian Council.

ANTHONY B. PINN is the Agnes Cullen Arnold Professor of Humanities and Professor of Religious Studies at Rice University. In 2007, he became the founding director of the Houston Enriches Rice Education Project, which develops creative approaches to re-envisioning Rice's relationship to the larger Houston community. The author/editor of twenty-four books, Pinn's areas of research include African-American humanism, liberation theologies, religion and aesthetics, and religion and popular culture. In addition, Pinn is the director of research for the Institute for Humanist Studies (Washington DC) and a member of the executive committee of the Society for the Study of Black Religion.

QIYAMAH A. RAHMAN, a native of Detroit, obtained a bachelor's in education and an MSW from the University of Michigan; an MDiv from Meadville Lombard Theological School; and a doctorate from Clark Atlanta University in Africana Women's Studies, with a major in gender and development and a minor in feminist/womanist theory. A Unitarian Universalist since 1992, when she was introduced to Frances Ellen Watkins Harper, her research has focused on black women in Unitarian Universalism, among other subjects. From 1999 to 2005 she served as district executive of the Thomas Jefferson district, the first African-American woman to hold the position of DE. Currently, she is the director of contexual ministry and senior lecturer at Meadville Lombard Theological School.

YVONNE SEON, ordained in 1981, is the Unitarian Universalist Association's first African-American female minister. Before that she worked in Africa as executive director of the Inga Dam Project; in Washington DC as a foreign affairs officer and later congressional aide; and in Ohio as an educator and pioneer in black studies. She earned a BA from Allegheny College (1959), an MA from American University (1960), a PhD from Union Graduate School in African and African-American Humanities (1974), and an MDiv from Howard University Divinity School (1981). Retired and living in Yellow Springs, Ohio, she is the founding director (retired) of Bolinga Black Cultural Resources Center in Yellow Springs.

WILLIAM SINKFORD is the senior minister of the First Unitarian Church of Portland, Oregon. He served as the seventh president of the Unitarian Universalist Association from 2001 until 2009. Previously, he had served as the UUA director of congregational, district, and extension services. Born in San Francisco in 1946, Sinkford was an active member of the First Unitarian Church of Cincinnati, Ohio, during his teenage years, serving as the president of Liberal Religious Youth, the continental UU youth organization. He graduated cum laude from Harvard in 1968. After college, Sinkford worked in the field of marketing, and later housing development, before entering Starr King School for the Ministry, where he earned his MDiv in 1995.

ACKNOWLEDGMENTS

The dedication of *Darkening the Doorways* requires an explanation. Over thirty years ago Will Frank and I began corresponding about the African-American Universalist presence in Virginia. Seventeen years ago Richard and Barbara Morris inquired about Don Speed Smith Goodloe; we have been in touch ever since. Fifteen years ago Nancy Doughty and I began our effort to uncover the story behind why the congregation in Detroit did not call Eugene Sparrow. Walter Herz first wrote to me about W.H.G. Carter in 2000. These collaborators are Euro-Americans who have a passion for uncovering the African-American history within our faith tradition and a commitment to helping Unitarian Universalism evolve into a more inclusive faith. When it came to me that I wanted to dedicate this book to them I grew teary. I saw that they have been my steadfast companions in this endeavor.

Mary Benard, the editorial director of Skinner House, hoped someone would take up this project; so did I. That changed when I began teaching UU African-American history at Meadville Lombard Theological School. Suddenly, I needed such a book. I am grateful to Mary for holding on to that vision. I am also grateful to Meadville Lombard's president, Lee Barker, for asking me to teach—and to my students for their responses to my lectures, our discussions about many primary documents, and their research uncovering more history.

This book would not exist if not for its sixteen contributors. Read about them under "About the Contributors." Many I have known for decades; others I came upon serendipitously. Regardless, whenever one of their manuscripts arrived—whether the first or fourth draft—I felt as though I was unwrapping a present. I was, and I am grateful to them all.

Access to archives has been crucial. I am thankful for the Meadville Lombard Library and its assistant librarian, Adam Bohanan, and my research assistant, Joe Cherry; the Andover-Harvard Theological Library and research librarians Gloria Korsman and Fran O'Donnell; All Souls Church, Unitarian, in Washington DC and its archivist, Molly Freeman; the Walter P. Reuther Library of Labor and Urban Affairs of Wayne State University, Detroit, Michigan; and the Schomburg Center for Research in Black Culture at the New York Public Library. I am also grateful to the families of Eugene Sparrow and Lewis and Marcella McGee, for working with me and for their permission to use the papers they donated to Meadville Lombard, and finally to the Barnstable Unitarian Church for permission to excerpt Margaret Moseley's memoir.

Many people helped me to ferret out and understand specific details of the history of African Americans within Unitarian Universalism. They include Mark Belletini, Charles Blackburn, Dick Gilbert, Edward Harris, Mwalimu Imara, Jacqui James, Richard Leonard, the late Dores McCree, Orloff Miller, Kay Montgomery, Clark Olsen, Robert M. Schacht, Betty Reid Soskin, Farley Wheelwright, Margaret Williams, Fred Wooden, Kathy Tew Rickey, and Gordon Gibson.

I am grateful to the UU Funding Panel of the UU Veatch Program of the Shelter Rock Unitarian Universalist Congregation for its support, to Meadville Lombard Vice President Debbie Bieber for administering its grant, and to the Women's Heritage Society for providing photographs.

In the end it came down to Skinner House Editor Marshall Hawkins, who made sure that everything was ready for production. Thanks.

The person who has had to live with my ups and downs, my obsessiveness and irresponsibility in regard to everything else—when for weeks at a time I would lose myself in this project—is my wife, Donna Morrison-Reed. I am thankful for her patience, support, and clear thinking when I really get stuck.

Picture Key

The Unitarians, page 1

Clockwise from top center:
Ethelred Brown
Frances Ellen Watkins Harper
William H. G. Carter
Fannie Barrier Williams
Don Speed Smith Goodloe
Center photo:
Peter H. Clark

The Universalists, page 87

Clockwise from top center:
Jeffrey W. Campbell
Mary J. Jordan
Thomas E. Wise
Annie B. Willis
Joseph Fletcher Jordan

The Empowerment Saga, page 151

Clockwise from top center:
Lewis Allen McGee
Mwalimu Imara
Wade H. McCree Jr.
Betty Reid Soskin
David Hilliard Eaton

Still Seeking a Way, page 231

Clockwise from top center:
Michelle Bentley
Thomas Eliron Payne
Yvonne Seon
William Roland Jones
Jacqui James
Center photo:
William Sinkford

Group Photo on Page 310

Left to Right

Front row: Om Prakash, Manish Mishra, Sofia Betancourt, Mark Morrison-Reed, Jessica York, Catie Olson

Second row: Addae Kraba, Aisha Hauser, Lilia Cuervo, Jacqueline Clement, Danielle DiBona, Hope Johnson, Marta Valentin, Monica Cummings, William Sinkford

Third row: Carlton Elliott Smith, Jennifer Ryu, Jonipher Kwong, Leela Sinha, India McKnight, Angela Henderson, Darrick Jackson, Alicia Forde, Janice Marie Johnson, Wendy Pantoja

Fourth row: Melvin Hoover, Rosemary Bray McNatt, Abhi Janamanchi, Leslie Takahashi Morris, Laura Spencer, Cheryl LeShay, Qiyamah Rahman, Walter LeFlore, Kathleen McGregor, Marla Scharf, Jodi Tharan, Mitra Rahnema, Clyde Grubbs

Last row: Leon Spencer, Archene Turner, Nayer Taheri Ghadiri

NOTES

The Unitarians

1 Earl Morse Wilbur, *A History of Unitarianism in Transylvania, England, and America* (Boston: Beacon Press, 1977), p. 436.

2 Theodore Parker, "John Brown's Expedition Reviewed," in *Autobiography and Miscellaneous Pieces: The Collected Works of Theodore Parker, Part Twelve*, Francis Power Cobbe, ed. (London: Trübner and Co., 1865), p. 173.

3 Franklin Southworth to Egbert Ethelred Brown, Feb. 4, 1903, Meadville Lombard Theological School Archives, Chicago.

A Cold Shoulder for William Jackson

1 William Jackson, *A Memoir of Rev. William Jackson*, Photoscript, private collection, p. 5. Jackson's memoir states that Taylor's arrest followed upon the Dred Scott decision, but that case was decided by the Supreme Court in 1857, by which time Jackson was living in New Bedford. The Fugitive Slave Law was enacted in 1850, at the time Jackson was in his second tenure as minister of Oak Street Baptist Church in Philadelphia.

2 Joan Beaubion of the New Bedford Historical Society attests to this and believes there is documentation.

3 George Willis Cooke, *Unitarianism in America* (Boston: American Unitarian Association, 1902), pp. 173–74.

4 "Autumnal Convention," *Christian Inquirer*, Oct. 20, 1860, p. 1.

5 Ibid.

6 Jackson, p. 15.

7 *New Bedford Evening Standard*, Oct. 11, 1860, p. 2.

8 *New Bedford Mercury*, Oct. 12, 1860, p. 2.

9 Douglas C. Stange, *British Unitarians Against American Slavery, 1833–65* (Rutherford, NJ: Fairleigh Dickinson University Press, 1984), p. 159.

10 *Christian Inquirer*, October 20, 1860, p. 2.

11 *New Bedford Mercury*, October 12, 1860, p. 2.

12 *New Bedford Evening Standard*, October 11, 1860, p. 2.
13 Douglas C. Stange, *Patterns of Antislavery among American Unitarians, 1831–60* (Rutherford, NJ: Fairleigh Dickinson University Press, 1977), p. 227.

Frances Ellen Watkins Harper

1 Ann Allen Shockley, *Afro-American Women Writers, 1746–1933: An Anthology and Critical Guide* (New York: Penguin, 1989), p. 190.
2 Some of these organizations included the Women's Christian Temperance Union, the American Equal Rights Association, the American Association for the Education of Colored Youth, the American Women's Suffrage Association, the Republican Party of the Civil War era, the John Brown Memorial Association of the Women's National Council of Negro Women, the American Missionary Association, the National Federation of Afro-American Women, and the Universal Peace Union.
3 Michael Stancliff, *An Historic Character: Frances Ellen Watkins Harper, African American Moral Reform and the Rise of a Modern Nation State, 1850–1898*. PhD dissertation, University of New York at Buffalo, 2001, p. 11.
4 William Still, "Introduction," in *Frances E. W. Harper, Iola Leroy, or Shadows Uplifted* (New York: Oxford University Press, 1990), p. 2; originally published, Philadelphia: Garrigues, 1893.
5 Frances Ellen Watkins Harper, "Duty to Dependent Races," delivered to the National Council of Women of the United States, Washington DC, Feb. 23, 1891; in Shirley Wilson Logan, ed., *With Pen and Voice: A Critical Anthology of Nineteenth-Century African-African Women* (Carbondale, IL: SIU Press, 1995), p. 42. Another well-known member of the First Unitarian Church of Philadelphia was Laura Matilda Townes, one of the first white northern women to travel south to teach freed children. She taught at Penn School, the first school for freedmen during the Civil War. Townes ran the school, which was located on St. Helena Island, South Carolina, until her death in 1901. While the Quakers like to claim Townes, she very specifically states in the only book written on her life that she was a Unitarian. Furthermore, she mentions Rev. Furness, her minister. Charlotte Forten (1837–1914), sometimes identified as a Unitarian but not substantiated, was also one of the first blacks to travel south to teach. Forten and Townes worked together and mention one another in their writings about Penn School. The Penn Center named its library after Townes and has retained some of her writings there.
6 The three most notable black Unitarian women during Harper's era included Florida Ridley Ruffin (1861–1943), a Boston socialite and activist; Fannie Barrier Williams (1855–1944), a Chicago activist and proponent of black women's rights; and Maria Louise Baldwin (1856–1922).

Peter H. Clark

1 For almost a half century, historians believed that Peter H. Clark's maternal grandfather was William Clark, the world-famous explorer who led the first overland expedition to the Pacific coast and back with Meriwether Lewis. This myth can be traced to a 1942 biography of Peter Clark in the *Negro History Bulletin* written by Dovie King Clark, his brother's daughter-in-law. The notion of this historical lineage, which may also have come from Peter himself as a way of furthering his reputation during his later years of living in St. Louis, was embraced by some white scholars as a comfortable explanation of how a person of color could possess such intelligence and leadership ability. In recent years, most researchers have dispelled any such genealogical link as having little to no basis in fact.

2 Walter Herz, "A Chronology of Peter H. Clark's Life," unpublished.

3 Walter Herz, "Peter H. Clark," in "Dictionary of Unitarian and Universalist Biography," www.25-temp.uua.org/uuhs/duub/articles/peterclark.html.

Fannie Barrier Williams

1 Mary Jo Deegan. *The New Woman of Color: The Collected Writings of Fannie Barrier Williams, 1893–1918* (DeKalb, IL: Northern Illinois University Press, 2002), p. 11.

2 In 1918, the Frederick Douglass Centre was added to the Wendell Phillips Social Settlement, which closed in 1925. The Frederick Douglass Center building became the headquarters for the National Urban League in Chicago.

3 Fannie Barrier Williams, "The Intellectual Progress of the Colored Women of the United States Since the Emancipation Proclamation," in Deegan, p. 27; originally published in *The World's Congress of Representative Women, 1894*, Vol. 2, pp. 696–711.

4 James Loewenberg and Ruth Bogin, eds, *Black Women in Nineteenth-Century American Life: Their Words, Their Thoughts, Their Feelings* (University Park: Pennsylvania State University Press, 1976), p. 279.

5 Fannie Barrier Williams, "Religious Duty to the Negro," in Deegan, pp. 73–75; originally published in J. W. Hanson, ed., *The World's Congress of Religions* (Chicago: W. B. Conkey, 1894), pp. 893–97.

6 Ibid., pp. 76–77.

7 Fannie Barrier Williams, "A Northern Negro's Autobiography," in Deegan, p. 13.

8 Ibid.

Don Speed Smith Goodloe

1 W.E.B. DuBois, *The Souls of Black Folk* (Toronto: General Publishing, 1994), pp. 25–35.
2 Wallis A. Goodloe, interview by Mark D. Morrison-Reed, Nov. 19, 1982, Goodloe Archives, Goodloe Memorial Unitarian Universalist Congregation, Bowie, MD.
3 Franklin Southworth to Ethelred Brown, Feb. 1903, Meadville Lombard Theological School Archives, Chicago.
4 *Kaldron*, yearbook of Allegheny College, 1906.
5 *Maryland Normal and Industrial School Catalog, 1911–1912*, Goodloe Archives, Goodloe Memorial Unitarian Universalist Congregation, Bowie, MD.
6 Jessie L. Nichols to D. S. S. Goodloe, December 28, 1920, Goodloe Archives, Goodloe Memorial Unitarian Universalist Congregation, Bowie, MD.
7 *The First Colored Professional, Clerical and Business Directory of Baltimore City, 1922–1923*, Vol. 502 (Baltimore, MD: R. W. Coleman, 1923), p. 104; Archives of Maryland Online, www.aomol.net/megafile/msa/speccol/sc2900/sc2908/000001/000502/html/am502—104.html.

Clarence Bertrand Thompson

1 Otey M. Scruggs and Laurence C. Howard, "C. Bertrand Thompson and Scientific Management: Relevance for the 21st Century," unpublished, 2003.
2 Ibid.
3 Ibid.
4 Minutes of Standing Committee of Peabody Unitarian Church, Massachusetts, Sept. 30, 1907, Peabody Unitarian Church Archives, North Shore UU Church, Danvers, MA.
5 Clarence Bertrand Thompson to Peabody Unitarian Church, Oct. 1, 1909, Peabody Unitarian Church Archives, Northshore UU Church, Danvers, MA.
6 Scruggs and Howard.

Rev. Ethelred Brown Is Symbol of Radicalism in Pulpits in Harlem

1 Arthur G. McGiffert Jr., *Pilot of the Liberal Faith: Samuel Atkins Eliot, 1862–1950* (Boston: Skinner House, 1976), pp. 20–21.
2 Louis Cornish to Mr. McDougall, Oct. 1921, Egbert Ethelred Brown file, UUA Inactive Ministers File, Andover-Harvard Theological Library, Cambridge, MA.

3 McGiffert, p. 107.
4 Anonymous letter to unknown recipient, n.d., Egbert Ethelred Brown file, UUA Inactive Ministers Files, Andover-Harvard Theological Library, Cambridge, MA.
5 Bertram Wolfe (1896–1977) was white. A scholar, journalist, and leader in the Communist Party of America, he was expelled from the CPA in 1928.

William H. G. Carter

1 W.H.G. Carter, *My Father's Business*, self-published, 1960, p. 3.
2 Ibid., pp. 68–69.
3 Morris W. Hudgins, "W.H.G. Carter: Pioneer Unitarian Minister," sermon delivered Jan. 7, 2001, at Northern Hills Unitarian Universalist Fellowship, Cincinnati, OH.
4 Carter, p. 10.
5 Lon Ray Call to George G. Davis, "Subject: Unitarian Brotherhood Church, Negro, Cincinnati, OH," Nov. 14, 1938, W. H. G. Carter file, Morrison-Reed Collection, Sankofa Archive, Meadville Lombard Theological School Library, Chicago.
6 Lon Ray Call to Mark Morrison-Reed, Feb. 11, 1984, W. H. G. Carter file, Morrison-Reed Collection, Sankofa Archive, Meadville Lombard Theological School Library, Chicago.
7 Ibid.

Resolution on Race Relations

1 Stephen H. Fritchman, *Heretic: A Partisan Autobiography* (Boston: Skinner House Books, 1977), pp. 65–66.

Why Brotherhood Week?

1 Robert Hill, ed., *The Marcus Garvey and UNIA Papers*, Vol. 10 (Berkeley: University of California Press, 1983), pp. 226–27.

1st Unitarian Uses Brotherhood Idea

1 Richard Henry to Mark Morrison-Reed, email correspondence, June 4, 2010.
2 Laurence C. Staples, *Washington Unitarianism* (Northampton, MA: Metcalf, 1970), p. 112.

The Candidacy of Eugene Sparrow

1 "Des Moines, Iowa," Memorandum from Dan Huntington Fenn, Nov. 7, 1945, Proposed Negro Unitarian—Des Moines, Iowa, file, Box 3, AUA Dept. Extension and Maintenance Sec. (George Davis) 1936–1945, Andover-Harvard Theological Library, Cambridge.

2 Grant Butler to Dan Fenn, June 18, 1946, Proposed Negro Unitarian—Des Moines, Iowa, file, Box 3, AUA Dept. Extension and Maintenance Sec. (George Davis) 1936–1945, Andover-Harvard Theological Library, Cambridge.

3 Frederick May Eliot to Randall S. Hilton, Jan. 3, 1950, Tracy Pullman File, First Unitarian Universalist Church of Detroit Archives.

4 Minutes of Church Council meeting, Jan. 1950, First Unitarian Universalist Church of Detroit Archives.

5 Minutes of Church Council meeting, May 1950, First Unitarian Universalist Church of Detroit Archive.

6 Helen Riebling, interviewed by Nancy Doughty, Jan. 1997, Audio Cassette file, Morrison-Reed Collection, Sankofa Archive, Meadville Lombard Theological School Library, Chicago.

7 Nancy Mercer, interviewed by Nancy Doughty, Jan. 1997, Audio Cassette file, Morrison-Reed Collection, Sankofa Archive, Meadville Lombard Theological School Library, Chicago.

8 Andee Seegar, interviewed by Nancy Doughty, Jan. 1997, Audio Cassette file, Morrison-Reed Collection, Sankofa Archive, Meadville Lombard Theological School Library, Chicago.

9 Louise Walters, interviewed by Nancy Doughty, Jan. 1997, Audio Cassette file, Morrison-Reed Collection, Sankofa Archive, Meadville Lombard Theological School Library, Chicago.

10 Seegar.

11 Ibid.

12 Phyliss Fenkse, interviewed by Nancy Doughty, Jan.1997.

13 Vivian Spaulding, interviewed by Nancy Doughty, Feb. 1997.

14 Edward H. Redman, "In Memory of Rev. Eugene Sparrow," delivered Sept. 9, 1978, Widener College, Sparrow file, Morrison-Reed Collection, Sankofa Archive, Meadville Lombard Theological School Library, Chicago.

15 John Evans, "Some Memories of Eugene Sparrow," delivered Feb. 20, 1990, Meadville Lombard Theological School, Sparrow file, Morrison-Reed Collection, Sankofa Archive, Meadville Lombard Theological School Library, Chicago.

16 Eugene Sparrow, "Why I Believe There Is a God," in *Why I Believe There Is a God: Sixteen Essays by Negro Clergymen* (Chicago: Johnson Publishing Company, Inc., 1965), p. 93.

On the Eve of Merger

1 Charles Lyttle, *Freedom Moves West* (Boston: Beacon Press, 1952), p. 58.
2 Edward H. Redman, "In Memory of Rev. Eugene Sparrow," delivered Sept. 9, 1978, Widener College, Sparrow file, Sankofa Archive, Meadville Lombard Theological School Library, Chicago.
3 "How 'Open' Is the Unitarian Door?" Report of the Commission on Unitarian Intergroup Relations, *Christian Register*, March 1954, pp. 10–18.
4 "Bell to Head Adult Education Council of Liberal Churches," *Universalist Leader*, December 1954, p. 290.
5 "The Role of the Negro in American Unitarianism—A Growing Participation," *Christian Register*, Sept. 1956, pp. 12–13.
6 Bylaws of the Unitarian Universalist Congregation at Shelter Rock, NY, p. 30.

The Universalists

1 Russell Elliott Miller, *The Larger Hope: The First Century of the Universalist Church in America, 1770–1870* (Boston: Unitarian Universalist Association, 1979), p. 579.
2 Richard Eddy, "Universalism in Gloucester, MA, An Historical Discourse on the One Hundredth Anniversary of the First Sermon of Rev. John Murray in that town," delivered in the Independent Christian Church, Nov. 3, 1874 (Gloucester, MA: Procter Bros., 1892), p. 188; Internet Archive: American Libraries, www.archive.org/details/universalisming00eddygoog.
3 Miller, p. 576.
4 Ernest Cassara, *Universalism in America: A Documentary History* (Boston: Beacon Press, 1971), p. 189.
5 Miller, p. 578.
6 Miller, p. 600.

Joseph Jordan

1 "Necrology," *Christian Leader*, No. 61, 1896, p. 100.

Mary J. Jordan

1 "J. F. Jordan," biographical statement, 1926, author unknown, Unitarian Universalist Special Collections, Unitarian Universalist Ministers and Lay Leaders file, Andover-Harvard Theological Library, Cambridge, MA.

Joseph Fletcher Jordan

1 "J. F. Jordan," biographical statement, 1926, author unknown, Unitarian Universalist Special Collections, Unitarian Universalist Ministers and Lay Leaders file, Andover-Harvard Theological Library, Cambridge, MA.

2 E. H. Lake, *Key to Truth; or, Expository Remarks on Biblical Phrases and Passages: Together with Brief Essays on Religious Subjects, Comprising Arguments in Favor of Universalism, and Objections to Endless Punishment* (Boston: Usher, 1855), cover page.

3 Ibid, p. 183.

4 Ibid., p. 179.

5 "J. F. Jordan."

6 Whereas Thomas Wise had opposed the attempts of white Universalist leaders to impose a Booker T. Washington approach on the Tidewater Mission Schools, Joseph Fletcher Jordan combined the DuBois and Washington approaches without controversy. The name of the school enshrined both, i.e., the Suffolk Normal (academic) Training (industrial) School, while it strove to encompass the gamut from Greek and Latin to sewing and mechanical crafts.

7 In chapters 23 and 24 of Russell Elliott Miller's *The Larger Hope: The Second Century of the Universalist Church in America, 1870–1970* (Boston: Unitarian Universalist Association, 1985), he describes Universalist missionary efforts in Japan. It was started at the same time as the Norfolk mission, but one significant difference was that the effort in Japan, after being debated for a decade, had evolved out of a denominational consensus, whereas the latter mission arose serendipitously, and the financial support it garnered was half-hearted. During the fifty-year Japanese endeavor, the mission, although always underfunded compared to other denominations, received hundreds of thousands of dollars.

8 Joseph Fletcher Jordan, "Universalism and the Negro," *Universalist Leader*, Apr. 27, 1912, pp. 527–28.

9 The rise of the Ku Klux Klan (KKK) was a pressing enough issue that a nine-page section about it entitled "For the Time Being at Least This Ends It" appeared in the *Universalist Leader,* Jan. 17, 1925 (pp. 14–22). The case for the KKK is presented and, apart from several supportive voices, is roundly denounced. The editor, John van Schaick, described the KKK as "a dangerous wrongheaded attempt to deal with . . . the race problem."

10 "A Friend," *Norfolk Journal and Guide,* May 11, 1929.

Annie B. Willis

1 Among the many loyal and outstanding teachers who worked with Miss Annie in support of the Jordan School were Ethel Whack, who enrolled in the social work program at Atlanta University in the summer term of 1939 to prepare for the change from school to social service provision, and Rose T. Hurst, who became co-director in 1949 and took over when Miss Annie retired in 1974.

Jeffrey W. Campbell and Marguerite Campbell Davis

1 Jeffrey W. Campbell, "Personality Not Pigmentation," *Christian Leader*, Feb. 24, 1940, pp. 180–83.

2 John van Schaick, "The Ballou Decision," *Christian Leader*, Mar. 25, 1939, p. 272.

3 John van Schaick, "The Editorial on the Ballou Decision," *Christian Leader*, Apr. 15, 1939, pp. 343–44.

4 John van Schaick, "Idealism and Realism in Mixed Marriages," *Christian Leader*, Aug. 12, 1939, p. 760.

5 John van Schaick, "Is Facing Facts Wrong?" *Christian Leader*, Sept. 2, 1939, p. 831.

6 John Murray Atwood, "Race Prejudice and Mixed Marriages," *Christian Leader*, Sept. 2, 1939, pp. 833–35.

7 John van Schaick, "Mr. Campbell's Article," *Christian Leader*, Feb. 24, 1940, pp. 176–77.

8 Campbell, "Personality."

9 John Murray Atwood, "Dean Atwood Reopens the Davis Case," *Christian Leader*, Apr. 4, 1942, p. 214.

10 John Murray Atwood to John M. Ratcliff, Feb. 6, 1942, Francis Elwin Davis file, UUA Inactive Ministers Files, Andover-Harvard Theological Library, Cambridge, MA.

11 Roger Etz to Harry Westbrook Reed, May 2, 1935, Jeffrey W. Campbell file, UUA Inactive Ministers Files, Andover-Harvard Theological Library, Cambridge, MA.

12 Jeffrey W. Campbell, interviewed by Mark Morrison-Reed, Putney, Vermont, July 1979.

13 Jeffrey W. Campbell to Leon Fay, Aug. 12, 1964, Jeffrey W. Campbell file, UUA Inactive Ministers Files, Andover-Harvard Theological Library, Cambridge, MA.

14 Ibid.

15 Jeffrey W. Campbell to O. Eugene Pickett and William F. Schulz, Nov. 26, 1979, Jeffrey W. Campbell file, UUA Inactive Ministers Files, Andover-Harvard Theological Library, Cambridge, MA.

Universalism's Theological Conundrum

1 Russell Elliott Miller, *The Larger Hope: The First Century of the Universalist Church of America, 1770–1870* (Boston: Unitarian Universalist Association 1979), p. 576.

2 George Rogers, *Memoranda of the Experience, Labor and Travels of a Universalist Preacher* (Cincinnati: John A. Gurley, 1845), pp. 218–19.

3 William Roland Jones, *Is God a White Racist? A Preamble to Black Theology* (Garden City, NY: Anchor Press, 1973), p. xiv.

4 Rogers, pp. 218–19.

5 Hosea Ballou, *A Treatise on Atonement* (Boston: Skinner House Books, 1986), p. 48; originally published 1892.

6 James Baldwin, *The Fire Next Time* (New York: Dial Press, 1963), pp. 44–45.

7 Russell Elliott Miller, *The Larger Hope: The Second Century of the Universalist Church of America, 1870–1970* (Boston: Unitarian Universalist Association, 1985), p. 362.

8 Ibid.

9 H. E. Williams, "The Suffolk Colored Mission," *Universalist Leader*, Oct. 12, 1912, pp. 1327–28.

10 Miller, *Second Century*, p. 412.

11 Ibid., p. 369.

12 Ernest Cassara, *Hosea Ballou: The Challenge of Orthodoxy* (Boston: Beacon Press, 1961), pp. 148–49.

13 Joseph Fletcher Jordan, "Universalism and the Negro," *Universalist Leader*, Apr. 27, 1912, p. 528.

14 Roger, p. 101.

15 Kimberly French, "The Gospel of Inclusion: A Black Pentecostal Bishop Embraces Universalism, Befriends a Unitarian Minister, and Shakes Up the Largest Congregation in the UUA," Fall 2009, *UU World*, www.uuworld.org/life/articles/145503.shtml. For more on this story, read Carlton Pearson, *The Gospel of Inclusion: Reaching Beyond Religious Fundamentalism to the True Love of God* (New York: Atria, 2006).

16 "Report of the Commission on National and International Relief," *1930 Universalist Yearbook* (Boston: Universalist Church of America), p. 71. This money was to aid Armenia and on the Commission was John van Schaik Jr., who opposed raising funds for the Suffolk Mission.

17 Jeffrey W. Campbell, interview by Mark Morrison-Reed, July 1979.

18 John van Schaick, "Idealism and Realism in Mixed Marriages," *Christian Leader*, Aug. 12, 1939, p. 760.

19 Miller, *Second Century*, p. 247.

20 "American Piety in the 21st Century: New Insights to the Depth of Religion in the U.S.: Selected Findings from the Baylor Religious Survey," 2006, www.baylor.edu/content/services/document.php/33304.pdf.

21 James Baldwin, *Notes of a Native Son* (New York: Bantam, 1964), p. 149.

The Empowerment Saga

1 Homer Jack, *Homer's Odyssey: My Quest for Peace and Justice* (Becket, MA: One Peaceful World Press, 1996), p. 318.

2 Charles Blackburn, email to Mark D. Morrison-Reed, Sept. 5, 2010.

3 Richard D. Leonard, *Call to Selma: Eighteen Days of Witness* (Boston: Skinner House Books, 2002), pp. 147–48. In addition to the 131 names of Unitarian Universalist ministers that Leonard lists, I have uncovered twelve others, plus two seminarians: Carl Bierman, Ernest Brown, David Bumbaugh, Joseph Ira Craig, Alan Deale, Jan Knost, Robert A. Kilgore, Charles McGehee, Kenneth T. MacLean, Ernie Pipes, Gene Reeves, Paul Sawyer, and students Ralph Mero and Jack Zylman.

4 Unitarian Universalist Association, *Report of the Committee on Goals* (Boston: UUA, 1967), p. 28.

5 Mwalimu Imara, email to Mark D. Morrison-Reed, Oct. 29, 2010.

Admission of Members Without Discrimination

1 Plenary Debate transcript, 1963, 1926–1976 AUA/UUA GA Resolution file, Morrison-Reed Collection, Sankofa Archive, Meadville Lombard Theological School Library, Chicago, pp. 139–40.

2 Ibid., pp. 185–86.

3 Minutes of the Second General Assembly, *1964 Unitarian Universalist Association Directory* (Boston: UUA, 1964), p. 58.

Last Exit to Grosse Point

1 Henry Hampton, interviewed by Carol Dornbrand, 1985, Boston.

Martin Luther King Jr.

1 Richard Boeke, "Three Little-Known Affirmative Actions," 2008, McGee file, Morrison-Reed Collection, Sankofa Archive, Meadville Lombard Theological School Library, Chicago.

I Cannot Approve

1 Wade H. McCree Jr., "Earnest but Mistaken," *Register Leader*, May 1968, p. 17.

David Hilliard Eaton

1 Allison Blakely, "A Leader for the Second Reconstruction: David Hilliard Eaton," unpublished, 1998, p. 3.
2 David H. Eaton, "The Road to Reconciliation," sermon delivered Feb. 13, 1972, All Souls Church, Unitarian, Washington DC.
3 Ibid.
4 Eaton, "The Road."
5 David H. Eaton, interviewed by Carol Dornbrand, 1985; copy of transcript in David Eaton file, Morrison-Reed Collection, Sankofa Archive, Meadville Lombard Theological School Library, Chicago.
6 Five months earlier, in May 1969, James Foreman, a leader of Student Non-Violent Coordinating Committee (SNCC), had interrupted a service at Riverside Church in New York City and delivered the Black Manifesto, which demanded reparations among other things.
7 Blakely, p. 4; cites David Eaton sermon on Oct. 12, 1969.
8 David H. Eaton, "Take the Blindfold Off the Lady," May 3, 1970, All Souls Church, Unitarian, Archives, Washington DC.
9 "Shooting at Sight," editorial, May 4, 1970, *Washington Post*.
10 *The Washingtonian*, Jan. 1972.
11 Eaton, interview.
12 Charles Howe, "David Eaton's All Souls Ministry," *Journal of Unitarian Universalist History*, 2000, Vol. XXVII, Unitarian Universalist Historical Society, pp. 97–98.
13 Stephanie Griffith, "Activist Pastor at All Souls Leaving Pulpit," *Washington Post*, section D, Mar. 30, 1992, pp. 1, 3.

The Black Humanist Fellowship of Liberation

1 Byron Edward Jackson, "History of the Unitarian Society of Cleveland," 1958, Unitarian Universalist Society of Cleveland Archives, Cleveland Heights, OH.
2 Farley Wheelwright to Joseph Barth, May 21, 1969, Unitarian Universalist Society of Cleveland Archives, Cleveland Heights, OH.
3 Ibid.
4 Contract between the Division of Ministry, Churchmanship, and Extension of the Unitarian Universalist Association and John Frazier, Sept. 19, 1969,

John Frazier Papers, Western Reserve Historical Society, Cleveland, OH.

5 In an unpublished interview with Gordon Gibson, Frazier reveals that he discovered the Jackson congregation through his relationship with Buford Posey. Posey, a member of the Jackson congregation and an associate of Medgar Evers, was the first white person in Mississippi to join the NAACP. After the murders of the civil rights workers James Chaney, Michael Schwerner, and Andrew Goodman in 1964, Posey did the unpardonable in the eyes of white Neshoba County and talked openly with the FBI. Shortly afterward, he left the state. For more information, see "Buford Posey and Johnny Frazier: A Unitarian Universalist Connection in Mississippi," by Gordon Gibson.

6 Hayward Henry, "Position Paper on BUUC Ideology: From Black Power to Black Nationalism," Humanist Fellowship of Liberation Papers, Western Reserve Historical Society, Cleveland, OH.

7 Farley Wheelwright to Board of Trustees of the Unitarian Society of Cleveland, Sept. 1, 1969, Unitarian Universalist Society of Cleveland Archives, Cleveland Heights, OH.

8 James Huston to the Members of the Unitarian Society of Cleveland, Sept. 10, 1969, Unitarian Universalist Society of Cleveland Archives, Cleveland Heights, OH.

9 Hayward Henry, "The Case for Black Unitarianism," delivered Oct. 5, 1969, Unitarian Universalist Society of Cleveland Archives, Cleveland Heights, OH.

10 Glover Barnes, "The Case for Integrated Unitarianism," delivered Oct. 12, 1969, Unitarian Universalist Society of Cleveland Archives, Cleveland Heights, OH.

11 Farley Wheelwright, "From the Minister's Study," *The Beacon*, Oct. 13, 1969, No. 886.

12 Donald Petarra, "A Viewpoint," Oct. 15, 1969, Unitarian Universalist Society of Cleveland Archives, Cleveland Heights, OH.

13 David Burwasser, "A Viewpoint," Oct. 20, 1969, Unitarian Universalist Society of Cleveland Archives, Cleveland Heights, OH.

14 Edith Gaines, "A Viewpoint," Oct. 10, 1969, Unitarian Universalist Society of Cleveland Archives, Cleveland Heights, OH.

15 Brenda Green, "A Viewpoint," Oct. 13, 1969, Unitarian Universalist Society of Cleveland Archives, Cleveland Heights, OH.

16 Ed and Anna Fritz, "A Viewpoint," Oct. 19, 1969, Unitarian Universalist Society of Cleveland Archives, Cleveland Heights, OH.

17 *William Mack v. James I. Huston*, pp. 1–2, No. 878, 886, Cuyahoga Cty., OH, Court of Common Pleas, 1970.

18 Farley Wheelwright, "An Open Letter to a Colleague," delivered Jan. 4, 1970, Unitarian Universalist Society of Cleveland Archives, Cleveland Heights, OH.

19 Donald Szantho Harrington to Farley Wheelwright, Jan. 7, 1970, Unitarian Universalist Society of Cleveland Archives, Cleveland Heights, OH.

20 "Finance Committee Report for Fiscal 1969—to the Annual Meeting Apr. 1970," "1970 Annual Meeting of the Unitarian Society of Cleveland—Apr. 24, 1970, Agenda," Unitarian Universalist Society of Cleveland Archives, Cleveland Heights, OH.

21 Mack v. Huston, p. 6.

22 Minutes of the Humanist Fellowship of Liberation, Nov. 29, 1970, Papers of the Humanist Fellowship of Liberation, Western Reserve Historical Society, Cleveland, OH.

The Empowerment Paradox

1 Benjamin F. Scott, "Thoughts on the Occasion of the Tenth Anniversary of the Vote to Fund the Unitarian Universalist Black Affairs Council," delivered June 11, 1978, the First Unitarian Society of Chicago, BAC/BAWA file, Morrison-Reed Collection, Sankofa Archive, Meadville Lombard Theological School Library, Chicago.

2 Holley Ulbrich, *The Fellowship Movement: A Growth Strategy and Its Legacy* (Boston: Skinner House Books, 2008), p. 42.

3 Victor H. Carpenter writes, "My being in South Africa during most of the 1960s had prevented my involvement in the American Civil Rights movement, thus curtailing the deep emotional attachment which many of my UU colleagues developed for the ideal of integration. Without that emotional attachment to racial integration, my eyes were open to the revolutionary redirection of liberal religion's social witness being demanded by black UUs at the Biltmore Hotel" (Victor H. Carpenter, *The Long Challenge: The Empowerment Controversy (1967–1977)*, Chicago: Meadville Lombard Theological School, 2003, p. 90). Because Selma became an icon symbolic of interracial solidarity, Carpenter misinterpreted its impact on the participants. The names of the ministers that went to Selma in March 1965 are listed in Richard D. Leonard's *Call to Selma: Eighteen Days of Witness* (Boston: Skinner House, 2002, pp. 147–48). Having reviewed this list, Gordon Gibson and James Hobart, both of whom were in Selma and later became BAC supporters, expressed the opinion that a majority of those listed later became BAC supporters. Harry A. Thor in 1999 wrote, "Probably, the reality of my experience in Selma made me a supporter of [BAC's] unpopular financial agenda [for] our denomination." Rather than increase UU ministers' attachment to

integration, Selma radicalized many—by revealing that the issue was one of poverty, prejudice, and an asymmetry of power—and gave them the experience of having to trust and follow black leadership. The appendix to *Call to Selma* also indirectly suggests this is true. It contains short testimonies written by those who went to Selma, and integration is not among the themes expounded upon.

4 Homer Jack, *Homer's Odyssey: My Quest for Peace and Justice* (Becket, MA: One Peaceful World Press, 1996), p. 120.

5 In 1927, Lewis Allen McGee, an AME minister, approached Unitarian minister Curtis Reese and was told, "if you want to be a Unitarian you'd better bring your own church." In 1930, the minister Harry V. Richardson was refused admission by the AUA. He graduated from Harvard Divinity School in 1932, earned a doctorate from Drew, and went on to found and be the first president of the Interdenominational Theological Center in Atlanta. Jeffrey W. Campbell, who held dual fellowship with the Universalist and Unitarian denominations, said that Frederick May Eliot would "start making excuses" as soon as he saw him at the end of the hallway.

6 "Special Report—The Emergency Conference on the Unitarian Universalist Response to the Black Rebellion: Proceedings," Oct. 23, 1967, UUA Department of Social Responsibility, Boston, MA, lists the following as members of the Black Caucus: Jules L. Ramey, Louis J. Gothard, Benjamin F. Scott, George T. Johnson, Henry Hampton, John Frazier, Jr., Thomas E. Payne, Jerry T. Jones, Marjorie Jordan, Barbara Jackson, Hayward Henry (later Mtangulizi Sanyika), Selina Reed, James Carter, Anna Hedgeman, Howard Traylor, LeRoy Cole, J. Clayton Flowers, William H. Johnson, Kenneth Knight, Charles W. Lee, Rochelle R. Lester, William R. Morris, Winifred Norman, Philip Rutledge, Juanita H. Simpson, Eugene Sparrow, Thomas C. Taylor, Carrie Thomas, Richard L. Traylor, S. J. Williamson, Jr., and John Young. Renford Gaines (later Mwalimu Imara), who is listed as a conference leader but not as a Black Caucus member, affirms that he did belong to the caucus. Also unlisted is Ann Reading—a member of the Student Caucus, she joined the Black Caucus on its second day. Althea Alexander's name also does not appear on the above list but does appear in the UUA Commission on Appraisal's report, *Empowerment: One Denomination's Quest for Racial Justice* (Boston: Unitarian Universalist Association, 1983, p. 26), where she is listed with Ramey and Gothard as one of "the young leaders from Los Angeles."

7 Jack Mendelsohn, "Black Power and the Liberal Church," delivered Nov. 5, 1967, Arlington Street Church, Boston, BAC/BAWA file, Morrison-Reed Collection, Sankofa Archive, Meadville Lombard Theological School, Chicago.

8 Scott, p. 2.

9 Mendelsohn.

10 John Wolf, "Black Power Comes to Unitarianism," delivered May 6, 1968, All Souls Unitarian Church, Tulsa, OK.

11 Kenneth Clark, "Racism for the UUA?" *Register Leader*, May 1968, pp. 11–12.

12 Whitney M. Young Jr., *Beyond Racism: Building an Open Society* (New York: McGraw Hill, 1969), p.102.

13 African-American Leadership in the UUA:

Board of Trustees
Wade McCree, 1965–1969
Edna Griffin, 1969–1977
Dalmas Taylor, 1971–1979
Gwendolyn Thomas, 1976–1987
Loretta Williams, 1978–1979
Gustavia Gash, 1983–1987
Norman Lockman, 1983–1986
Winnifred Norman, 1983–1991
Edward Simmons, 1987–1995
Leon Spencer, 1991–1999
William Jones, 1993–2001
Norma Poinsett, 1995–2003
Adele Smith-Penniman, 2001–2002
William Sinkford, 2001–2009
Tamara Payne-Alex, 2000–2009
Charles Redd, 2003–2005
Rosemary Bray McNatt, 2007–2010

Commission on Appraisal
Joseph Samples, 1969–1975
Harold Wilson, 1969–1970
Norma Poinsett, 1971–1981
Dalmas Taylor, 1979–1987
Mark Morrison-Reed, 1983–1991
O'Ferrell Nelson, 1987–1991
Marjorie Bowens-Wheatley, 1993–1999
Charles Redd, 1999–2003
Janice Marie Johnson, 2001–2005
Arthur Morrison, 2005–2006
Jacqui C. Williams, 2006–2011

Nominating Committee
Henrietta McKee, 1969–1970
Jack O. LeFlore, 1969–1973
William M. Scott, 1969–1973
Cornelius McDougald, 1969–1973
Winnifred Norman, 1973–1977
Gustavia Gash, 1981–1983
Etta Green Johnson, 1983–1987
David Eaton, 1985–1989
Sayre Dixon, 1989–1993
Charles Yielbonzie Johnson, 1991–1995
Daniel Aldridge, 1993–1997
Michelle Bentley, 1993–1997
Laura Spencer, 1997–2001
Hope Johnson, 2005–2009
James Coomes, 2003–2007
Leon Spencer, 2007–present

14 When the jurisdiction of the Suffolk Normal and Training School was turned over to the General Sunday School Association (GSSA) in 1917, the school became a living model for interracial understanding and respect to the Sunday school children of Universalist churches. The GSSA increased its support of the mission by annually using a month-long American Missionary (later Friendship) Program in Universalist Sunday schools. Produced between 1939 and 1966, the New Beacon Series curriculum occasionally touched on race. Stories from Africa were included in Sophia Lyon Fahs's *From Long Ago and Many Lands* (Boston: Beacon Press, 1948) and *Beginnings of Life and Death* (Boston: Beacon Press, 1938). The beginning of the AME church is mentioned in the first edition of Reginald D. Manwell and Sophia Lyon Fahs's *The Church Across the Street* (Boston: Beacon Press, 1947) and expanded upon in a revision. *In Worshipping Together with Questioning Minds* (Boston: Beacon Press, 1965), Sophia Lyon Fahs devoted four chapters to the life of George Washington Carver. Therefore, in 1968, when Hayward Henry, the chair of the Black Unitarian Universalist Caucus, claimed that nowhere in the religious education curricula were black contributions to American society studied, it was hyperbole—not none, but not enough. A curriculum team was appointed to address the issue of racism. However, after a difficult field test and a subsequent decade-long effort by Mary Small, the monumental thousand-page project was stillborn. Long, very didactic, expensive to produce, and reflective of a dated pedagogical approach, it was never published. The major religious education curricula to be issued by the

UUA in the early 1970s was the controversial *About Your Sexuality*. Regarding race, it should be noted that the book did use multicultural models. Published in 1978, a curriculum for five to seven year olds was entitled *The Adventures of God's Folk*—written by Joseph A. Bassett, it included a two-session unit on "Harriet Tubman, the Beautiful Black Moses" and another on "Sacajawea, the Remarkable Woman Who Accompanied Lewis and Clark." Regarding race, nothing educationally substantive for adults appeared until 1984, when the COA disseminated a companion discussion guide to its report on empowerment, a year after the report itself came out. In 1985, the UU Identity Curriculum team was established. Staffed by Elizabeth Anastos, this team, in addition to helping Mark Morrison-Reed develop *How Open the Door?: Afro-Americans' Experience in the UUA* (UUA, 1989), made sure that African-American content was part of all the curricula it developed: Peg Gooding's *Growing Up Times* (UUA, 1988) and *The Stepping Stone Year* (UUA, 1989), which included a lesson on Lewis Latimer; Elizabeth Strong's *Messages in Music* (UUA, 1993), which encouraged youth to embrace all forms of music, including soul, blues, and jazz; and Lois Eklund's *Travel in Time* (UUA, 1989), which included a story about Errold Collymore, the first black AUA board member. The intention of this approach was to offer the stories and culture of African Americans as an integral part of the UU story as opposed to a topic treated separately. In addition, the *In Our Hands* social justice series of curricula released during the same years touched on the theme of diversity. Subsequently, the elementary-grade curriculum *Rainbow Children*, written by Norma Poinsett and Vivian Burns (UUA, 1995), was produced, as was *Race to Justice: A Racial Justice and Diversity Program for Junior High* (UUA, 1995), written by Jose Ballester and Robin Gray. In 1996, the adult curriculum *Weaving the Fabric of Diversity* was developed by Jacqui James and Judith Frediani (UUA, 1996).

15 Scott, p. 3.

16 Jean Ott, title of unpublished adult education class.

Still Seeking a Way

1 Bill Schulz, Preface, in Mark Morrison-Reed, *Black Pioneers in a White Denomination* (Boston: Skinner House Books, 1980), p. ix. Note: this essay appears only in the first edition of this book.

William Roland Jones

1 William R. Jones, *Is God a White Racist? Preamble to Black Theology* (Boston: Beacon Press, 1997), p. viii.

2 Ibid., p. ix.
3 William R. Jones, interview by Anthony B. Pinn, Aug. 28, 2009.
4 William R. Jones, "The Case for Black Humanism," in William R. Jones and Calvin Bruce, eds., *Black Theology II: Essays on the Formation and Outreach of Contemporary Black Theology* (Lewisburg, PA: Bucknell University Press, 1978), p. 222.
5 Ibid.
6 Jones, interview.
7 Christopher L. Walton, "Awards and Commendations: UUA Honors Courage and Long Service," *UU World*, Sep./Oct. 2001, www.uuworld.org/2001/04/gaawards.html.
8 Warren R. Ross, "Confronting Evil: Has Terrorism Shaken Our Religious Principles?" *UU World*, Jan./Feb. 2002, www.uuworld.org/ideas/articles/5787.shtml.
9 William R. Jones, "The New Three R's," in Dan O'Neal, Alice Blair Wesley, and James Ishmael Ford, eds., *The Transient and Permanent in Liberal Religion: Reflections from the UUMA Convocation on Ministry* (Boston: Skinner House Books, 1995), pp. 162–63.
10 William R. Jones, "Towards a New Paradigm for Uncovering Neo-Racism/Oppression in UUism," paper given to the author by William R. Jones.
11 Jones interview.

Thomas Eliron Payne

1 Thomas Eliron Payne, "UUA Biographical Information Supplement," c. 1967, Payne file, Morrison-Reed Collection, Sankofa Archive, Meadville Lombard Theological School Library, Chicago.
2 Thomas Eliron Payne, "Thomas Eliron Payne," c. 1988, Payne file, Morrison-Reed Collection, Sankofa Archive, Meadville Lombard Theological School, Chicago.
3 Commission on Appraisal, *Empowerment: One Denomination's Quest for Racial Justice, 1967–1982* (Boston: Unitarian Universalist Association, 1983), p. 20.
4 Payne, "Thomas Eliron Payne."
5 Thomas Eliron Payne, "Soulful Journeys: The Faith of African-American Unitarian Universalists," Melvin Hoover and Jacqui James, eds. (Boston: Unitarian Universalist Association, 2002).
6 Thomas Eliron Payne, unsigned theological reflection, AAUUM Meeting, November 1990, Tulsa, OK.

Afterword

1 William Ellery Channing, *The Works of William E. Channing, D.D.* (Boston: American Unitarian Association, 1875), p. 838.

2 John van Schaick, "Is Facing Facts Wrong?" *Christian Leader*, Sept. 2, 1939, p. 831.

3 This number comes from the 2009 Berry Street Essay by Paul Rasor. Entitled "Ironic Provincialism or Engaged Multiculturalism? A Unitarian Universalist Turning Point," *www.olduuma.org/BerryStreet/Essays/BSE2009.htm* (p. 14). An excerpted version was published in *UU World* (Spring 2010, p. 35) as "Can Unitarian Unitarianism Change?" Rasor, having surveyed UUA data and the raw data from the Pew Forum's Religious Landscape Survey, argues for the number 91.5 percent Euro-Americans. This is significantly lower than the 97.6 percent quoted in the 1997 UUA "Fulfilling the Promise" survey (which was nearly identical to the 97.5 percent reported in the 1989 Commission on Appraisal survey, "The Quality of Religious Life in Unitarian Universalist Congregations," p. 56).

4 "Report of the Committee on Goals," Boston: Unitarian Universalist Association, 1967, p. 30.

5 "The Quality of Religious Life in Unitarian Universalist Congregations," Commission on Appraisal survey, Unitarian Universalist Association, Boston, 1989, p. 16.

6 William G. Sinkford, "Our Calling: Opportunity and Redemption," *UU World*, Summer 2007, p. 7.

7 "Historical Trends II: The Educational Progress of African Americans," www.jointcenter.org/DB/factsheet/historical-trendsII.htm.

8 Patricia Jimenez, "Facing the Challenge, Dreaming the Possible," delivered at the Urban Church Conference, 1988, Baltimore, MD, in Leslie Takahashi Morris, Chip Roush, and Leon Spencer, *The Arc of the Universe Is Long: Unitarian Universalists, Anti-Racism and the Journey from Calgary* (Boston: Skinner House Books, 2009), pp. 290–91.

9 William F. Schulz, Preface, in Mark D. Morrison-Reed, *Black Pioneers in a White Denomination* (Boston: Skinner House Books, 1980). Note: this essay appears only in the first edition of this book.

INDEX